❧ · *A TASTE OF RUSSIA* · ❧

A Taste of Russia

· A COOKBOOK OF · RUSSIAN HOSPITALITY

DARRA GOLDSTEIN

Harper Perennial

A Division of HarperCollins*Publishers*

A hardcover edition of this book was published in 1983 by Random House under the title *A La Russe*. It is here reprinted by arrangement with Random House.

A TASTE OF RUSSIA. Copyright © 1983 by Darra Goldstein. All rights reserved. Printed in the United States of America. No part of this book may be used or reproduced in any manner whatsoever without written permission except in the case of brief quotations embodied in critical articles and reviews. For information address HarperCollins Publishers, 10 East 53rd Street, New York, NY 10022.

First HarperPerennial edition published 1991.

Library of Congress Cataloging-in-Publication Data
Goldstein, Darra.
A taste of Russia : a cookbook of Russian hospitality / Darra
Goldstein. — 1st HarperPerennial ed.
p.   cm.
Reprint. Originally published: A la russe. 1st ed. New York :
Random House, c1983.
Includes index.
ISBN 0-06-097385-4 (pbk.)
1. Cookery, Russian.   I. Title.
TX723.3.G64   1991
641.5947—dc20   90-55984

91 92 93 94 95 HC 10 9 8 7 6 5 4 3 2 1

To My Russian Friends

When you come for a visit, we'll give you melons the likes of which you've never tasted! And you'll find no better honey in any other village. Why, when we bring in the honeycomb, the scent fills the room! You can't imagine it, our honey is pure as the Tsarina's tears, or the clear crystal of her earrings. And the pies, what pies my old lady will feed you! If you only knew, they're sugar, pure sugar! and the butter brims on your lips when you bite into them! Wizards these old ladies are! Did you ever drink kvass made from pears and blackthorn berries? or vodka infused with raisins and plums? Have you eaten frumenty with milk? My friends, what glorious flavors there are in the world! Once you start eating, you can hardly stop . . . ah, sweet nectar of life! Why, only last year . . . But what am I prattling on about? You'll just have to come see us, come soon! We'll feed you such treats you'll tell all the world.

—Rudi Panko, beekeeper, in Gogol's
Evenings on a Farm Near Dikanka

PREFACE

My interest in Russian cuisine stems from two sources. As a student of literature, I was eager to satisfy my curiosity about the preparation of foods described in Russian novels and short stories. More deeply rooted in me, however, were memories from childhood—the dishes I first tasted from my grandmother's spoon.

My grandmother came to America from Byelorussia in the early part of the century. We called her Baba, and whenever she came to visit, her favorite pastime (her only pastime!) was cooking and baking for her grandchildren. I could spend hours at her side in the kitchen, watching her fingers deftly rolling out the dough for my favorite jam-filled cookies, *rogaliki*. She would let me choose the jam and spread it on, and I always opted for a mixture of plum and cherry. Baba made the cookies early in the morning so we could have them fresh for lunch. As soon as they were safely baking in the oven, she would start preparing the evening meal. It might be *golubtsy*, "little doves," a mixture of ground beef and rice carefully rolled up in cabbage leaves and simmered in a spicy tomato sauce, or a tender pot roast flavored with rum, or chicken stewed for long hours with prunes and sometimes apricots. Baba never followed a recipe, but as I grew older I would query her as she cooked, hoping to be able to reproduce her delicious meals once she was gone.

Later, when I began studying Russian literature, I was struck by the number of references to food in obscure tales as well as in the classics. The opulence of the aristocratic tables thrilled and enchanted me, while the descriptions of thick soups and chewy breads—tne foods I had grown up on—invariably sent me running to the kitchen for a snack. Luckily, not all of my pleasure was vicarious. I was fortunate to be able to experience Russian food in its natural habitat, first as a student in Leningrad and later as a guide for a traveling exhibit that toured several Soviet cities. People from Odessa to Alma-Ata generously opened their homes to me, and my hosts were always eager to share their treasured recipes. From them, I learned how the culinary art had evolved from the nineteenth-century extravaganzas described in literature to the monumental *zakuska* buffets of today. Each new family I met asserted that *theirs* was the best kvass, *theirs* the best *golubtsy*. And when I think of the friends behind each recipe, each does seem like the best to me.

Other recipes in this book were given to me by émigré friends, and I combed old Russian cookbooks for the interesting and the unusual. I wanted to share my love of the Russian people and their cuisine. I wanted to write a cookbook that not only described how to prepare traditional foods but also painted the Russian life and culture corresponding to them.

One word of warning is in order, lest the delicacies presented cause the reader to assume that *kulebyaka* and champagne-sturgeon soup are the usual fare of Russians today. The Soviet Union suffers from a chronic food shortage, and Russians more often dine on buckwheat groats, canned peas and cabbage soup than on a cut of meat. Food distribution is based on a system of hierarchies, in which Moscow, most prominent and visible to Western eyes, receives priority over all other Soviet cities. Next on the ladder come the capitals of the larger republics, along with the military and scientific centers, and so on down the rungs, until the smallest rural villages receive their meager allotments, which provide for only the barest necessities. A common sight on the Moscow subway is peasant women, laden with sacks of produce and sausage, heading home to their villages after buying up food for their families, friends and neighbors. Muscovites blame their shortages on the hordes of peasants who arrive daily and buy up the stock.

Even within these city allotments, there exists a hierarchy of privileged positions and special stores. The system is a complicated one, but the point is that some people are able to eat much better than others. And the reason is not simply a matter of money, as in Western society, but rather of influence or pull, or *blat,* as it is called in Russian. In Moscow especially, there are special stores closed to the general public that sell everything from fresh caviar to ketchup. The food in these stores is purchased with coupons, not money, and very few people have access to the coupons. In addition, there are foreign-currency stores that stock imported delicacies—but of course it's illegal for a Soviet citizen to possess foreign currency.

Yet the Russians are nothing if not resourceful, and even the average citizen knows how to obtain good food. There is an extensive system of barter, for one thing. If, for example, Natalia Fyodorovna works at a meat store, she can reserve for her friends the ground beef that has just arrived. Her friend Sofia Pavlovna, who works in the dairy store, returns the favor, and when good butter comes in, she sets it aside. Virtually any foodstuff can be had in this manner, trading what one can get for what one cannot; it is simply a matter of knowing the right people, cultivating good connections. When I was in the Soviet Union, I didn't immediately understand why the stores had nothing at all on the shelves, while I was served all kinds of meat and fish at people's homes. The reason is simple: most of the food exchange goes on *under* the counter, not across it. Even the vocabulary is expressive of this fact of Russian life. Most products cannot simply be "bought" (*kupit'*), but they *can* be "obtained" (*dostat'*).

So while it is possible to eat well in the Soviet Union today, one must not forget the extremes of inconvenience, connivance and expense people are often driven to for items as basic as a few oranges, sausages or even a liter of milk. The effort of shopping is enormous, making the Russians' hospitality all the more generous. One wonders how many Western families would regale guests so lavishly if they had to go to even half the trouble.

And in spite of all the difficulties, the Russians still take great pleasure in preparing a good meal. Even if ingredients are nearly impossible to obtain, even if meals at state-controlled restaurants are uncertain at best, the art of Russian cooking is still thriving.

Apart from Russian friends who helped (immeasurably!) in the creation of this book, I would also like to acknowledge the aid of the following people: Brett Singer, for that initial elbow in my side; Elaine Markson, my kind and enterprising agent; Jill Norman and Anne Freedgood, my wise and discerning editors; George Curth, for his help at every stage; Helen Haft and Irving Goldstein, my parents, for their endless encouragement and cheerful labors in the kitchen; and my husband, Dean Crawford, for his unflagging support, ideas, *mots justes*—and for staying with me despite all those beets.

CONTENTS

PREFACE · ix

INTRODUCTION · 3

I · THE *ZAKUSKA* TABLE · 17

II · IN THE DAYS OF THE TSAR: CLASSIC RECIPES · 57

III · HOLIDAY CELEBRATIONS · 121

IV · AT THE DACHA: RUSSIAN HOME COOKING · 151

V · FROM THE PANTRY · 195

VI · SPECIALTIES FROM THE REPUBLICS · 227

VII · SITTING AROUND THE SAMOVAR · 269

INDEX · 293

❧ · *A TASTE OF RUSSIA* · ❧

INTRODUCTION

There is an old Russian saying that goes something like this: "You can rack your brains, but you can't beat hospitality!" Odd as the saying may be, it does capture the Russian sentiment toward guests, whom they love to regale with food and drink. As an American living in the Soviet Union, I was invited to countless homes. In most cases I hardly knew my hosts, but the moment I entered their doors I became their *dorogoi gost'*, their "dear guest," and was treated to all they could lavish upon me throughout the evening. Their hospitality extended beyond the offering of physical sustenance. The Russians love to bestow gifts, and the uninitiated had better be careful not to admire openly anything in a Russian home: within minutes it will be quietly offered along with the food. The gift of hospitality is felt all the more keenly in the Soviet Union of today, where obtaining even a good piece of meat is a considerable feat. Yet somehow the Russians manage, and it is their greatest joy to present a well-laden table to their guests, especially to those who have come from afar.

Hospitality is a long-standing tradition in Russian culture. The reader of Russian literature is apt to find his mouth watering at the abundant feasts and simple peasant meals so richly described by classic Russian authors. At least one favorite character, Oblomov of Goncharov's novel of the same name, does nothing in almost 500 pages but lounge in bed, daydream and eat sumptuous meals. Unfortunately, being so lethargic, Oblomov rarely entertains; thus he neglects the Russian custom of sharing one's larder with guests both anticipated and unexpected, and suffers accordingly. A prescribed etiquette exists for sharing food with guests. In Gogol's "Ivan Fyodorovich Shponka and His Aunt," Shponka drops in on his neighbors unexpectedly. The hostess asks him if he'd like some vodka, for which she is severely rebuked by her son: "You're not yourself, Mother!" cried Grigory Grigorevich. "Whoever asks a visitor whether he wants anything? You just give it to him, that's all." An old Russian saying affirms that only the ailing should be asked if they want to eat, because the healthy undoubtedly will. In Russian and Soviet society it is not thought impolite to drop in unannounced at a neighbor's or friend's home, even at suppertime—the host can then take delight in begging one to stay and share the evening meal. The presence of a guest is still considered an honor: it is the host who should thank his guests for coming, not the other way around.

There are many superstitions and customs about the receiving and entertaining of guests: greetings must take place either within the apartment or outside in the hall since it is unlucky to shake hands or embrace over the threshold; at the table, wine must be poured from the bottle in a certain way in order not to tempt ill fate; unmarried women should never take the last morsel of food from a platter, lest they become old maids; a cigarette should never be lighted from a candle flame; before embarking on a journey, family and friends must gather and sit down in silence, wishing the traveler godspeed. The Russians love ritual—it is a large part of their daily lives even today—and hospitality is the foremost ritual in which standards of perfection must be met.

The Russian word for hospitality, *khlebosol'stvo,* is formed from two words, *khleb,* "bread," and *sol',* "salt." Together the words mean regaling with bread and salt. To offer one's bread is to honor one's guest, and no Russian meal is complete without several richly flavored loaves. In old Russia it was the custom to present the guest with a loaf of freshly baked bread (usually rye), lavishly decorated with cut-out bits of dough. This loaf, the *karavai,* often grew to immense proportions. A wooden dish of salt was offered along with the bread. Sometimes the salt dish was even placed in a special indentation in the center of the loaf. As soon as the guests appeared, the ornate *karavai* was brought to the table, and the guest cut the first slice of bread to dip in the salt, saying *Khleb da sol'!,* "Bread and salt!" or, less literally, *Bon appétit!* This ritual of sharing bread and salt at the table came to be synonymous with the Russian concept of hospitality—hence the word *khlebosol'stvo*. To this day the Russians are capable of eating an astounding amount of bread: a family of four easily consumes two to three loaves a day, and if guests are coming, the number increases substantially. But this should come as no surprise: Russian bread has always been among the best in the world.

The old Russian ritual of hospitality was not confined to bread and salt, however. A samovar, an urn for hot water, was always kept heated, ready for the arrival of unexpected guests. Guests were always accorded the best and most comfortable seats in the house. Here a distinction must be made between the prerevolutionary gentry and nobility and the peasantry.

The gentry usually received guests in the drawing room, in the Western manner. From there the party would move on to another chamber, where all could feast on *zakuski,* an elaborate array of hors d'oeuvres, until the servants announced that dinner was ready in the dining hall. The origins of the *zakuska* table can be traced back to Scandinavia through the dynasty of Rurik, who came to rule the heathen Slavic tribes in the ninth century A.D. The *zakuska* table proved well suited to the practical needs of the Russian way of life. Owing to bad weather and poor roads, houseguests invariably arrived late. With a large *zakuska* table set and ready at all times, the cold and hungry guests could refresh themselves immediately after their journey, and dinner was not jeopardized by standing around too long.

It was a different matter in the homes of the peasantry. Peasant cottages often consisted of only one room, most of which was taken up by the marvelous, versatile Russian stove, the *pech'*. The stove had two ovens: one for slow simmering and one for quick baking. It was enormous, occupying up to a third of the entire living area, because not only was the stove used for heating and all kinds of cooking and baking, it was also equipped with a sleeping ledge, the coziest spot in the cottage. The ledge was usually reserved for old grandmothers with aching bones, but lazy children loved to scramble up onto it and try to loll away the day there undetected. Russian fairy tales abound in stories of evil stepmothers who lie around on the stove all day while their long-suffering stepdaughters work. Noble estates also housed large stoves with sleeping space, but the ledge was relegated to the maidservants, as the gentry preferred the luxury of goose-down mattresses and comforters on a wooden bedstead.

The guest in the peasant cottage was invited to make himself comfortable in one of two honored spots: on top of the stove or in the icon corner. The icon corner was usually situated opposite the stove, and at least one icon hung there—often more, depending on the family's affluence—along with a constantly burning lamp. Beneath the icons stood the only table in the cottage, and there the guests were most often invited to sit. This corner was known as the *krasnoye mesto,* "beautiful spot." The Russian language has a rich storehouse of sayings to describe these places of honor for guests. A typical greeting was "Welcome to our cottage! Our beautiful spot is for our beautiful guest." Or "Make yourself at home! Climb up onto the stove!" And once a guest actually had clambered up onto the stove, he was considered one of the family.

· FOOD IN RUSSIAN LITERATURE ·

These rituals of hospitality were all preliminaries leading up to the main attraction, the meal itself. This meal could range from a simple, yet thoroughly satisfying bowl of *borshch* (beet soup), served up with black bread and home-cured pickles, to a lavish feast of many courses, including such delicacies as *ryabchik* (hazel hen) in a sour-cherry sauce, or the roe of sturgeon, better known as caviar. Obviously the gentry ate a great variety of foods and enjoyed all kinds of delights, while the peasantry knew little other than their repertoire of hearty soups and *pirogi* (pies). Russian literature is rich in descriptions of food because to a Russian, cooking and eating are vital concerns. Great moments in literature often coincide with an account of what is being—or about to be—consumed. This practice extends to even the most spiritual of Russian writers. In the chapter entitled "A Scandal" in Dostoevsky's *The Brothers Karamazov,* Fyodor Pavlovich Karamazov has been invited to the Father Superior's room at the monastery. The initial description of the room focuses on a lavishly set table, dazzling the eye:

> . . . but the main splendor at the moment was the luxuriously set table: the cloth sparkled, the china shone. There were three kinds of superbly baked breads, two bottles of wine and two of the monastery's own wonderful *kvas,* renowned throughout the region. There was no vodka. . . . Five courses were prepared for dinner: *ukha* with sterlet and *pirozhki* with fish; poached fish, prepared in a special, delicious way; salmon cutlets; ice cream and compote; and finally a fruit pudding, like blancmange.

The Russian Orthodox monasteries enforced an injunction against eating game killed by snare, so no wild fowl was served. And since no meat is featured at the Father Superior's table, we realize that this is a Lenten menu. Still, the food is tempting, in spite of the religious proscriptions; but true to Dostoevskian form, the meal remains untouched because Fyodor Pavlovich makes a scene, the "scandal" of the chapter title: the visitors eventually leave without ever having sat down to the table.

Many of the gentry emulated foreign mannerisms and foreign food, and entire meals were prepared à la française or à l'anglaise. When, in Tolstoy's *Anna Karenina*, Oblonsky invites Levin to dine at one of Moscow's most fashionable restaurants, he displays his refined taste by ordering a totally French meal: *soupe printanière, turbot, sauce Beaumarchais, poularde à l'estragon, macédoine de fruits*. Levin, very much a Tolstoyan character, would rather eat a simple bowl of overwhelmingly Russian *shchi* (cabbage soup) and *grechnevaya kasha* (buckwheat groats). The dichotomy between the two men, and between the two opposing camps in Russia—the Westernizers and the Slavophiles—is dramatized throughout the passage by the food they order. Even at "French" meals, however, the service remained traditionally Russian. The various courses were brought to the table separately; only desserts and flowers were allowed to remain on the table throughout the meal. These desserts were often sculpted and used as centerpieces.

It is a bit ironic that the nineteenth-century Russian gentry worked so hard at being worldly: the French, meanwhile, were adapting to the idea of dining à la russe! French society first became enthralled with Russian culture around 1811, when Tsar Alexander I sent one of his court favorites to Paris as ambassador. This ambassador was a renowned epicure, and since Napoleon and his troops marched on Russia shortly thereafter, it can be surmised that the ambassador was more skilled in gustatory than diplomatic affairs. But in spite of the hostilities, the Russian gastronomic romance with things French reached its zenith under the same Alexander I, when the great Carême was invited, at Prince Bagration's request, to serve as the tsar's personal chef. Carême served well, if condescendingly, but after being forced to prepare the victory banquet celebrating Napoleon's defeat by the Russian army, he refused to cook for the tsar any longer. Carême's legacy to the Russian cuisine is the *sharlotka,* better known under its French name as *charlotte russe*.

As mentioned earlier, Russian service differed from French service in that each course was brought to the table separately, the second course not appearing until the first had been cleared away, and so on throughout the meal. At formal dinners even the china and cutlery were replaced as the meal progressed. Service *à la russe* ensured steaming hot soups, juicy roasts and refreshingly chilled puddings. Besides, the diner could enjoy each course in turn and anticipate the next, without the distraction of having to face it on the table before him, cooling and congealing in its own gravy. French service, by contrast, relied on a feast for the eye: as the diners entered the hall, they were struck by an abundantly laden table—the myriad foods, displayed with beauty and grace, eliciting sighs and salivations and designed to dazzle. But unfortunately, such awesome arrays of food frequently had been sitting out for some time, and what tempted the eye all too often disappointed the palate. The Russians, of course, deemed their service superior, especially since their copious *zakuska* table also fulfilled the function of the French *joie pour les yeux*. Gradually Russian service took hold, and by the late 1850s much of fashionable Europe was dining *à la russe*. Charles Dickens, an innovator in gastronomy as well as in literature, entertained in the Russian style, offering his critics a chance to censure him for more than his tales. The Russian table, once considered so uncouth, even barbaric, by the "civilized" Europeans, soon became the dominant mode; our modern-day table service, although modified, is its direct descendant.

It must be stressed that only the Russian upper class dined so extravagantly. Some aristocrats who affected French manners eschewed the dishes of their own native cuisine, leaving the exploration of this simpler food to the petty landowners who ran small estates in the backwoods of Russia and the Ukraine. This class of Russians also knew how to dine well. The management of their estates occupied their lives: they kept kitchen gardens, and they dried, salted and preserved the fruits and vegetables against the bitter Russian winter. Two such typical landowners, husband and wife, provide the theme for Gogol's "Old-World Landowners." In the story the couple's life revolves around food. It is the panacea for all complaints, real or imagined, as long as they have each other. Gogol's tale captures the essence of rural life in Russia and the Ukraine: one can almost smell the curd pies sizzling in freshly churned butter; the sour aroma of cabbage put up in large oaken barrels lined with black-currant leaves; the spicy scent of wood grouse roasting in the oven, its garnish of gooseberries imparting a tartness to the air. The tale's heroine is the lady of the house, Pulkheria Ivanovna.

For Pulkheria Ivanovna, housekeeping meant continually locking and unlocking the pantry, salting, drying and preserving an endless number of fruits and vegetables. Her house was like a chemical laboratory. A fire was constantly tended under the apple tree; and the kettle or copper vat—filled with jam, jelly, or confections made with honey, and sugar, and I can hardly remember what else—was almost never removed from its iron tripod. Under another tree, in a copper cauldron, the coachman was forever distilling vodka with peach leaves, with bird-cherry blossoms, with centaury or cherry pits, and by the end of the process he was in no condition even to lift his tongue, muttering such nonsense that Pulkheria Ivanovna couldn't understand a thing. Then he'd always head for the kitchen to sleep it off. Pulkheria Ivanovna always liked to prepare more than was needed, to have some on hand, and so much stuff was preserved, salted and dried, that it would have buried the entire estate, had not the maidservants eaten a good half of it, sneaking into the pantry and stuffing themselves to such an extent that for the rest of the day they'd groan and complain about their stomachs.

As Gogol's narrator states, "Both of the old people, in the time-honored tradition of old-world landowners, loved to eat." The story goes on to describe a typical day of eating: an early breakfast with coffee; a mid-morning snack of lard biscuits, poppy-seed pies and salted mushrooms; a late-morning snack of vodka, more mushrooms, and dried fish; a dinner at noon of various porridges and stews, their juices tightly sealed in earthenware pots; an early afternoon snack of watermelon and pears; a midafternoon snack of fruit dumplings with berries; a late-afternoon snack of yet other delicacies from the larder; supper at half past nine; and finally, long after they'd retired to bed, a midnight snack of sour milk and stewed dried pears, calculated to relieve the stomachache brought on by the excesses of the day. Other characters in Gogol face the same problems: the narrator in "A Bewitched Place" boasts that "sometimes we'd eat so many cucumbers, melons, turnips, onions, and peas, that I swear you'd have thought there were cocks crowing in our stomachs." No detail is overlooked in describing the foods these typical landowners enjoyed, foods influenced not at all by the French mode of the time. It was hard work being the mistress of an estate, and those who managed it well were highly regarded, and of course well fed.

For an accurate sense of the social importance of food and the extent of Russian hospitality, one can read almost any nineteenth-century classic of Russian literature. Taken as a whole, the books cover a broad spectrum of Russian life. Tolstoy describes magnificent repasts in the French style among the nobility. Chekhov takes us into the sitting rooms of the gentry where elegant teas are served. Gogol's narrator, speaking of the old-world landowners, relates: "But the old couple seemed most interesting to me when they had guests. Then everything in their house took on a new air. One might say that these kind people lived for their guests. They brought out the best of all they had and vied with one another in regaling you with everything their household produced."

In *The Gulag Archipelago,* Solzhenitsyn adds another lament to the already unbearable lives of political prisoners caught in a Catch-22 situation: they craved books to read, yet if they managed to get hold of Gogol or Chekhov, their position often became even harder to endure: "And it was harder still to be betrayed by an author whose books you'd loved— if he started drooling over food in great detail, then away with him! Get away from me, Gogol! The same with you, Chekhov! Both of them had just too much food in their books."

· REGIONAL SPECIALTIES ·

The state of the culinary art in Russia remained virtually the same from the time of Carême until the 1917 October Revolution. Then, in gastronomy, as in all other aspects of life, things changed suddenly and radically. There were no more gentry to lazily pass long summer days directing servants in the art of preserving. Most women began to work outside the home, and little time remained for complicated culinary endeavors. The peasantry thronged to the cities, where they found housing in cramped apartments, often sharing one small kitchen with several other families. There were no large pantries, no Russian stoves to simmer stews or bake the hearty breads. People stopped eating the way they once had, although interest in food did not diminish. Instead, the Russians began to adapt to the new conditions by developing a less complex cuisine. One favorable result was that yearly trips to the spa to "cure" the liver from an overdose of rich food became less frequent. The contemporary visitor to the Soviet Union will still find Chicken Kiev on most restaurant menus, but in a Soviet home one is more likely to be served chicken stew or spicy meatballs.

As if to compensate for the diminishing treasures of their own cuisine, the Russians have eagerly adopted regional specialties from the other republics. Technically speaking, Russia is only one of the fifteen republics that make up the Soviet Union; just over half of the Soviet Union's total population is ethnically Russian, and each republic has maintained its own culinary tradition. The Soviet cuisine is varied indeed when one considers that the republics extend from the Baltic Sea (where food is rich in butter, cream, and eggs) to the mountains bordering China (where standard fare is fermented mare's milk and exotic lamb stews) to the Sea of Okhotsk (where local delicacies include *balyk* and *vesiga*— the dried and salted fillet and backbone of the sturgeon) to the far north beyond the arctic circle (where the inhabitants feast on *stroganina*— frozen raw fish).

The Russians especially love the cookery of Georgia, a southern republic in the Caucasus, where fresh fruits grow year-round—a source of wonder and longing to the Russians trapped for long months in frost and ice. Ever since the first half of the nineteenth century, when Mikhail Lermontov romanticized the Caucasus in his poetry and prose, the Russians have felt a deep attraction for the dark-eyed Georgian people, with their fiery temperaments and fiery food. The blander Russian cuisine has eagerly adopted many exotic, spicy southern specialties, such as *shashlyk* (skewered lamb) with pomegranate sauce, *tabaka* (pressed and grilled chicken), and *kharcho* (a soup spiced with coriander).

The Georgians are famed not only for their culinary expertise, but for their business acumen as well. They are notorious entrepreneurs, lacking neither the goods—fresh lemons, tangerines, pomegranates, dates—nor the market. Snowbound Russians are willing to pay almost any price and stand in lines of almost any length to buy even a single yellow lemon to brighten the gray winter skies and perk up the ubiquitous cabbage soup. Each Soviet city has a large central market, and even far north of the Caucasus it is not uncommon to see ferocious-looking Georgian farmers, with long mustaches and high, conical Astrakhan hats, selling fruits out of the cotton string bags used to transport them. These bags crowd the aisles of airplanes and trains, holding the promise of fast fortune for the farmers. I can remember lemons in December selling two for 2 rubles 50 kopeks, or about $3.50 apiece, in the Moldavian capital of Kishinev. Farther north they command even higher prices.

· ENTERTAINING RUSSIAN STYLE ·

As in the days of the tsar, the Russians still love to entertain, and the center of any home is still the table, which stands in the largest room of the apartment, often in the middle of the floor. The Russians have a great knack for seating a large number of people around a small table. No one minds bumping elbows or knees: there is an intensity and excitement in such close contact. The table is spread with a clean linen cloth, and small plates are set at each place. Most of the table is taken up by bottles and glasses. Each setting requires a small shot glass, or *ryumochka,* for vodka and another for cognac, a goblet for wine or champagne, and a glass for juice, kvass (home-brewed beer) or mineral water. Bottles of each of these libations are placed directly on the table and remain there throughout the meal. All of the bottles are opened before the meal even begins: an impossible amount to imbibe, it would seem. But Russian meals last for hours on end, and invariably, by the end of the meal, all the bottles are empty, some having even been replaced.

The table is also laden with an assortment of five to ten *zakuski,* both hot and cold, accompanied by the mandatory loaves of bread. There is usually a choice of rye or white. The Russians consider the white bread fancier and more suitable for guests, but I always chose the rye, finding the blander white bread fit only for slathering with fresh caviar, where it does not compete with the subtle flavor of the roe. As part of the *zakuska* there are often several salads drenched with sour cream, composed of cucumbers and radishes in the winter, tomatoes and scallions in the summer. Crystal dishes hold pickled tomatoes and marinated wild mushrooms. Several varieties of fish are offered: canned sardines or mackerel in oil; herring in various sauces; hot-smoked and cold-smoked sturgeon fillets, the likes of which I have never tasted since. There are prepared dishes, such as vegetable caviars and piping-hot *pirozhki*—pies with meat or vegetable fillings, baked or deep-fried. It is very important (and very hard) for the novice at Russian dining to bear in mind that this is only the *zakuska* spread, that the main meal has not yet arrived. Still the temptation is too great to pass up anything, and the hostess will invariably press second helpings, saying *Esh'te, esh'te na zdorov'ye!* "Eat, eat to your health!"

Eating always starts off with a round of vodka or, out of deference to any more timid guests, cognac. The *ryumochki* are filled almost to overflowing, and the host proposes the first toast—usually to his guests. Then everyone clinks glasses and downs the vodka *zalpom,* in a single chug. No place for cowards here! To survive the toasting and remain alert at least until the main course, one must do as the Russians do: immediately grab a *buterbrod* (bread spread with butter and topped with smoked fish) and eat it. At the very least, reach for a slice of bread and a pickle. By always eating something after each gulp of vodka, one can drink a great deal without getting drunk, or at least before realizing one's true condition. With the first toast, the meal has formally begun, and the *zakuski* are assaulted in earnest. Next comes the *vtoroye,* or main course, for which meat, poultry or fish may be served. Russians like particularly to serve chicken to guests, because for them it's a luxury. There might be a regional specialty, such as *pel'meni* (Siberian dumplings) or *plov* (rice pilaf). Soup is served at midday, but rarely, if ever, at the evening meal. It goes without saying that more drinking accompanies the main meal. I was dismayed to find that even when excellent Georgian wines are served, they are chugged Russian-style, like vodka.

But no matter how fast one drinks, one must try to eat slowly, because once one's plate is empty, it will be heaped again with more food before one has a chance to protest. The Russians still equate a large belly with good health. They say: "If you want to be well-fed, sit next to the hostess; if you want to get drunk, sit next to the host." Both host and hostess are compulsive about refilling glasses and plates. And each time a glass is refilled, a new toast must be raised. A full glass calls for a new toast, and each toast justifies a new glass, so either way the final outcome is inevitable. A guest's foolish smile and lethargic gait at the end of the evening indicate to his hosts that they have served him well.

Following the main course, the table is cleared of everything except bottles and glasses, but this is often a delayed process. Since there is no living room *per se* in Russian apartments, the whole evening is spent around the table. Often neighbors from upstairs or down the hall will drop in, and room is always made for them, chairs are always found. The hostess busies herself in the kitchen preparing tea, or sometimes coffee, though the Russian tea is far better. Many homes have small electric samovars to set on the table for a distinctive touch. (The old-fashioned coal-heated samovar has long since disappeared from Russian homes, except as an ornament.) Along with the tea, an assortment of pies, cakes, sweet breads and chocolates is presented. There are rarely fewer than three desserts to choose from, and usually one must taste a little of each. Although the Russians are great tea drinkers, they often have only one cup before continuing to work on the vodka, wine or cognac that is still standing on the table. Or they will bring out a treasured liqueur— a homemade cordial or a hard-to-obtain distillation, such as Riga's famed Balsam, with the scent and flavor of pine resin.

The Russians love to entertain at home, but sometimes they go out to restaurants, often in large parties, placing their orders in advance. When they arrive at the restaurant, the tables are already set with *zakuski,* artistically displayed, and with a range of sparkling bottles and glasses. After the marvelous *zakuski,* restaurant second courses always disappointed me, as did the inevitable restaurant atmosphere. The Soviet conception of a chic restaurant is the opposite of ours: a live band playing Western pop music at ear-splitting levels is invariably offered as the evening's entertainment, making conversation almost impossible. And judging by Soviet reaction, the louder the music, the more chic the restaurant.

· SHOPPING FOR FOOD ·

The center of activity in any Soviet city is the marketplace. The market opens around six in the morning, when women on their way to work will stop and buy fresh produce for the evening meal. Later in the day the old grandmothers, the *babushki,* appear for their shopping. Worldly-wise Soviet citizens carry an expandable string bag at all times. The bag is jocularly referred to as an *avos'ka,* a "just-in-case"—just in case something good should appear at the market or on the street that day. The market is lined with rows of stalls manned by country folk selling the vegetables they have grown on the tiny private plots allotted them by the state. Selling at the market is lucrative for them, since their goods command a high price. Most shoppers still prefer the expensive market to the cheaper state-run stores, where produce is generally of poor quality and where one can find only old onions, carrots, turnips and cabbage.

At the market old men sit behind large burlap sacks bursting with sunflower seeds. (Russians chew these seeds all day: the floors of buses and public buildings are littered with the hulls.) There are mounds of freshly ground spices: paprika in graduated degrees of piquancy and color; *khmeli-suneli,* a wonderfully fragrant Georgian spice mixture with coriander, dill and pepper; aromatic nutmeg and cinnamon for baking pies and breads. Bunches of fresh parsley, dill and coriander are splayed randomly along the counters. Scallions, cucumbers, cabbages and root vegetables create a medley of color and form. Honey glistens golden in the comb or in crystals; it can also be had boiled if one brings one's own jar. Live geese and ducks lie with feet bound to prevent their escape;

pig's heads and pig's feet startle the casual shopper. Fresh sour cream and cottage cheese lend a heady smell to the air, along with salted cucumbers and mushrooms and soused apples soaked in their own juice. Springtime is the best season at the marketplace: the air is redolent with the blossoms of thousands of lilacs, peonies and carnations.

Since Russians have very little storage space and only tiny refrigerators at home, they go to the market almost every day. They buy bread daily, too, but it never lasts long enough to grow stale. Recently, self-service grocery stores have appeared in the Soviet Union, considerably easing the burden of buying food, but the majority of groceries, or *gastronomy,* still require laborious shopping. The system is such that one must wait in several lines to buy even a single item: first, to see what's available; next, to pay the cashier; and finally, to relinquish the cash receipt to the salesgirl in exchange for the purchase. Sometimes it's easier to seek out a *kulinariya,* where one can buy a few ready-made products like risen dough ready for baking, prepared beet and potato salads, and frozen *pel'meni* all set for the pot.

If one feels like eating during the day, there are innumerable street stands to satisfy all sorts of cravings. The most popular are the ice-cream stands. Even in the dead of winter, when the temperature drops well below zero, bare hands eagerly clasp *trubochki* or *batonchiki* and icy lips happily lick the frozen mass. Even in subzero temperatures Russian ice cream is delicious! After being chilled by a cone, frozen fingers can be warmed on a steaming hot *pirozhok* from another stand. The *pirozhki* on the streets are juicy fried morsels of ground meat wrapped in dough. They are often greasy but nonetheless satisfying in the icy air. There are kiosks that sell all kinds of cookies and rusks, and kiosks that sell chocolates, caramels and bonbons. I always found it amusing to watch the candy vendor weigh out my purchase: if the scale registered 210 grams instead of the 200 I'd asked for, she'd simply lop off a corner of one of the candies, wrapper and all, to make the weight exact. I never minded this, as it gave me an excuse to eat the damaged piece right away.

My favorite outdoor stand in Moscow was opposite the Kursk Railway Station. (Sadly, it was replaced by a Pepsi stand for the 1980 Olympics.) When the kiosk was open and the vats in operation, a cloud of hot steam rose up into the cold air, beckoning from a good distance away. Here they made the best *ponchiki* (doughnuts) in Moscow: piping hot balls dripping with fat and liberally sprinkled with powdered sugar. The vendor filled a paper cone with doughnuts and offered hot coffee. High tables are still set in the ground in front of the kiosk, but one can no longer stand there and eat doughnuts to one's heart's content.

Passing through the countryside and the seasons, one is well advised to arrive in Kiev in the summertime. There, old women in brightly colored scarves almost hiding their creased faces display homemade *medivnyk* (honey cake). The cakes are so rich in honey that swarms of bees always surround them. One takes a slight risk in reaching for a slice—but it's well worth it! Finally, as in every city, rows of automated machines dispense *gazirovannaya voda* (carbonated water), a favorite Russian refresher. A glass of plain soda water costs only 1 kopek, but for 3 kopeks the machine mixes in some flavored syrup. Unfortunately, the machines use only one glass. After inserting money in the slot, one must hold the glass upside down over a brush that ostensibly washes the lip of the glass—with cold water. No one *seems* to get sick (at least not on the spot), although I have encountered prudent old women who carry their own glasses around with them. With luck one can find a *babushka,* instead of a machine, selling the *gazirovannaya voda,* and even a glass of plain soda water seems tastier when prepared by a grandmother's hands.

I

THE *ZAKUSKA* TABLE

o a Russian, dinner is unthinkable without *zakuski,* those imaginative "little bites" that make up the first course of a Russian meal.

The range of *zakuski* is almost infinite, from simple smoked sprats on black bread to the gray pearl of the Caspian, Beluga caviar; from sliced beet vinaigrette to button mushrooms drenched in spicy marinade. Salade Olivier (Russian Salad), savory stuffed eggs, shimmering pork brawn, tender kidneys in Madeira, eggplant caviar with its pungent tang—all these delights belong to the diversity of the *zakuska* spread.

This first course may offer only a few modest dishes to whet the appetite, or it may feature a stunning array of twenty or more items, both hot and cold, each designed to complement, not overshadow, its neighbor. *Zakuski* may be as straightforward as bread smeared with herbed butter, or they may require hours of preparation, as does cold fish in aspic. But whether humble or grand, *zakuski* are the *sine qua non* of the Russian table, integral to the spirit of Russian dining.

In any discussion of Russian hors d'oeuvres, what comes to mind first is caviar, the near-legendary roe of the sturgeon. Fresh caviar is indeed sumptuous enough to serve alone as a featured first course, and should one wish to dine in the style of the tsars, it is still very nearly possible to do so. First, one must procure the freshest available caviar, preferably the large-grained gray Beluga. (The tsars themselves often dined on a rare variety of golden caviar from the prized Volga sterlet, but as this great waterway has since been polluted and the fish stocks depleted, we must substitute the hardly less exquisite Beluga.)

The caviar should be served with a silver spoon in a crystal or silver bowl over ice—any other metal will interfere with the delicate taste of the roe. Next to the caviar place rounds of French bread, the nearest approximation to the Russian *kalach* (fine ring-shaped loaf). A small tub of unsalted butter should also be provided, but true aficionados scorn the lemon, chopped onion and egg that often accompany the lesser grades of caviar.

Now this royal *zakuska* is halfway complete, needing only a beverage to complement the slightly salty taste of the roe. And what could be more fitting for tsars than sparkling champagne? Here, the contemporary consumer is in luck, for the firm that once purveyed champagne to the tsars of Russia now makes it available to the Western world. This champagne is Louis Roederer Cristal, said by many to be the finest in the world. While most champagne comes in bottles tinted green, with a punt, or indentation, in the bottom to catch the sediment, Roederer's bottle is crystal clear, with a flat, puntless, bottom. According to one account, Roederer developed his unusual bottle especially for Tsar Alexander III, who was ever fearful for his life after his father's assassination. Alexander wanted his favorite champagne to be immediately recognizable, lest someone try to poison him. Hence Roederer's clear crystal bottle (alas, now made of glass). But the punt caused some worry, too: an anarchist might slip a homemade bomb into the bottle's depression, and the champagne, wrapped in a linen napkin for serving, would still look innocuous. And so the puntless bottom was born. Following the October Revolution, Roederer stopped supplying the Russians with champagne because they failed to pay their bills, but he did not stop producing his original bottles. It is interesting to note that the Soviets today produce, in very limited quantities, an exceptional champagne (their *zolotoye,* "golden") in clear glass bottles with completely flat bottoms.

For those of us without the pocketbook of a tsar, however, there are other, less expensive caviars, and Russian vodka to accompany them. Only one step down from the Beluga is the black Osetrova caviar, smaller-grained but with a magnificent taste. The *osyotr* sturgeon itself is smaller, weighing on the average 700 pounds, while the beluga sturgeon can weigh up to several thousand pounds and yield 200 pounds of roe. The Osetrova caviar is followed in grade by Sevryuga, which comes from the smallest sturgeon, the stellate, and hence has the smallest grains of all the fine caviars.

One can also find *payusnaya* caviar, highly thought of in the Soviet Union, though less appreciated in the West. This pressed caviar is made from damaged eggs, which are crushed to form a rather sticky paste, less subtle in flavor than the undamaged roe. *Payusnaya* caviar has traditionally served as soldiers' rations during their long stints at the front, as it is much less perishable and consequently less expensive than the fresh caviar.

Some roe lovers favor the brightly colored eggs of the salmon, ranging in hue from deep orange to soft red. While black caviar calls for white bread, salmon roe tastes best on black, and a little chopped onion and lemon juice here are no crime. Russian émigrés living in Scandinavia enjoy the tiny golden *löjrom* from whitefish, which they mix with fresh cream and serve over toast. It is unfortunate that the dyed lumpfish roe produced mainly in Iceland so often substitutes for the real thing, as the taste of lumpfish roe is in no way comparable to that of fresh caviar. Sadly, even in the Soviet Union caviar is becoming more and more scarce. (It is ironic that the seventeenth-century nobility found it so plentiful that they often boiled it in vinegar or poppy-seed milk for a change of pace.) One hopeful sign is the development of a caviar industry in western America, which promises to make real caviar more accessible to all.

If caviar comes to mind first for getting a Russian meal off to a good start, then vodka is not far behind, and when a liberal amount of the potent stuff is supplied to guests, the meal not only will be off to a fast start, but to a rollicking one as well. Russians love their vodka, a fact apparent in the word itself, for *vodka* is an affectionate diminutive of *voda,* "water," the most elemental substance of all.

Strong drink has always been important to the Russian people, even as far back as the tenth century A.D., when Grand Prince Vladimir, the first ruler of unified Russia, was searching for a religion under which to govern his still-heathen land. Vladimir called in representatives of the Islamic and Christian faiths for consultation and was all set to accept Islam as the new faith of Rus' when he learned that religious law forbade the consumption of alcoholic beverages. Vladimir was appalled. Hardly hesitating at all, he declared Christianity the new faith of his nation, proclaiming, "Drinking is the joy of Rus'!" Little has changed since those ancient days: drinking is still Russia's joy, as well as its bane. Recently, factories have begun installing samovars to encourage the drinking of tea over vodka, but it does little good. Once a Russian is drunk, his only recourse, by popular belief, is to cure himself with the hair of the dog that bit him, which leads only to more drinking.

But vodka should not be blamed. It is an excellent beverage and, taken in moderation, provides a perfect balance to the salty tidbits of the *zakuska* table. A proper *zakuska* course should offer at least several different varieties of well-chilled flavored vodkas. Many of these are easy to prepare at home by infusing a good-quality plain vodka with fresh herbs or citrus peel, or with golden strands of saffron or crushed cherry pits. Less common are such specialties as a dusky, mauve vodka made from litmus (a lichen extract), or garnet *ryabinovka,* infused with the autumnal berries of the mountain ash tree. Some connoisseurs prefer pale-blue cornflower vodka, others *kedrovka,* with its startling essence of cedar. In Gogol's food-heavy tale "Old-World Landowners," Pulkheria Ivanovna presents her own array of healthful vodkas at the *zakuska* table.

Pulkheria Ivanovna was most entertaining when she led her guests to the *zakuska* table. "Now this," she would say, removing the stopper from a flask, "is vodka infused with St. John's wort and sage. If the small of your back or your shoulder blade aches, it really hits the spot. This vodka over here is made with centaury. If you've got a ringing in your ears or shingles on your face, it's just the thing. And this one's distilled from peach pits— here, take a glass, what a wonderful smell! If you've bumped your head against the corner of a cupboard or the table when getting out of bed, and a lump's sprung up on your forehead, then all you have to do is drink a glassful before dinner. The minute you take your hand away, the lump will disappear, as if it had never been there at all."

While not all vodkas are guaranteed to heal, it is true that they'll take the pain away. Of the clear vodkas, the best is *pshenichnaya,* distilled from grain rather than potatoes, with a taste as pure as liquid crystal. Unfortunately, this vodka is rarely found outside the Soviet Union, but other good Russian or Polish vodkas make excellent substitutes. It is best to shun the cheaper American brands, as they taste overwhelmingly of alcohol and are impossible to drink straight, well suited as they may be for mixed drinks. Russian vodka is drunk *only* straight, never mixed with other beverages—unless one is intent upon getting drunk fast and opts for the old Russian *yorsh,* a blending of vodka and beer designed to make one's hair stand on end (in imitation, no doubt, of the fish of the same name with protruding spines on its fins).

Vodka should be kept in the freezer at all times, ready for the unexpected guest. Its high alcohol content keeps it from freezing, while the liquid turns delightfully viscous. (The sensation of thick, ice-cold vodka surging down one's throat is not soon forgotten.) Besides being drunk very cold, vodka is customarily gulped down in a single swallow, the liquid tossed far back into the mouth. The reason is a practical one: if vodka is sipped, one inhales the fumes, and the fumes are what cause drunkenness faster than the drink itself. Or so the Russians claim. In Chekhov's "The Siren," the court stenographer explains the proper way to approach vodka:

> . . . when you sit down you should immediately put a napkin around your neck and then, very slowly, reach for the carafe of vodka. Now you don't pour the dear stuff into any old glass . . . oh no! You must pour it into an antediluvian glass made of silver, one which belonged to your grandfather, or into a pot-bellied glass bearing the inscription "Even Monks Imbibe!" And you don't drink the vodka down right away. No, sir. First you take a deep breath, wipe your hands, and glance up at the ceiling to demonstrate your indifference. Only then do you raise that vodka slowly to your lips and suddenly—sparks! They fly from your stomach to the furthest reaches of your body.

There are many rituals associated with the drinking of vodka. Traditionally, on the eve of his wedding, a Russian bridegroom was made to drink vodka from full glasses spelling out the name of his sweetheart. Woe to him if her name was Apollinaria! In Fyodor Sologub's novel *The Petty Demon,* guests of the wily host Skuchaev find themselves participating in a strange game called Pour and Drink Up, in which Skuchaev serves his unwitting guests vodka from glasses whose bases have been sharpened to a narrow point, so that it is impossible to set them down without their toppling over. As long as the guest holds an empty glass (as he inevitably does, since the vodka is downed in a single swig), hospitality demands that it be refilled, and so Skuchaev has come up with a sure way to get his guests drunk.

In literature the most famous *zakuska* table is no doubt the one set by the Chief of Police in Gogol's novel *Dead Souls.* Intended to impress, the meal is ordered on the spur of the moment, and impress is exactly what it does. The spread includes several varieties of fresh sturgeon, including beluga, also smoked salmon, freshly salted caviar and pressed caviar, herring, all sorts of cheeses, smoked tongue, salt-dried sturgeon fillets, an amazing fish pie (*pirog*) made from the head and cheeks of a 325-pound sturgeon and another pie stuffed with choice wild mushrooms. This *zakuska* menu more than reflects the Russian love of fish; today it would be balanced by more meat and vegetable dishes. But if one gets the impression that the "small bite" of the *zakuska* is often a feast in itself, that's not at all incorrect. Indeed a delightful way to entertain Russian-style is to set up a large *zakuska* table around which guests can circulate freely before heading into the dining room for the proper main course.

There are a few basic rules to follow in laying a *zakuska* table, not the least of which concerns the shape of the table itself. It should be oval or round and placed away from the wall, so that all foods are accessible to all guests at all times. Small plates, forks and napkins are arranged at opposite ends of the table so that service may start simultaneously from both sides. Along the outer edges of the table are placed the various *zakuski,* hot along one side, cold on the other. Beyond the *zakuski,* closer in toward the center of the table, are baskets or plates piled high with bread, both black and white, and mounds of unsalted butter molded in fancy shapes. In the very center of the table stand carafes of flavored vodka surrounded by small shot glasses, or *ryumochki.* Cognac may also be provided for the more timid guests.

The recipes in this chapter cover a wide range of *zakuski,* which may be served singly as the opening to a simple meal, or in pairs, or as part of a more impressive board. But they are only a small sampling of all the possibilities for *zakuska,* as the range of this first course is limited only by one's imagination. And while such dishes as pâté of meadowlark and wild boar's jaws *en gelée* are no longer required for the table's diversity, a fine array may be made by using recipes from this book. For an even grander display, the homemade *zakuski* may be supplemented by prepared specialties from the delicatessen. Here are a few suggestions:

Cured fish and meats of all kinds, particularly hot-smoked and cold-smoked sturgeon; smoked eel layered with lemon slices; thin wafers of smoked salmon; sardines in oil and in various sauces; kippered herrings; Norwegian anchovies (*kil'ki*); sliced beef tongue; cured ham (Polish-style and Westphalian); smoked turkey; roast beef or chicken shaped into thin rolls; head cheese; Russian bologna; various salamis and sausages;

Marinated vegetables, such as pickled beets; pickled green tomatoes; green olives and black olives; pickled hot peppers;

Hard cheeses of all types, sliced very thinly;

Fresh seafood, such as oysters on the half shell; crab legs with mayonnaise; bay shrimp with homemade tartar sauce;

Cocktail meatballs (*tefteli*) in tomato sauce;

Freshly boiled potatoes tossed with dill.

In addition, the following recipes from other chapters of this book are also excellent on the *zakuska* table:

Armenian Flat Bread
Barrel-Cured Sauerkraut
Barrel-Style Dill Pickles
Beet Salad
Buckwheat Groats with Mushrooms and Cream
Carrot Salad
Celeriac Salad
Cold Stuffed Eggplant
Cottage Cheese Tartlets
Coulibiac of Salmon
Cranberry-Horseradish Relish

Cucumbers in Sour Cream
Dried Fish
Estonian Potato Salad
Fresh Ham Cooked with Hay
Georgian Cheese Pie
Georgian-Style Kidney Beans
Mushrooms in Sour Cream
Pickled Eggplant
Pirozhki with Savory Filling
Prepared Horseradish
Radishes in Sour Cream

Russian Black Bread
Russian Pancakes (*blini*)
Rye Bread
Salted Mushrooms
Sour Cabbage
Sourdough White Bread
Soused Apples
Spiced Pickled Cherries
Stuffed Cabbage Leaves
Wine Bowl

NOTE: In the pages that follow, recipes are, as you will see, set in italics. Sometimes the name of a recipe is given that is set in roman; this means that it is given elsewhere in the book and may be looked up in the Index.

FLAVORED VODKAS

The following flavored vodkas are simple to prepare at home. After infusing, keep them in the freezer for best results.

Anise Vodka/
Anisovaya: Place 2 teaspoons whole anise seed in 1 pint of plain vodka and infuse at room temperature for 24 hours. Strain.

Apricot Vodka/
Abrikosovaya: Place one dozen apricot kernels in 1 pint of plain vodka and infuse at room temperature for 24 hours. Strain.

Black-Currant-Bud
Vodka/
Smorodinovka: Pick the buds of black currants when they are still sticky. Place a handful in 1 pint of plain vodka and infuse at room temperature for 24 hours. Strain. An alternative method is to make a very strong infusion in only ¼ pint of vodka and then add 10 to 12 drops of the essence to a bottle of plain vodka.

Cherry Vodka/
Vishnyovka: Crush 36 cherry pits and place them in 1 pint of plain vodka. Infuse at room temperature for 24 hours. Strain.

Coriander Vodka/
Koriandrovaya: Place 2 teaspoons of coriander seed, slightly crushed, in 1 pint of plain vodka and infuse at room temperature for 24 hours. Strain.

Garlic-and-Dill
Vodka/
Chesnochnaya: Place 1 clove of garlic, slightly crushed, 1 sprig of fresh dill and 3 white peppercorns in 1 pint of plain vodka. Infuse at room temperature for 24 hours. Strain. A small bit of dill may be left in the vodka, if desired.

Herb Vodka/
Travnik: Place a few sprigs of a favorite herb, such as

tarragon or basil, in 1 pint of plain vodka and infuse at room temperature for 24 hours. Strain. A small bit of the herb may be left in the vodka.

Lemon or Orange Vodka/*Limonovka:*

Remove the rind from ½ large lemon or from 1 orange in a single strip, taking care to avoid the bitter white pith. Infuse in 1 pint of plain vodka at room temperature for 24 hours. (Do not leave the peel in longer, or the vodka will turn bitter.)

Pepper Vodka/ *Pertsovka:*

Place 30 black peppercorns and 30 white peppercorns in 1 pint of plain vodka and infuse at room temperature for 24 hours. Strain.

Saffron Vodka/ *Shafrannaya:*

Place ¼ teaspoon saffron threads in 1 pint of plain vodka and infuse at room temperature for 24 hours. Strain.

Tea Vodka/ *Chainaya:*

Place 4 teaspoons black tea leaves, preferably fruit-scented, in 1 pint of plain vodka and infuse at room temperature for 24 hours. Strain.

Buffalo Grass Vodka/ *Zubrovka:*

Place 8 blades of buffalo grass in 1 pint of plain vodka and infuse at room temperature for 24 hours. One blade of grass may be left in the vodka after straining.

FRESH SALMON ROE CAVIAR
🦂 *KRASNAYA IKRA* 🦂

This recipe has traveled the globe. It came to me by way of Alla Avisov, a charming Russian woman who came to America via Germany and Venezuela. Alla loves to cook and has a file full of recipes gleaned from family and friends. Every year during the salmon spawning season, Alla and her husband delight their guests with this fresh caviar made from salmon roe.

1 sac fresh salmon roe	*2 tablespoons salt*
1 quart water	

Place the sac of salmon roe in a sieve, then place the sieve over a large bowl.

Bring the water to a boil. When it boils, add the salt. The water will foam up. Pour the boiling water over the roe immediately, shaking the sieve as you do so (it helps to have two people to carry out this task).

Lower the sieve into the water in the bowl, shaking it lightly from time to time. This process causes the roe to be released from the membranous sac enclosing it. With a wooden skewer, carefully separate the individual eggs.

With a slotted spoon, lift the roe from the water and place it in a jar. The caviar will keep in the refrigerator up to 1 week. If you wish to keep it longer, rinse the roe a second time with a salt solution and pour a little vegetable oil over the top of the caviar in the jar.

NOTE: If fresh whitefish or sturgeon roe is available, it may be substituted for the salmon.

HERRING
♯ SELYODKA ♯

The most essential ingredient of the *zakuska* table is herring, its saltiness stimulating the need for ever larger doses of vodka. In Russia herring is prepared in many different ways. It may be pickled or served with savory sauces. It may be finely chopped, then molded to resemble a whole fish and garnished with a real head and tail. Or it may be fried in pieces and served with a tomato dressing. A fancy *zakuska* table boasts several of these preparations, several alternatives, but at least one is mandatory.

One of Chekhov's most delightful stories is "The Siren," in which a hungry court clerk tries to speed up a diligent judge's decision by tormenting him with a mouth-watering account of a real Russian dinner: "The best appetizer, if you'd like to know, is herring. Imagine you've eaten a bite of it with onion and mustard sauce. Just imagine! . . . Then, my benefactor, while you're still feeling sparks in your stomach, you must immediately eat some caviar, either plain or, if you prefer, with lemon; and then some radishes with salt, then some more herring . . . ," droning on and on until the poor judge, now ravenous, can bear no more and troops off to dinner, leaving his work undone.

The recipes that follow are calculated for salt herring, which must be soaked overnight before using. But if you are lucky enough to have access to fresh herring, by all means use it. It need not be soaked beforehand.

· I ·
PICKLED HERRING
☼ SELYODKA MARINOVANNAYA ☼

1 2-pound herring	4 to 6 hot dried peppers
2 cups cider vinegar	4 bay leaves
1 cup water	1½ teaspoons mustard seed
¾ cup sugar	2 teaspoons coriander seed
	24 black peppercorns
1 large onion, thinly sliced	⅔ cup black olives
1 large carrot, scraped and cut into rounds	

If using salt herring, soak it overnight in milk or buttermilk to cover. The next day, rinse it and pat it dry. Cut off the head and remove the fins. Slice the herring down the belly and open it flat. Remove the backbone, and cut the fish on the diagonal into 1-inch slices.

In a saucepan bring the vinegar, water and sugar to a boil. Cook until the sugar dissolves. Set aside.

In 2 large preserving jars layer the remaining ingredients with the slices of herring, making sure that the spices are evenly distributed. Pour the marinade over all.

Close the jars tightly and leave the herring to age in the refrigerator for at least 5 days before serving. To serve, place the herring in decorative bowls and garnish with the onion slices, olives and some of the marinade.

Yield: 10 to 12 *zakuska* servings.

· II ·

HERRING IN SOUR CREAM
🌸 *SELYODKA V SMETANE* 🌸

1 recipe Pickled Herring *(see above), drained*
¼ cup pickling liquid from the herring

1 cup sour cream

Onion slices, olives

Arrange the pickled herring on a dish.

Mix together the pickling liquid and the sour cream. Pour the mixture over the herring and garnish with a few onion slices and olives.

Yield: 10 to 12 *zakuska* servings.

· III ·

HERRING IN DILL SAUCE
🌸 *SELYODKA POD UKROPNYM SOUSOM* 🌸

1 pound herring
½ cup olive oil
¼ cup red wine vinegar

2 tablespoons snipped fresh dill (or 2 teaspoons dried dill)
2 teaspoons sugar

Prepare the herring as for pickling, cutting it diagonally into 1-inch slices.

Mix together the remaining ingredients and pour the sauce over the herring slices. Chill for several hours before serving.

Yield: 6 first-course servings; more as a *zakuska*.

· IV ·
HERRING IN MUSTARD SAUCE
❀ *SELYODKA S GORCHICHNOI PRIPRAVOI* ❀

1 pound herring	*3 tablespoons sour cream*
6 tablespoons olive oil	*2 teaspoons capers, drained*
3 tablespoons prepared mustard	*(reserve a few for garnish)*

Prepare the herring as for pickling, cutting it diagonally into 1-inch slices.

Mix together the olive oil and mustard. Stir in the sour cream and capers. Pour the sauce over the prepared herring and chill for several hours before serving.

Yield: 6 first-course servings; more as a *zakuska*.

MARINATED SMOKED SALMON
SYOMGA MARINOVANNAYA

Marinating such delectable (and expensive) fish may seem like a sacrilege, but the end result need only be tasted to prove its worth.

½ pound smoked salmon, in
  slices
1 large Bermuda onion, sliced
  and separated into rings
8 black peppercorns
1 large bay leaf, crushed

¼ teaspoon mustard seed
½ cup olive oil
½ cup vegetable oil
½ cup white wine vinegar
2 cloves garlic, crushed
1 teaspoon salt

In a 1-quart jar alternate layers of the smoked salmon, onion rings, peppercorns, bay leaf and mustard seed.

In a small bowl mix well the oils, vinegar, garlic and salt.

Pour the dressing over the salmon layers. Seal the jar and store in the refrigerator for at least 1 week before serving. Have plenty of black bread on hand to serve with the salmon.

Yield: 8 zakuska servings.

CANAPÉS OF SMOKED SALMON
🐟 *BUTERBROD S SYOMGOI* 🐟

Black beads of caviar are highlighted against the brilliant pink of smoked salmon in these lovely hors d'oeuvres, which take only minutes to prepare. They may be held in the refrigerator for several hours, covered, before serving.

¼ cup heavy cream
1 tablespoon prepared
  horseradish
6 pieces of thinly sliced black
  bread, cut into quarters

¼ pound smoked salmon,
  sliced
3 tablespoons sour cream
4 teaspoons black caviar
Parsley

Whip the cream until it forms soft peaks. Fold in the horseradish. Spread each quarter of bread with some of this mixture.

Top the whipped cream with a thin slice of smoked salmon.

Top each slice of salmon with a dab of sour cream, and then sprinkle a little caviar over the sour cream, pressing down lightly so it will stay in place.

Tuck a tiny piece of parsley into the whipped cream on each square. Chill.

Yield: 2 dozen canapés.

SMELTS IN TOMATO SAUCE
🦐 KORYUSHKI V TOMATNOM SOUSE 🦐

The slightly sweet tomato sauce masking these fried smelts provides a nice balance for a *zakuska* table laden with pickled fish and vegetables. If frozen smelts are available, they may be used directly from the freezer. This is an excellent appetizer.

½ pound smelts
1 egg
1 tablespoon cold water
⅓ cup fine dry bread crumbs
¼ cup olive oil

2 tablespoons olive oil
2 medium onions, sliced
  paper-thin
2 medium carrots, scraped and
  sliced into ¼-inch-thick
  rounds

½ cup tomato paste
1 cup chicken stock
1 teaspoon salt
2 tablespoons dark brown sugar
¼ cup red wine vinegar
8 slices of lemon, each ⅛-inch
  thick

Parsley

Beat together the egg and cold water. Dip the smelts in this mixture and then in the bread crumbs until well coated. Heat the ¼ cup of olive oil in a large frying pan and fry the smelts until golden on both sides, about 5 to 6 minutes. Do not overcook.

Remove the smelts from the frying pan and set aside. Wipe the skillet and then pour in the remaining 2 tablespoons of olive oil. Fry the onions and carrots in the oil until tender, about 15 minutes. Stir in the remaining ingredients and simmer, covered, for 15 minutes. Cool the sauce to room temperature.

After the sauce has cooled, remove the lemon slices. Arrange the smelts on a plate and pour the sauce over them, turning them once to coat. Chill for several hours before serving, garnished with parsley.

Yield: 4 servings.

TURBOT IN DILL MARINADE
🎏 *PALTUS V MARINADE S UKROPOM* 🎏

Here is an interesting way to use up the leftover brine from a jar of dill pickles. This spicy fish may be served either plain or on squares of black bread.

2 pounds turbot fillets	⅛ teaspoon mustard seed
Salt, freshly ground black pepper to taste	2 teaspoons snipped fresh dill (or ½ teaspoon dried dill)
1 onion, sliced into very thin rings	4 cups brine from jar of dill pickles
1 clove garlic, minced	
1 bay leaf	Lemon, thinly sliced
8 black peppercorns	Minced parsley
¼ teaspoon crushed dried red pepper	Fresh dill

Preheat the oven to 350°F. Season the fish with salt and pepper. Lightly grease an oven-proof dish and place the fish in it. Sprinkle the onion, garlic and spices evenly over the fish fillets. Pour the dill brine over all.

Cover the dish. Bring the fish to a simmer over medium heat on top of the stove, then transfer the dish to the preheated oven. Poach the fish for about 15 minutes, depending on the thickness of the fillets, until the fish is flaky but still holds its shape.

Cool the fish to room temperature in its marinade, then chill overnight. The next day, remove the fish from the marinade, cut the fillets into bite-sized pieces and arrange them on a glass plate, garnished with thinly sliced lemon, minced parsley and sprigs of fresh dill.

Yield: 10 *zakuska* servings.

NOTE: If an even spicier dish is desired, add more crushed red pepper and mustard seed.

The fish may also be served hot from the oven as a main course, in which case the fillets are left whole to make 4 servings.

COLD FISH IN ASPIC
❧ RYBA ZALIVNAYA ❧

This poached fish in aspic is a mosaic of color and form, as though seen through the surface of a pond. A stunning addition to the *zakuska* table.

1 3-pound fish (any firm white-fleshed fish will do; I often use red snapper)	¼ cup dry white wine
	4 teaspoons tomato paste
	4 egg whites, lightly beaten
6 cups cold water	3 packages unflavored gelatin
2 cups dry white wine	(¾ ounce)
1 onion, quartered	½ cup cold water
1 carrot, scraped	
3 sprigs parsley	Sliced dill pickles
2 sprigs dill (or ½ teaspoon dried dill)	Sliced olives
	Capers
1 bay leaf	Lemon slices
10 white peppercorns	Pimiento
1½ to 2 teaspoons salt	

In a stockpot place the water, the 2 cups of wine and the onion, carrot, parsley, dill, bay leaf, peppercorns and salt. Bring to a boil over high heat and then simmer, covered, for 20 minutes. This is the poaching liquid.

Place the fish in a poacher along with the poaching liquid (court bouillon). Poach until tender, about 25 minutes. Carefully remove the fish and set aside to cool. Strain the liquid, reserving the carrot.

Remove the skin, head, tail and bones from the fish. With a fork, gently separate the flesh into fairly large pieces. Do not flake it finely.

Place the strained fish stock in a large kettle. Add the ¼ cup of wine, tomato paste, egg whites and gelatin, which has been dissolved in the ½ cup of cold water. Stir well. Bring the liquid to a rolling boil and remove from the heat. Let stand for 15 minutes. Then strain. The liquid should now be completely clear.

Lightly grease a 2-quart mold with vegetable oil. (I like to use a large, shallow round one, about 12 inches in diameter.) Pour in about 1 cup of the warm aspic* and set the pan in the refrigerator until the aspic has jelled.

On the jelled aspic arrange the carrot, which has been chopped, and the pickles, olives, capers, lemon slices and pimiento in a decorative pattern. Carefully pour enough warm aspic over the vegetables to cover them. Set the pan in the refrigerator and chill until this layer has hardened.

Place the fish in a single layer on the jelled layer of aspic, then pour the remaining liquid over it. Chill for at least 4 hours, until completely firm.

To unmold, run a knife around the edges of the mold to loosen, then dip the mold very briefly in hot water. Invert onto a plate.

Serve the aspic with spicy Russian-Style Mustard or with Mayonnaise and Sour Cream Sauce (see below).

Yield: 12 to 16 servings.

* The amount of aspic poured into the bottom of the mold depends on the size and shape of the mold. There should be only a thin layer so that the pattern of vegetables will clearly show through once the aspic is inverted. If you are using a deep mold with a smaller diameter, pour in just enough aspic to cover the bottom in a thin layer. You may also want to add the fish in several layers alternating with aspic, instead of just one.

MAYONNAISE AND SOUR CREAM SAUCE
✿ SOUS PROVENSAL' ✿

2 egg yolks	1 cup (or more) olive oil
1 teaspoon prepared mustard	
2 tablespoons wine vinegar	5 egg whites
1 teaspoon salt	1½ cups sour cream

In a bowl mix the egg yolks, mustard, vinegar and salt. Slowly, drop by drop, beat in the olive oil with a steady motion, until a good thick mayonnaise is formed, adding more oil if necessary.

Beat the egg whites until stiff but not dry. Fold them into the sour cream. Add the sour cream mixture to the mayonnaise mixture and stir well. Chill.

RUSSIAN LIVER PÂTÉ
❦ PASHTET IZ PECHONKI ❦

Once, as I entered a Moscow restaurant, my attention was riveted by the *zakuski* displayed on a long table. There appeared to be tiny hedgehogs arranged in conversational clusters on a bed of chopped scallion, as if at a garden party. However, closer inspection revealed them to be molded out of liver pâté, with whole cloves for the eyes and piped butter for the quills. Although aware of the Russian penchant for small woodland creatures, I was still surprised at the strange shape that fancy took. Personally, I prefer the excellent Russian liver pâté served plain and unadorned, rather than in the shape of small animals. But that, of course, is a matter of taste. The *pashtet* may be prepared from either chicken or calf's liver.

1 pound chicken livers (or calf's liver, cut into strips)	*1 large egg*
⅓ cup butter	*2 slices home-style white bread, crusts removed*
2 large onions, thinly sliced	*½ cup rich chicken stock*
1 teaspoon salt	
⅛ teaspoon freshly ground black pepper	

Melt the butter in a large frying pan, add the onions and cook until golden. Add the chicken livers and continue cooking for about 10 minutes, or until the livers are no longer pink.

In a food processor or blender combine the cooked onions, livers, salt, pepper, egg, bread and stock. Chop very fine, until the texture is smooth.

Preheat the oven to 350°F. Grease a 9-inch loaf pan and spoon the liver mixture into it.

Bake for 45 minutes. Cool the pâté to room temperature, then chill thoroughly before serving. Either turn the pâté out onto a plate or spoon it into a bowl.

Yield: 8 first-course servings; more as a *zakuska*.

ROAST MEAT AND HERRING SOUFFLÉ
⚔ *FORSHMAK* ⚔

This is a mixture of minced cooked meats and herring, blended with eggs to make a pudding not unlike a heavy soufflé. As so often happens in cross-lingual borrowings, the German *Vorschmack* ("foretaste" or "foreboding") has come to mean "appetizer" in this Russian dish. *Forshmak* is substantial enough to serve for a luncheon, but I prefer it as a *zakuska,* baked in a hollowed-out French loaf as in the Variation below.

1 pound roast meat (beef, veal or lamb in any combination)	3 eggs, separated Salt, freshly ground black pepper to taste
1 large onion, chopped	
2 tablespoons butter	
½ salt herring (6 ounces), soaked overnight, bones removed	2 tablespoons grated Parmesan cheese
3 potatoes, boiled and peeled	2 tablespoons fine dry bread crumbs
½ cup sour cream	2 tablespoons butter

Soak the salt herring overnight in milk or water to cover. The next day pat it dry and, after removing all the fins and bones, chop it coarsely. It does not have to be skinned.

Fry the onion in the 2 tablespoons of butter until golden.

In a meat grinder or food processor, grind together the roast meat, sautéed onion, chopped herring and boiled potatoes finely. Then stir in the sour cream and the egg yolks. Season to taste, but be careful with the salt, as the herring will still be rather salty.

Beat the egg whites until stiff but not dry.

Preheat the oven to 400°F. Grease a 2-quart oven-proof baking form.

Fold the egg whites into the meat mixture and turn the mixture into the greased form. Sprinkle with the grated cheese and bread crumbs. Dot with the remaining butter. Bake for 35 to 40 minutes, until puffed and brown.

Yield: About 10 servings.

VARIATION: To make *forshmak v kalache* (*forshmak* baked in a loaf), scoop the soft insides out of a loaf of French bread, a ring-shaped one if possible. Fill the hollow with the prepared *forshmak* mixture. Bake as directed above.

CHICKEN AND MUSHROOMS *EN COCOTTE*
☙ *ZHUL'YEN KURINYI V KOKOTNITSAKH* ☙

A French dish adapted for the Russian table.

½ pound cooked chicken
1 large onion
¼ pound mushrooms, trimmed
4 tablespoons butter
Salt, freshly ground white
  pepper to taste

3 tablespoons sour cream
Freshly grated nutmeg

½ cup grated Swiss-style cheese
1 tablespoon butter

Mince the chicken and set aside. Mince the onion and mushrooms.

In a frying pan melt the 4 tablespoons of butter. Cook the onion for about 5 minutes, until it begins to soften, then stir in the mushrooms and chicken. Continue to cook for about 5 minutes more, adding salt and pepper to taste.

Remove the pan from the heat and stir in the sour cream. Add nutmeg to taste.

Preheat the oven to 400°F. Divide the chicken mixture among four greased ramekins. Top each ramekin with 2 tablespoons of grated cheese and a dab of butter. Bake for 10 minutes, or until bubbly. Serve hot.

Yield: 4 servings.

KIDNEYS IN MADEIRA
❧ POCHKI V MADERE ❧

The railway buffet at Tsarskoye Selo, the royal retreat, was famed for its version of these succulent kidneys. Ironically, in Andrei Belyi's novel *Petersburg,* they were also the dish chosen by Nikolai Apollonovich at a moment of high suspense, when he might be revealed as a political terrorist. But politics aside, Kidneys in Madeira is a lovely *zakuska,* befitting the tables of both anarchists and tsars.

3 veal kidneys (or 6 lamb kidneys)	1¼ cups Madeira
Salt, freshly ground black pepper to taste	½ cup beef or chicken stock
Flour	6 tiny new potatoes, boiled and peeled
8 tablespoons butter	Minced parsley
¼ pound mushrooms, trimmed and sliced	

Remove the membranes from the kidneys, then soak the kidneys in cold water for 30 minutes. Pat dry. Cut the kidneys crosswise into ¼-inch-thick slices. Season with salt and pepper and dredge with flour.

Melt half of the butter (4 tablespoons). Quickly fry the mushrooms in the butter, for only about 4 minutes, then transfer them to a dish. Place the remaining butter in the pan. Add the kidney slices and brown them quickly over high heat, about 5 minutes. Transfer to the dish with the mushrooms.

Add ¼ cup of the Madeira to the pan to deglaze it. Then stir in the stock and the remaining wine. Return the kidneys and mushrooms to the pan and simmer gently for 15 minutes.

Just before serving, stir in the peeled potatoes. Serve from a chafing dish, garnished with parsley.

Yield: 6 *zakuska* servings.

EGGPLANT CAVIAR
🐟 BAKLAZHANNAYA IKRA 🐟

For those unable to afford the luxury of fish roe at their tables, this finely chopped eggplant dish presents a tasty alternative—hence its nickname "poor man's caviar." This spicy "caviar" originated in the Caucasus and was adopted by the Russians into their own cuisine. It is best served on thick slices of black bread. Try to resist eating the caviar right away so the flavors can meld overnight in the refrigerator.

3 small eggplants (about 2½ pounds)
½ cup olive oil
2 medium onions, finely chopped
1 green pepper, finely chopped
4 cloves garlic, crushed
3 large tomatoes, peeled and finely chopped (or 1 28-ounce can of plum tomatoes, drained and finely chopped)
1 generous teaspoon honey
1 tablespoon salt
Freshly ground black pepper to taste

Juice of 1 lemon

Place the eggplants in a baking dish and bake in a preheated 375°F oven until tender, about 45 minutes. Set aside to cool.

Meanwhile, sauté the onions in the olive oil until soft but not brown. Then add the chopped green pepper and the garlic and cook until the green pepper begins to soften.

Peel the baked eggplants and chop the pulp finely. Add to the frying pan along with the chopped tomatoes, honey, salt and pepper. Bring the mixture to a boil, cover, and reduce the heat to low. Simmer for about 1 hour.

Remove the cover from the frying pan and continue to simmer the mixture until all the excess liquid has evaporated from the pan and the mixture is thick but not dry. Stir occasionally. This final simmering will take 20 to 45 minutes, depending on the consistency of the vegetables. When the mixture is ready, stir in the lemon juice and taste for seasoning. (I usually add black pepper liberally here.)

Transfer the caviar to a bowl and chill, covered, in the refrigerator for several hours or overnight.

Yield: 8 generous first-course servings; or more as a *zakuska*.

VARIATION: Yellow (Crookneck) Squash or Zucchini Caviar/*Ikra iz kabachkov*

Squash is a favorite vegetable in southern Russia. The Russian word for squash, *kabachok,* also means "little tavern." The mass of tiny seeds clustered in the flesh of the vegetable is said to be reminiscent of people clustered in a tavern.

This is a good way to use up overabundant squash from a summer garden. Simply follow the directions above for Eggplant Caviar, substituting 2½ pounds yellow squash or zucchini for the eggplants. Do not peel the squash. Bake the squash for only 15 to 20 minutes in the oven, then proceed as directed above.

NOTE: Olive oil *must* be used in these recipes for "caviar."

PORK OR VEAL BRAWN
☙ *STUDEN'*, or *KHOLODETS* ☙

This classic Russian appetizer is none other than meat (or sometimes poultry) molded in aspic. The names *studen'* and *kholodets* both derive from Slavic roots meaning "chill" and "cold," and indeed the aspic must be thoroughly chilled before unmolding. Served on a decorative platter, *studen'* is a notable addition to the *zakuska* table.

4½ quarts cold water	8 black peppercorns
2½ pounds calf's feet (or pig's feet)	1 generous tablespoon salt
1 pound lean beef chuck, plus bone (or pork loin)	2 bay leaves
1 pound chicken necks, skin removed	1 whole head garlic
	2 teaspoons salt
	½ teaspoon freshly ground
1 medium onion	black pepper or to taste
1 medium carrot	3 hard-boiled eggs

In a large stockpot heat the water until warm. Then add the calf's feet, beef and chicken necks. Bring to a boil, then immediately reduce the heat to a simmer. Skim off the foam as it rises to the surface.

When the foam has stopped rising, add the onion, carrot, peppercorns and the tablespoon of salt. Partially cover the pot and cook the broth over very low heat, at a gentle simmer, for 6 hours, until the broth is rich. It should be reduced by about one half.

One hour before the broth is ready, add the bay leaves.

After 6 hours, strain the liquid through several layers of cheesecloth into a clean pot. There should be about 2 quarts.

Discard the carrot and onion. Remove the meat from the chicken necks and shred it along with the beef.

Peel the whole head of garlic and press the cloves through a garlic press. Stir in the 2 teaspoons of salt and the black pepper. Mix well with the shredded meat.

Prepare 4 1-quart molds by brushing them very lightly with vegetable oil. Pour in enough broth to cover the bottom of the mold generously, then refrigerate until the broth has jelled. Top the jelled layer with sliced hard-boiled eggs and other garnish, if desired. Place a layer of meat on top of the eggs and pour on the remaining broth to cover.

Place in the refrigerator and allow to chill for 8 hours or overnight. Scrape off any fat that has formed on the surface.

To unmold, run a knife carefully around the edges of the jelly to loosen it. Wrap the mold for just a moment in a hot dish towel, place a serving platter over it and invert the *studen'* onto the plate. Serve the *studen'* well chilled, with a pot of spicy Russian-Style Mustard on the side.

Yield: 12 to 16 servings.

COCKTAIL SAUSAGES IN TOMATO SAUCE
🦐 *SOSISKI SOUS-TOMAT* 🦐

Always a favorite.

½ pound cocktail sausages	*Freshly ground black pepper*
1 small onion, chopped	*to taste*
2 tablespoons butter	*Dash of cayenne pepper*
½ cup tomato puree	*2 tablespoons vodka*
¼ cup beef stock	
¼ teaspoon salt	*1 tablespoon chopped parsley*

Fry the onion in butter until soft but not brown. Add the sausages and fry them until browned on all sides. Then transfer the sausages to a chafing dish to keep warm, leaving the onions and butter in the pan.

Stir the tomato puree into the onions and butter. Add the beef stock, salt, black pepper and cayenne. Then stir in the vodka. Return the sausages to the pan and heat them gently for about 15 minutes. Serve from a chafing dish, garnished with parsley.

Yield: 4 servings.

MUSHROOM CAVIAR
🗡 GRIBNAYA IKRA 🗡

This version of "caviar," made with finely chopped mushrooms and sour cream, is hardly inferior to the real thing. Thrifty cooks used to use leftover mushroom trimmings to make this dish, but it tastes even better with fresh caps and stems.

3 large scallions (including green tops), finely chopped	Cayenne pepper to taste
3 tablespoons butter	⅔ cup sour cream
¾ pound mushrooms, trimmed and finely chopped	3 tablespoons snipped fresh dill (or 1 tablespoon dried dill)
Juice of half a large lemon	
Salt, freshly ground pepper to taste	Parsley
	Tomato slices

Briefly sauté the scallions in the butter. Add the mushrooms and lemon juice. Season to taste. Cook over medium heat, stirring occasionally, for 5 minutes. Remove from the heat and stir in the sour cream and dill. Check for seasoning. Set aside to cool to room temperature.

Serve the "caviar" at room temperature, garnished with parsley and tomato slices.

Yield: 6 to 8 servings.

NOTE: Make sure not to chop the mushrooms and scallions too finely, or you will end up with a sauce instead of "caviar."

MARINATED MUSHROOMS
𝕏 *GRIBY, MARINOVANNYE V TOMATNOM SOUSE* 𝕏

Every *zakuska* table should offer at least one mushroom dish. This recipe is particularly well suited for the champignons one regularly buys at the grocery, since the marinade lends great flavor to the mild mushrooms. Although they may be eaten after only a 12-hour rest in the refrigerator, they taste best when allowed to soak for a full week. Any leftover marinade may be used as a rich dipping sauce for thick chunks of black bread.

4½ pounds button mushrooms, wiped and trimmed*
½ cup olive oil
6 tablespoons freshly squeezed lemon juice

6 tablespoons olive oil
3 large onions, sliced
5 cloves garlic, crushed
1 teaspoon freshly ground black pepper
¾ teaspoon thyme
¾ teaspoon marjoram

4 bay leaves
3½ pounds canned plum tomatoes (4 generous cups), drained (reserve the juice) and chopped
¾ cup juice from the tomatoes
1½ cups red wine vinegar
1½ teaspoons sugar
¼ teaspoon hot pepper sauce or cayenne pepper
Salt to taste

Heat the ½ cup of olive oil in a large frying pan. Add the mushrooms (in batches, if necessary) and sauté until just tender, before they begin to shrink. Transfer the mushrooms to a large bowl and toss with the lemon juice.

Add the 6 tablespoons of olive oil to the frying pan. Sauté the sliced onions and garlic until soft, but not browned. Add the pepper and herbs; sauté another minute more. Stir in the tomatoes, then add the juice from the tomatoes and the vinegar, sugar, and hot pepper sauce or cayenne pepper. Simmer, covered, for 25 minutes.

* Larger mushrooms may be used if they are sliced, but they are not as nice for the *zakuska* table.

Pour the sauce over the mushrooms and season with salt to taste. Add more black pepper, if desired. Let the mushrooms cool to room temperature and then chill, covered, for at least 12 hours, or up to 10 days, in the refrigerator. Bring to room temperature before serving.

Yield: 6 cups of mushrooms.

RUSSIAN SALAD
✠ *STOLICHNYI SALAT,* or *SALAT OLIV'YE* ✠

This famous Russian salad is actually the brainchild of a French chef, Olivier, who caused a sensation in Moscow in the 1860s when he concocted a salad of cooked chicken and potatoes masked with mayonnaise. For many years the matrons of Moscow society vied with one another in hiring Olivier as chef for their elaborate banquets, and his restaurant, Olivier's Hermitage, remained in vogue well into the 1890s.

Since Olivier's initial inspiration, the salad has evolved into the complex combination of meat and vegetables that is served today. Its close cousin is Salade Bagration, which is named after Prince Pyotr Bagration, who led his Russian troops to victory over Napoleon at Eylau, and which is made with boiled macaroni instead of potatoes.

½ pound cooked chicken, cut into bite-sized pieces	*2 tablespoons white wine vinegar*
2 pounds boiling potatoes (4 medium)	*½ cup mayonnaise*
	½ cup sour cream
1 large carrot, scraped	*Salt, freshly ground white pepper to taste*
¾ cup freshly shelled peas	
1 orange	
*2 tart apples, cored but not peeled**	*¼ cup mayonnaise*
	¼ cup sour cream
2 whole scallions	*1 tablespoon olive oil*
	1 tablespoon white wine vinegar
3 hard-boiled egg yolks	
2 tablespoons olive oil	*Fresh parsley or dill*

*Either red or green apples may be used, but the red will add more color to the salad.

Boil the potatoes in salted water until just tender; drain and peel. While still warm, cut them into chunks.

In a separate pot, boil the carrot until just tender; drain and cut it into rounds, setting a few rounds aside for the garnish.

Boil the peas in salted water for 5 minutes; drain.

Peel the orange and remove all of the white membrane. Cut the orange into 1-inch chunks. Chop the apples and scallions.

Mix all the vegetables together with the cooked chicken in a large bowl.

Prepare the dressing. Press the hard-boiled egg yolks through a fine sieve. Mix in the 2 tablespoons of olive oil until a smooth, creamy paste is formed. Stir in the 2 tablespoons of vinegar and ½ cup each of the mayonnaise and sour cream. Season to taste.

Pour the dressing over the warm vegetables and toss to mix thoroughly. Turn the salad into a clean bowl and chill, covered, overnight.

To serve, form the salad into a high mound on a decorative platter. Mix together the remaining mayonnaise, sour cream, olive oil and vinegar. Pour this dressing over the top of the mound so that it cascades down the sides. Garnish the salad with the leftover carrot rounds and with fresh parsley or dill.

Yield: 8 to 10 servings.

NOTE: The ingredients for this salad may be varied. Try substituting fresh peaches in season for the oranges, or crab meat for the chicken.

VARIATION: Salade Bagration

2 cups uncooked elbow macaroni	3 hard-boiled egg yolks
1 cup cooked chicken or turkey, cut into bite-sized pieces	3 tablespoons olive oil
½ cup cooked ham, cut into bite-sized pieces	3 tablespoons white wine vinegar
2 tart apples, cored and chopped, but not peeled	¾ cup mayonnaise
2 whole scallions, chopped	¾ cup sour cream
¾ cup freshly shelled peas	¼ cup chili sauce
½ cup chopped black olives	Salt, freshly ground white pepper to taste

Basically, this salad is prepared in the same way as Russian Salad above. Boil the macaroni in salted water until just tender. Drain. While the macaroni is still warm, toss it with the prepared meats, apples, scallions, peas, and olives and pour over it the dressing, which has been made by beating together the egg yolks, oil, vinegar, mayonnaise, sour cream and chili sauce. Season to taste, then chill overnight before serving.

Yield: About 10 servings.

PINK POTATO SALAD
𝕏 VINEGRET IZ KARTOFELYA I SVYOKLY 𝕏

There are many variations of the Russian potato salad. Some include meat or fish; others use only mayonnaise instead of sour cream; still others have an oil base. The salad offered here is a basic one, made festive by the addition of beets, which turn the potatoes a lovely deep rose color. It is sure to attract attention.

2 pounds potatoes	2 tablespoons olive oil
1 large beet	3 tablespoons white wine
3 hard-boiled eggs, chopped	vinegar
1 large cucumber, diced	1 teaspoon salt
½ cup dill pickle, diced	Freshly ground black pepper
3 scallions, including the green	to taste
tops, chopped	½ teaspoon dried dill
1 heaping tablespoon capers	½ cup sour cream

In separate pots, boil the potatoes and the beet until just tender. Drain and remove the skins. Chop the potatoes into coarse chunks; dice the beet. Put into a large bowl.

Add the eggs and the cucumber, pickle, scallions and capers. Mix well. Mix in the olive oil, vinegar, salt, pepper and dill. Finally, stir in the sour cream, mixing well to make sure each piece of the salad is coated. Chill, covered, overnight in the refrigerator before serving.

Yield: 8 to 10 servings.

RUSSIAN EGG SALAD
🏮 SALAT IZ YAITS 🏮

This strongly flavored salad is a must for the *zakuska* table. The egg slices are traditionally spread out in a long oval or rectangular cut-crystal dish, then masked with mayonnaise, rather than being mixed together with it.

6 hard-boiled eggs
½ cup mayonnaise (preferably homemade)
⅓ cup sour cream
1 small garlic clove, crushed
¼ teaspoon hot Russian-Style Mustard

¼ teaspoon salt
2 tablespoons finely chopped scallion tops

Carrot or pimiento

Slice the eggs thinly. Mix together the mayonnaise, sour cream, garlic, mustard and salt. Mask the eggs with this mixture. Sprinkle the chopped scallion on top. Garnish with a little carrot or pimiento for color.

Yield: 4 servings.

MUSHROOM-STUFFED EGGS
❦ YAITSA, FARSHIROVANNYE GRIBAMI ❦

Stuffed eggs complement any *zakuska* table. They may be filled with whatever is on hand, from leftover Russian Salad, to smoked fish and mayonnaise, to glistening grains of caviar. Here, the eggs are stuffed with a savory mixture of minced mushrooms and egg. For a stunning effect, mound the filling high in the cradles of egg.

4 hard-boiled eggs	*Freshly ground pepper to taste*
4 tablespoons butter	*A few drops of hot pepper*
1 small onion, minced	*sauce*
½ pound mushrooms, trimmed	
and minced	*4 teaspoons mayonnaise*
	2 teaspoons sour cream
2 tablespoons parsley	*Pinch of salt*
2 teaspoons fresh dill (or ½	
teaspoon dried dill)	*Pimiento (optional)*
½ teaspoon salt	

Sauté the onions in 2 tablespoons of the butter until golden. Add the remaining butter and the mushrooms and cook for 5 to 8 minutes more. Remove from the heat.

Peel the hard-boiled eggs and cut them in half lengthwise. Scoop out the yolks and chop them finely. Add them to the mushroom mixture, along with the parsley, dill, salt, pepper and hot pepper sauce.

Mix together the mayonnaise, sour cream and pinch of salt.

Fill the eggs with the mushroom mixture, mounding it high to form tall peaks. Dribble the mayonnaise mixture over the top so that it runs slightly down the sides. Garnish with a little pimiento, if desired.

Yield: 4 servings.

SWEET AND SOUR BEETS
🦂 *SVYOKLA V TOMATNOM SOUSE* 🦂

Even inveterate beet haters will eat this salad with surprise and pleasure. The deep red of the beets merges with the orange of the carrots to yield a beautiful ruby color. The salad tastes slightly more sweet than sour. If any is left over, it will keep well in the refrigerator for up to a week.

1 pound fresh beets	*2 cups* Basic Tomato Sauce
1 pound carrots	*(see below)*
1 large onion	
6 tablespoons olive oil	*1 tablespoon red wine vinegar*
	2 teaspoons sugar

Peel the beets and carrots. Grate them together with the onion. (This is most easily done with the shredding disk of a food processor.)

In a large frying pan heat the olive oil. Add the shredded vegetables, mixing well. Sauté the vegetables over medium-high heat for 10 to 12 minutes, until just barely tender. Stir in the tomato sauce, vinegar, and sugar. Continue to cook over medium heat, stirring occasionally, until all the moisture evaporates, about 20 to 25 minutes. Transfer to a dish and chill before serving.

Yield: 8 to 10 servings.

BASIC TOMATO SAUCE
⚙ *TOMATNYI SOUS* ⚙

2 tablespoons olive oil	*½ teaspoon dried basil*
1 large onion, coarsely chopped	*A few drops of hot pepper*
1 large clove garlic, crushed	*sauce*
1½ pounds ripe tomatoes,	
quartered	*1 tablespoon butter*
1 small green pepper	*1 tablespoon flour*
1 teaspoon salt	*1 tablespoon tomato paste*
Freshly ground black pepper	*½ teaspoon sugar*
to taste	

Sauté the onion and garlic in the olive oil until soft but not brown. Stir in the tomatoes, green pepper, salt, black pepper, basil and hot pepper sauce. Cover the pan and simmer for 30 minutes. Then put the mixture through a vegetable mill.

In a saucepan melt the butter. Stir in the flour, then cook for a few minutes. Stir in the pureed tomato mixture, then add the tomato paste and sugar. Simmer for 10 minutes.

Yield: 2 cups.

VINAIGRETTE OF BEETS
☙ VINEGRET IZ SVYOKLY ❧

Lest you wince at the sight of another recipe for beets, it's best to keep in mind the old adage, "Beets make the blood rich." And if that isn't justification enough, this savory salad should speak for itself.

1 pound beets
¼ cup olive oil
¼ cup red wine vinegar
1 teaspoon hot Russian-Style
    mustard

Salt, freshly ground black
    pepper to taste

Minced parsley

Preheat the oven to 375°F. Bake the unpeeled beets for 1 to 1½ hours, until tender. (If in a hurry, the beets may be boiled, but their flavor will not be as good.)

Meanwhile, mix together the remaining ingredients. When the beets are tender and cool enough to handle, but still warm, slip off the skins and slice. Cover the slices with the vinegar and oil mixture. Chill before serving. Garnish with minced parsley.

Yield: 4 to 6 servings.

CAULIFLOWER WITH MAYONNAISE
TSVETNAYA KAPUSTA POD MAYONEZOM

Here are two ways of preparing cauliflower to brighten the *zakuska* table. In both recipes the cauliflower is left whole and crowned with a colorful dressing: a golden mustard and horseradish mayonnaise or a brilliantly tinted beet mayonnaise. Both preparations look very festive and, of course, taste delicious.

· I ·
CAULIFLOWER WITH MUSTARD AND HORSERADISH MAYONNAISE

1 head cauliflower
⅓ cup mayonnaise (preferably homemade)
⅓ cup sour cream
2 tablespoons Russian-Style Mustard
1 teaspoon fresh lemon juice

⅛ teaspoon salt
White pepper to taste
½ teaspoon prepared horseradish

1½ tablespoons minced parsley

Steam the whole head of cauliflower over boiling water for 10 minutes. Drain and chill thoroughly in the refrigerator.

Just before serving, mix together the mayonnaise, sour cream, mustard, lemon juice, salt, pepper and horseradish, blending well. Spread this mixture over the top and sides of the chilled cauliflower, masking it completely. Sprinkle the minced parsley over the top.

To serve, cut the cauliflower in wedges with a sharp knife.

Yield: 6 servings.

· II ·
CAULIFLOWER WITH BEET MAYONNAISE

1 head cauliflower
1 tiny beet (about 1 ounce)
⅔ cup mayonnaise (preferably
   homemade)
2 teaspoons prepared
   horseradish

½ teaspoon fresh lemon juice
Salt to taste

Snipped fresh dill

Steam the whole head of cauliflower over boiling water for 10 minutes. Drain and chill thoroughly in the refrigerator.

Meanwhile, boil the beet until tender. Peel it and put it through a fine strainer. Mix together the sieved beet and the mayonnaise, horseradish, lemon juice and salt.

Just before serving, mask the chilled cauliflower with the beet mayonnaise, covering the top and sides. Garnish with snipped fresh dill.

Cut into wedges to serve.

Yield: 6 servings.

NOTE: Be sure not to overcook the cauliflower. It must remain firm.

DILLED ONIONS
☙ LUK MARINOVANNYI ☙

The perfect complement to a glass of vodka!

1 1-pound jar pearl onions,
   drained
1 cup cider vinegar
½ cup sugar
1 teaspoon salt
2 tablespoons snipped fresh dill
   (or 1 teaspoon dried dill)

1 teaspoon caraway seed
1 teaspoon crushed hot dried
   pepper
12 black peppercorns

Place the drained onions in a 1-quart jar. Combine the vinegar, sugar, salt, herbs and spices in a medium saucepan. Bring to a boil, then pour the mixture over the onions. Close the jar tightly and cool to room temperature. Refrigerate the onions for two weeks before serving.

Yield: 1 quart onions.

OPEN-FACED RADISH SANDWICHES
☙ BUTERBRODY S REDISKOI ☙

Russians love radishes, from the mild red garden variety to the huge thick-skinned black balls, and the versatile vegetable is firmly rooted in the Russian cuisine. One old adage even testifies to its ubiquity: "We've had seven meals, and it's radishes still: radishes in thirds and slices; radishes with butter and kvass; radishes in bits and pieces; and radishes just as they are." Here, red radishes are finely chopped and mixed with cream cheese for a canapé spread that is as lovely to look at as it is to eat.

6 pieces thinly sliced black
  bread, cut into quarters
8 red radishes (⅓ cup), finely
  chopped
4 ounces cream cheese
1 teaspoon lemon juice

1 teaspoon snipped fresh dill
  (or ¼ teaspoon dried dill)
½ teaspoon coarse salt
1 tablespoon chopped parsley

8 red radishes, thinly sliced

In a small bowl cream the cream cheese. Add the chopped radishes, then stir in the lemon juice, dill, salt and parsley.

Spread the mixture on the slices of bread. On top of each canapé place overlapping slices of radish from the remaining 8 radishes.

Yield: 2 dozen canapés.

GARLIC-CHEESE SPREAD
SYR I CHESNOK POD MAYONEZOM

The garlic available in the Soviet Union is of a very pungent variety— no wonder Russia is a nation of garlic lovers! And after tasting this excellent garlic-cheese spread, one can hardly remain impartial to the tasty cloves for long. This spread can also be used as the base for delicious *buterbrody:* try it over a slice of ham on black bread, or generously topped with watercress.

8 ounces Muenster cheese
3 large cloves garlic, crushed
5 tablespoons mayonnaise

1 tablespoon snipped fresh
  chives
Sprinkling of salt

Grate the cheese into a medium-sized bowl. Add the garlic. Stir in the mayonnaise, mixing thoroughly with a wooden spoon until creamy. (A few lumps are all right.) Stir in the chives; sprinkle with salt. Blend well.

Refrigerate the cheese spread. Serve at room temperature with thin slices of black bread or lightly toasted rounds of French bread.

Yield: About 2 cups.

NOTE: The spread must be served at room temperature for the best flavor.

‽❀‽

II

IN THE DAYS
OF THE TSAR:
CLASSIC RECIPES

◊⟩

*R*ussian cookery had its heyday in the late-nineteenth-century court of the tsar and the homes of the gentry and nobility, when fantastic dishes were created to please discerning masters—Salad Demidoff, Pheasant Souvoroff, Veal Orloff, Beef Stroganoff, Nesselrode Pie. The fanciest chefs were all French, and the fanciest dishes resulted from a mixture of traditional French cookery and native Russian methods, as the original Russian foods received a flair they had previously lacked.

Still, Russian cookery did not blossom overnight. It took many years before gastronomy in Russia reached that state of refinement we consider its *haute cuisine* today. This evolution seems striking when one considers that the early Slavic tribes subsisted mainly on coarse gruels and primitive brews. The first written account of food occurs in the Russian *Primary Chronicle,* a history set down by a clerical scribe in Church Slavonic, a language now dead for many centuries. This entry is dated A.D. 997; the scene is the ancient town of Belgorod.

Heathen Pecheneg tribes laid siege to the town, and Belgorod was beset by famine. When the inhabitants learned that Grand Prince Vladimir was unable to come to their aid, they began to despair. They were on the verge of surrender when a sage old man formulated a plan to trick the Pechenegs. He bid the townspeople to gather all the oats, wheat and bran to be found and brew them into a porridge (*kasha*), then to gather as much honey as possible and dilute it to make mead. The grains were mixed with water and poured into a tub; so was the honey. Then the tubs were set in large pits in the ground, and a messenger invited the Pechenegs to send envoys to the town. The Pechenegs, expecting to find the townsfolk ready to surrender, were astonished to see them eating copious amounts of boiled *kasha* and mead. Between mouthfuls, the people informed their enemies that they received their sustenance from the earth itself, and even if the Pechenegs were to besiege them for ten years, they would not starve. Thus the siege was lifted, thanks to simple food and drink and the cunning of a wise old man: an apocryphal tale to be sure.

As the years passed, the status of *kasha* rose from plebeian to plush. By the twelfth century we find the grand princes of Russia dining on buckwheat porridge at their feasts, using the spoon as their utensil. (Even when the fork was introduced several centuries later, people balked, saying, "A fork's like a fishing rod, but a spoon's a net!" Apparently, the idea was to load as much food as possible into a single mouthful.) Buckwheat continued to be food for the wealthy until the sixteenth century, when the nobles discovered diversity and the coarse groats finally became accessible to the common man. Since that time buckwheat has become part of the peasant tradition, the upper classes turning instead to such delicacies as sturgeon roe and breast of chicken—but never entirely scorning their buckwheat.

The elaborate feasts of the boyars in the sixteenth-century court of Ivan the Terrible, vividly described by Count Aleksei Tolstoy in his historical novel *Prince Serebryanyi,* bear witness to the new diversity in food among the well-to-do. These feasts stretched on for six to eight hours at a time. The guests were regaled with ten different courses, each consisting of up to twenty distinct dishes of a given type: there might be ten roasts of wild fowl and five varieties of fish. Each course was presented separately at the table, until an array of sculpted masterpieces for dessert signaled the ending of the meal. Considering the massive amounts of food people consumed in those days, it is hardly surprising that their life expectancy was short.

By the late eighteenth century the standard feast menu had been sensibly toned down, offering only eight different courses with just one dish for each course. The order was as follows: hot soup, cold soup, roast meat or fowl, poached or baked fish, *pirog,* buckwheat, sweet pastry and sweetmeats. Such a progression of courses did not seem extreme at the time; if anything, the nobility found it restrained. Even so, the gifted eighteenth-century poet Gavrila Derzhavin felt inspired to write a cautionary ode entitled "Invitation to Dinner," which opens with a description of the delights of the dinner table awaiting the guests, but ends with the grave admonition that bliss is not to be found in sensual delights, for "moderation is the best of feasts." The Russians were finally learning from the Greeks.

Perhaps Derzhavin's words were taken to heart. Eating habits gradually became more temperate. By the time of Tolstoy, a wide choice of menu was available to the connoisseur, depending on how fancy a meal was desired. Dinners could range from two courses (soup and roast) to twelve (several different soups, roasts, fish, *entremets*, vegetables and desserts), the most common consisting of six: a hot soup, a cold soup, fish, roast meat or fowl, vegetable or salad—always served as a separate course—and dessert. A strict progression of wines from soup to dessert was observed throughout the meal. The cookbooks of the time show that for those who had money, a great diversity of products, both wild and cultivated, was available in the larger cities of Moscow, St. Petersburg and Kiev. English lamb imported from London was considered the finest, while native Ukrainian pork was said to be surpassed by no other pig. For beef, the Circassian meat from the Caucasus was believed superior. In Turgenev's novel *Fathers and Sons,* it is not unrealistic that when a special meal is prepared, a servant is dispatched at dawn for Circassian beef, while the bailiff of the estate is sent to fetch fresh fish and crayfish from the local waters.

Each area of Russia enjoyed the fish from its own rivers and lakes, and these local delicacies often could not be had outside a small radius. The people of St. Petersburg ate fish from the Neva River and the Gulf of Finland, which harbored trout, salmon, whitefish, burbot, bream, ruff, perch, eel, pike, smelt, crayfish and other delights too numerous to name. High-living members of society paid exorbitant prices to import the prized Volga sterlet to St. Petersburg in special tanks kept at carefully controlled temperatures. Most families enjoyed wild fowl, such as capercaillie, blackcock, pheasant, hazel hen, woodcock, snipe and quail. Those lucky enough to know a hunter feasted on bear cub and wild boar, both great delicacies of the time. More easily obtainable were elk, wild goat, deer and hare (the russet variety was reputed tastier than the white). Domestic geese and turkeys, often bought live and fattened at home, complemented the heavier wild fowl.

The nineteenth-century table took excellent advantage of the abundance in Russia's forests and waterways. And as the influence of French taste on Russian life grew, so did the interest in food and its fine preparation. Yet while many dishes gained new refinements (and some, fancy new French names), their bases remained typically Russian. Those who carried the French mode of the day too far were often ridiculed, as in Tolstoy's *Anna Karenina,* when Princess Myakhkaya tells in a loud voice of a dinner she and her husband attended where a fancy sauce ostensibly costing 1,000 rubles was served. "It was a green mess!" the Princess declares. Nevertheless, according to etiquette, the dinner invitation had to be reciprocated. The Princess retaliated (and claims to have triumphed) by making a Russian sauce for only 85 kopeks, which tasted far better. Tolstoy himself detested pretensions to the French style, preferring instead the native Russian fare as served by his hero Levin at his country estate: fresh bread and dairy butter, smoked goose and salted mushrooms for an appetizer, followed by a soup of wild nettles with *pirozhki,* then roast chicken with white sauce, served with a white Crimean wine, and finally a draft of homemade herb vodka. In spite of the influx of French wines, vodka still remained the preferred beverage, even among cosmopolitans. Shunning the more common wine cellar, Tsar Alexander II was said to have had a vodka cellar of 750,000 bottles.

One of the landmarks of traditional Russian dining in the mid-nineteenth century was Moscow's famed Merchants' Club. In the 1840s the club took over an old noble establishment, transforming its modish French menu into a splendid Russian table. Suckling pigs were ordered from the restaurateur Testov, well known in his own right for hand-feeding his piglets and keeping them in pens so small they could barely move their feet. Capons and *poulardes* were brought in from Rostov-Yaroslavsky, and milk-fed veal from the Trinity Monastery. The popular late-night dinners at the Merchants' Club are described by Vladimir Gilyarovsky in his entertaining book *Moscow and Muscovites.* These "second" dinners often included fish soup (*ukha*) with sterlet, sturgeons two arshins (almost five feet) in length, beluga sturgeon in brine, "banquet" veal, walnut-fed turkeys "as white as cream," fish pies (*rasstegai*) with burbot liver and sturgeon, suckling pig with horseradish and suckling pig with *kasha.* After the last toast ("To excess!"), the diners retired to the parlor, where they sipped coffee and liqueurs. If they were lucky, Nikolai Agafonych might appear and take orders for their favorite drinks. Nikolai Agafonych was the Merchants' Club's master brewer of kvasses and fruit drinks, for which the club was renowned. The diners, languorously reclining in easy chairs after the night's immoderations, would perk up the moment Nikolai Agafonych appeared and began calling out their orders for drinks infused with black-currant buds, so aromatic that the scent of early spring lingered long in one's nostrils; for nectars of ruby-red cherries or delicate raspberries; for kvass brewed from white bread instead of the usual black. Some hearty souls swore by Nikolai Aga-fonych's *kislye shchi,* a fermented brew so gaseous that it had to be kept in tightly stoppered bottles to avoid explosions. The Merchants' Club's notorious cook, the 360-pound Lyonechka, drank the *shchi* alongside frozen champagne, claiming that *kislye shchi* "might sock you in the nose, but it socks out drunkenness too!"

This Lyonechka was the inventor of a fabulous twelve-layered *kule-byaka,* which could be had only at the Merchants' Club or Testov's Tavern. Enclosed in his rich pastry crust were generous layers of meat, fish, mushrooms, chicken and all sorts of game. Lyonechka's creation was so elaborate that it had to be ordered a good twenty-four hours in advance.

Entertainment at these meals was usually provided by Russian, Hungarian or Gypsy singers and dancers. A touch of the exotic was much sought after by Muscovites of the time. One legendary merchant, Misha Khludov, regularly held lavish banquets, at which he always appeared in different wild garb accompanied by his pet tiger. By contemporary accounts, the ladies of Moscow were thrilled to see him as a Roman gladiator, clad only in a tiger skin that revealed the tautness of his physique; but they were probably less thrilled by the inevitable tiger stalking among them, sniffing at their plates.

In spite of all the hoopla of many nineteenth-century dinners, there was also a very serious side to Russian dining, one impelled by the deep religious feelings of the people. What determined the character of the Russian table more than anything else was the strict progression of feast and fast days in the Russian Orthodox religious year, which most Russians observed. Because there were so many fast (*postnyi*) days, when all meat, egg and milk products were proscribed (from 192 to 216 days of the year!), the feast (*skoromnyi*) days turned into extravaganzas—hence the liberal use of butter-rich foods in Russian cookery. Cooks had to be inventive to come up with tasty dishes for the many lean days of the year, and this fact accounts for Russia's wonderful fish and mushroom preparations. In addition, many ordinary foods could still be enjoyed on fast days if the ingredients were changed slightly, and such experimentation ultimately enriched the cuisine. Hemp, mustard, or nut oils were found to be substitutes for butter in cooking; pastries and breads were baked with almond milk or rose water instead of milk from cows.

To help guide cooks and homemakers through the maze of religious rules and direct them in the use of the abundant ingredients, many popular cookbooks appeared in the mid-1800s. But as early as the sixteenth century, a book had appeared offering advice on food preparation and preserving. This was the *Domostroi,* or book of Household Order, attributed to the monk Sylvester from Novgorod, a city with a large and prosperous middle class. In an attempt to reach beyond the ecclesiastical community, the *Domostroi* was written in conversational style. It contains chapters on brewing beer and *sbiten'* (a hot, spiced honey drink), chapters on putting up preserves and storing vegetables ("when others must go to the market, you need only go as far as your cellar"), instructions for making *shchi,* and tips on preparing other such ultra-Russian foods as *kisel'* (fruit pudding), *blini, pirogi* and *kasha.* Naturally, the *Domostroi* dwells rather tediously on the importance of keeping the fast and feast days, but it also gives sound advice on how to observe them most pleasantly. Even today it's a delightful document, affording much insight into sixteenth-century life.

In 1816, the first actual cookbook appeared in Moscow, *The Russian Kitchen,* written by a chef named Levshin. But the most popular of all— Elena Molokhovet's *A Gift to Young Housewives; or a Means of Reducing Household Expenses*—did not appear until 1861. What began as a personal collection of favorite recipes turned into a best seller, going through twenty-eight editions between 1861 and 1914. For the first time in a Russian cookbook, Molokhovets carefully detailed the ingredients and procedures necessary for the success of a myriad of dishes. Besides providing over 4,000 diverse recipes, she included menu suggestions and tips on household economy. Her book is still considered a classic in the Soviet Union today, where the contemporary housewife can read with longing of larders stocked with foods she has never seen, let alone tasted. Because of the expectations such reading material might engender, *A Gift to Young Housewives* has never been reprinted in the USSR and has long since disappeared from the shelves of antique-book sellers, as each treasured volume is passed down through family generations.

Molokhovets's cookbook was a tribute to the abundance and fine preparation of Russian food. Ironically, within ten years of its final edition, people throughout the newly formed Soviet Union were brewing "tea" from carrots and making bread out of coarse grains and sawdust. Of course, the food situation gradually stabilized, but the era of surfeit had finally come to an end, to be replaced by what Nabokov has termed "the sadness of balanced meals." It is true that the standard Russian meal of today is more balanced, more "sensible" than its counterpart one hundred years ago, but much of its éclat has been lost. This chapter, then, is intended to resurrect the glories of the Russian cuisine as they were once prepared for banquets and colorful feasts, when cooking and dining were both highly prized arts, when calories did not count.

STURGEON SOUP WITH CHAMPAGNE
⚶ SUP IZ OSETRINY S SHAMPANSKIM ⚶

This soup, a favorite of the empress Catherine the Great, is very elegant—and very expensive. Legend has it that Catherine planned a visit to her consort, Count Potemkin, at a time when no sturgeon was to be had in all of Moscow. Potemkin, never one to give up easily, sought out a cunning fishmonger who supplied him with enough fish for the soup. But it cost him dearly. In exchange for the sturgeon, Potemkin relinquished a painting he had recently purchased for 10,000 rubles. But when Catherine the Great is coming for dinner, what else can one do?

In old Russia a whole fillet of sturgeon was placed in each soup bowl and the broth poured over it. The diners sipped the broth and then attacked the fish with knife and fork. The method presented here is more streamlined—and more economical.

3 cups Basic Fish Stock
1 pound fresh sturgeon,
   trimmed and cut into cubes

1 cup dry champagne

Lemon slices
Chopped scallions

Place the fish stock and the cut-up sturgeon in a stockpot and bring to a boil. Simmer gently for about 10 minutes, until the fish is cooked.

Pour the champagne into the fish soup and just barely heat through. Ladle the soup into individual bowls and garnish each with some thin lemon slices and chopped scallions.

Yield: 4 servings.

CLEAR FISH SOUP
☙ *UKHA* ☙

Ukha is the Russian fisherman's soup, traditionally prepared by simmering the catch of the day over a wood fire on the sandy banks of the shore. No doubt it is these bucolic associations that make Russians sigh when *ukha* is mentioned, for they rarely make the soup at home. Basically, *ukha* is a clear fish broth, with potatoes sometimes added to fill it out. Almost any fish may be used, as long as it is very fresh, since old fish turns the soup cloudy. The Russians claim that "bony fish make *ukha* sweet." They themselves favor the *omul'* (arctic cisco), a fish of the salmon family that emits a weird cry when caught.

2½ quarts cold water
2 pounds fish (including some trimmings), cut into serving-sized pieces
1 onion, quartered
3 sprigs parsley

2 bay leaves
5 white peppercorns plus ground white pepper to taste
1½ tablespoons salt
2 potatoes, peeled and cubed (optional)

In a large kettle place the water and the fish. Such fish as perch, flounder, and sea bass are all good in this soup, and a mixture of fish is to be preferred, but avoid using cod.

Bring the fish and water to a boil, skimming the foam from the surface. Then add the remaining ingredients. Cover the kettle and simmer for 1 hour.

To serve, place a piece of fish in each bowl and pour broth over it.

Yield: 6 to 8 servings.

NOTE: Although purists insist that *ukha* must be made with a variety of fish and without any potatoes, my friend Klara makes an excellent version using 2 pounds of salmon (including some salmon collars) and 2 potatoes. Proceed as directed above.

RUSSIAN LEMON SOUP
❧ *LIMONNYI SUP* ❧

An unusual and delightful soup.

¼ cup raw rice	Juice and finely grated rind of
2 tablespoons butter	1 large lemon
½ cup clear chicken broth	
	Lemon slices
4 cups clear chicken broth	Minced parsley
½ cup heavy cream	

In a medium-sized saucepan cook the rice and the butter in the ½ cup of chicken broth until tender, about 20 minutes. Stirring the rice with a fork, gradually add the remaining chicken broth. Bring just to the boiling point.

Stir in the cream, then the rind and juice of the lemon. (If an even tarter taste is preferred, more lemon juice may be added.)

When the ingredients are well blended, ladle the soup into individual bowls, making sure that some rice is placed in the bottom of each bowl. Garnish with thin slices of lemon and minced parsley.

Yield: 4 servings.

VARIATION: To serve the soup cold, cook the rice as directed above and then stir in the remaining broth. Chill. Skim off any fat that has hardened on the surface, and then add the cream and lemon juice and rind. Chill well before serving.

KIDNEY AND DILL PICKLE SOUP
☙ RASSOL'NIK ☙

The classic Russian sour soup, provocative in both flavor and scent.

1 veal kidney (or 2 lamb
  kidneys)
Flour
1 large carrot, scraped
1 medium leek
1 medium potato, peeled
4 tablespoons butter

12 cups beef stock
3 dill pickles, insides scraped
  out, cut into julienne strips

¼ cup raw pearl barley
¾ teaspoon salt
Freshly ground black pepper
  to taste
2 tablespoons brine from the
  pickle jar

Sour cream

Remove all membrane from the kidney and soak the kidney in cold water for 30 minutes. Then pat dry and cut into slices. Dredge with flour.

Meanwhile, prepare the vegetables. Cut the carrot, leek and potato into julienne strips. Melt 2 tablespoons of the butter in a large stockpot and sauté the vegetables in it for 10 minutes.

In a small frying pan melt the remaining butter and brown the kidney slices in it over high heat, about 5 minutes.

To the vegetables in the stockpot, add the fried kidney slices and the stock. Then add the pickles, barley, salt and freshly ground pepper. Bring to a boil, skimming off the foam that rises to the surface. When the foam has subsided, cover the pot and simmer the soup for 45 minutes.

Stir in the pickle brine. Test for seasoning. At this point, sour cream may be stirred into the soup before serving, or it may be passed at the table and the soup served clear.

Yield: 4 to 6 servings.

COLD RASPBERRY SOUP
🎋 MALINNIK 🎋

A lush and elegant soup.

1 pound fresh raspberries
½ cup sugar (or more, to taste,
depending on the sweetness
of the berries)

2 cups claret
2 tablespoons sparkling water

Put 12 ounces of the berries through a vegetable mill, reserving the remaining 4 ounces (1 cup) for garnish. Stir in the sugar and then add the claret. Chill well.

Just before serving, stir in the sparkling water and the reserved berries. This soup looks lovely when presented in a glass bowl. A dollop of whipped sweet or sour cream may be placed in each portion, if desired. Serve plain biscuits on the side.

Yield: 4 to 6 servings.

NOTE: If fresh raspberries are not available, 2 10-ounce packages of frozen raspberries in syrup may be substituted. In this case, eliminate the sugar entirely.

RUSSIAN PIES
🎋 PIROZHKI 🎋

The Russian pie (*pirog* or *pirozhok*) is as ubiquitous in Russian life as it is in literature. Street corners are dotted with hawkers selling their pies hot from portable ovens; cafés offer meat pies along with bowls of soup. The importance of the *pirog* cannot be underestimated: in one of Gogol's *Dikanka* tales the narrator is alarmed to find that his wife has made off with half the pages of his book to use as baking paper for her pies, which, he confesses, are indeed the tastiest around.

The practice of enclosing all sorts of fillings, both savory and sweet, in an envelope of dough is an old one, and very characteristic of the Russian cuisine. The pies range from the complex and extravagant (the many-layered salmon *kulebyaka,* for instance) to the simple and plain (deep-fried half-moons of dough stuffed with leftovers). The large pies are called *pirogi.* They are usually square or rectangular in shape. Their diminutive cousins, the *pirozhki,* are pocket-sized and oval. All can be made from a variety of doughs—yeast, short or flaky pastry—depending on which suits the filling best.

The word *pirog* comes from *pir,* "feast": *pirogi* were, and still are, integral to Russian-style entertaining. The recipes below are for some of the more popular pie fillings, but improvisation is encouraged, as the possibilities are endless.

DOUGH

· I ·

BASIC RAISED PIROZHKI DOUGH
❀ *DROZHZHEVOYE TESTO* ❀

1 package active dry yeast	*2 teaspoons sugar*
¼ cup warm water	*1 whole egg*
1 cup milk	*2 egg yolks*
8 tablespoons butter, cut into bits	*4½ to 5 cups flour*
1 teaspoon salt	*1 whole egg, beaten*

Dissolve the yeast in the warm water. Heat the milk to lukewarm and add the butter to it. Stir the milk and butter mixture into the yeast. Add the salt, sugar, egg and egg yolks, mixing well. Gradually stir in enough flour to make a soft dough.

Turn the dough out onto a floured board and knead it lightly until smooth and elastic. Place in a greased bowl, turning dough to grease the top, and cover with a clean towel. Let rise in a warm place until doubled in bulk, about 1½ hours.

Punch down the dough and divide it into 48 balls of equal size. On a floured board roll each ball out to a circle 3½ inches in diameter. Place a heaping tablespoon of filling on each circle, then press the edges of the dough together firmly to seal. Gently shape the pies into elongated ovals.

Place the pies seam side down on a greased baking sheet. Cover and let rise until they are just doubled in bulk, about 40 minutes. Preheat the oven to 350°F.

Brush each pie with the beaten egg. Bake for 20 minutes, or until golden.

Yield: 4 dozen *pirozhki.*

VARIATIONS:

1. To make a sweet raised dough for dessert *pirozhki,* increase the amount of sugar to 2 tablespoons. Proceed as directed above.

2. The *pirozhki* may be deep-fried instead of baked, and then they are usually shaped into round balls instead of ovals. After the *pirozhki* have risen on the baking sheet, drop them, a few at a time, into deep hot fat (350°F) and fry them until golden, about 5 minutes, turning them once. Drain on paper towels and serve immediately.

3. To make 2 large *pirogi,* divide the risen dough into 4 pieces. Roll out each piece of dough into a 10-inch square. Spread 2 of the pieces with the desired filling, and then top each filling with the remaining squares of dough. Turn the bottom edge of the dough up over the top piece to seal. Shape any leftover scraps of dough into fancy shapes and affix them in a decorative pattern to the top of the *pirogi* with beaten egg. Let the *pirogi* rise in a warm place, covered, until doubled in bulk. Brush them with beaten egg and bake in a preheated 350°F oven for about 45 minutes, or until golden.

4. A four-cornered *pirog* is made for special occasions (such as a Name Day): roll out the dough as for the 2 large *pirogi* above, but instead of using only 1 filling, spread the bottom squares of dough with 4 different fillings, using 1 filling to cover each corner. Top with the remaining dough and proceed as directed above.

· II ·

SOUR CREAM PASTRY FOR PIROZHKI
❁ *BEZDROZHZHEVOYE TESTO* ❁

3 cups flour   *1 cup plus 2 tablespoons butter*
¾ teaspoon salt   *¾ cup sour cream*
2 tablespoons sugar

In a medium-sized bowl mix together the flour, salt and sugar. Cut in the butter until the dough is the consistency of cornmeal. Add the sour cream, mixing well. Wrap the dough in waxed paper and chill in the refrigerator for 2 hours.

Roll the dough out ⅛ to ¼ inch thick. With a round cookie cutter, cut out circles 4 inches in diameter. Place a generous tablespoon of filling on one half of each circle; fold the other half over to form half-moons. Crimp the edges together with a fork to seal.

Preheat the oven to 375°F. Place the *pirozhki* on a very lightly greased baking sheet and bake them for 20 minutes, or until golden.

Yield: 2 dozen *pirozhki.*

VARIATION: For sweet *pirozhki,* increase the amount of sugar to 6 tablespoons and proceed as directed above.

· III ·
SHORT DOUGH FOR SWEET PIROZHKI
☼ *SLADKOYE BEZDROZHZHEVOYE TESTO* ☼

Sweet *pirozhki* made from this dough are irresistible, as the servant Natasha in Fyodor Sologub's novel *The Petty Demon* knows. She wants to steal a *pirozhok* and eat it on the sly, but because the pastries are so rich they leave a trace on the baking sheet, and Natasha's suspicious mistress always examines the sheet to see if the number of buttery patterns left on it matches the number of *pirozhki* brought to the table. Natasha is afraid of being caught, so she doesn't yield to temptation—at least not this time.

3 cups flour	*½ cup sour cream*
½ teaspoon salt	*2 whole eggs*
¾ cup sugar	
½ teaspoon baking soda	*1 whole egg, beaten*
8 tablespoons butter	

Follow exactly the same procedure as for the Sour Cream Pastry (see above), but brush these *pirozhki* with beaten egg before baking.

Yield: 2 dozen *pirozhki.*

VARIATION: This dough may also be used to make small cookies called "pigtails" (*kosichki*): Roll the dough out ⅛ inch thick. Cut it into strips ½ inch wide and 5 inches long. Take 3 strips and braid them together, repeating until all the dough has been braided. Place the "pigtails" on a lightly greased baking sheet, brush them with beaten egg, and sprinkle them with poppy seeds. Bake in a preheated 375°F oven for 15 minutes. These make a good plain cookie for tea.

Yield: 2 dozen biscuits.

SAVORY FILLINGS FOR PIROZHKI

· I ·
BEEF FILLING
✸ *NACHINKA IZ RUBLENOGO MYASA* ✸

2 large onions, minced
2 tablespoons butter
1 tablespoon olive oil
1 pound lean ground beef
2½ teaspoons salt
Freshly ground black pepper
* to taste*

2 tablespoons snipped fresh dill
* (or 2 teaspoons dried dill)*
2 hard-boiled eggs, minced
2 tablespoons sour cream

Sauté the onions in the butter and oil until transparent. Stir in the beef and cook it until no trace of pink remains. Then add the remaining ingredients, mixing well. Set aside to cool before using as filling.

Yield: Filling for 4 dozen *pirozhki* or 2 *pirogi*.

· II ·
CABBAGE FILLING
✸ *NACHINKA IZ KAPUSTY* ✸

4 tablespoons butter
2 tablespoons olive oil
2 large onions, minced
1 pound cabbage, finely
* shredded*
1½ tablespoons snipped fresh

dill (or 1¼ teaspoons dried
dill)
1 tablespoon salt
Freshly ground black pepper
* to taste*
2 hard-boiled eggs, minced

Sauté the onions in the butter and oil until transparent, then add the cabbage and continue cooking for 15 to 20 minutes more, until the cabbage is tender but not browned. Stir in the remaining ingredients, mixing well. Let cool slightly before using.

Yield: Filling for 4 dozen *pirozhki* or 2 *pirogi*.

• III •
MUSHROOM FILLING
❁ *GRIBNAYA NACHINKA* ❁

8 tablespoons butter
2 medium onions, minced
1 pound mushrooms, minced
2 hard-boiled eggs, minced
¼ cup raw rice, cooked
   according to package
   directions

6 tablespoons minced fresh
   parsley
1 teaspoon salt
Freshly ground black pepper
   to taste
2 tablespoons snipped fresh dill
   (or 2 teaspoons dried dill)

Sauté the onions in the butter until soft but not brown. Stir in the mushrooms and cook for 5 minutes more. Remove from the heat and stir in the remaining ingredients, mixing well. Let cool slightly before using.

   Yield: Filling for 4 dozen *pirozhki* or 2 *pirogi*.

• IV •
SCALLION FILLING
❁ *NACHINKA IZ ZELONOGO LUKA* ❁

6 to 8 large scallions, finely
   chopped
¾ cup butter
1 cup minced fresh parsley
4 hard-boiled eggs, finely
   chopped

3 tablespoons snipped fresh dill
   (or 1 tablespoon dried dill)
2 teaspoons salt
Freshly ground black pepper
   to taste
¼ cup sour cream

Sauté the scallions in the butter for 5 minutes. Remove from the heat and stir in the remaining ingredients, mixing well. Let cool slightly before using.

   Yield: Filling for 4 dozen *pirozhki* or 2 *pirogi*.

· V ·
CARROT FILLING
❁ *NACHINKA IZ MORKOVI* ❁

6 medium carrots, scraped
8 tablespoons butter
1 scallion, finely chopped
3 slices day-old home-style
   white bread, crusts removed,
   crumbled
2 tablespoons snipped chives

1½ teaspoons salt
Freshly ground black pepper
   to taste
3 tablespoons sour cream
6 tablespoons minced fresh
   parsley

Boil the carrots in salted water until tender, then chop finely. Sauté them for 5 minutes in the butter, along with the scallion and the bread crumbs. Remove from the heat and stir in the remaining ingredients, mixing well. Let cool slightly before using.

Yield: Filling for 4 dozen *pirozhki* or 2 *pirogi*.

SWEET FILLINGS FOR PIROZHKI
· I ·
APRICOT FILLING
❁ *ABRIKOSOVAYA NACHINKA* ❁

1 pound dried apricots, cut into
   fairly small pieces

2 cups sugar

Place the apricot pieces in a large kettle and add just enough water to cover them. Let soak overnight.

The next day, stir the sugar into the apricots and water. Bring the mixture to a boil over medium heat. Then cook slowly, stirring, until the apricots are soft, about 30 minutes. Cool before using.

Yield: Filling for 2 dozen *pirozhki* or 1 *pirog*.

• II •
APPLE FILLING
⚙ *YABLOCHNAYA NACHINKA* ⚙

1½ pounds tart cooking apples,   *1 tablespoon flour*
   peeled and cored
Juice of 1 lemon   *3 tablespoons butter*
⅔ cup sugar   *1 egg, beaten*
¾ teaspoon cinnamon   *Sugar*
½ teaspoon (scant) cardamom
   (or less, to taste)

Grate the apples coarsely and immediately mix them with the lemon juice in a large bowl. Stir in the sugar, cinnamon, cardamom and flour. Place a heaping tablespoon of the filling on each round of dough. Top the filling with a dot of butter.

Brush the dough with beaten egg and sprinkle each pie lightly with granulated sugar before baking.

Yield: Filling for 2 dozen *pirozhki* or 1 *pirog*.

• III •
POPPY-SEED FILLING
⚙ *MAKOVAYA NACHINKA* ⚙

⅔ cup almonds, very finely   *¼ cup unsalted butter*
   chopped   *¼ cup honey*
¾ cup poppy seeds   *White of 1 large egg*

Toast the almonds for 10 minutes at 300°F until lightly browned. Grind the poppy seeds. Cream together the butter and honey, then stir in the almonds and poppy seeds. Whip the egg white until stiff and fold into the poppy-seed mixture. Place a heaping tablespoon of the filling on each round of dough.

Yield: Filling for 2 dozen *pirozhki* or 1 *pirog*.

· IV ·
WALNUT-HONEY FILLING
❀ OREKHOVAYA NACHINKA ❀

An especially good filling for the Short Dough (see above).

2 cups walnut halves, finely chopped	¼ cup honey
¼ cup sugar	¼ teaspoon cinnamon
	Grated rind of 1 lemon

Mix together the sugar and honey, then stir in the cinnamon. Add the walnuts and the lemon rind, mixing well. Place a heaping tablespoon of the filling on each round of dough.

Yield: Filling for 2 dozen *pirozhki* or 1 *pirog*.

SMALL FISH PIES
🐟 RASSTEGAI 🐟

These charming pies are the traditional accompaniment to fish broth, *ukha*. Their name comes from the Russian *rasstegnut'*, "to come undone," because the pies' fanciful shape (with their filling exposed) makes one suspect they've popped open in the baking.

In the past, when appetites were larger, *rasstegai* were often made the size of a salad plate. One noted Moscow tavern, Yegorov's, claimed to serve the best *rasstegai* in town. When these fish pies were ordered, the *ukha* came free. It was Yegorov's showy waiter Pyotr Kirilych who perfected the serving of *rasstegai* at the table. With a bold flourish of knife and fork, he frenetically attacked the warm pastry, then stood back to admire his workmanship: ten thin slices artistically stretching out from the center of the pie to its well-browned edges. This method of slicing soon became the rage in Moscow, but no one could do it quite as stylishly as Pyotr Kirilych.

½ package active dry yeast
2 tablespoons warm water
Pinch of sugar
2 tablespoons butter, melted
2 egg yolks
¼ teaspoon salt
6 tablespoons milk
2 cups flour

¼ pound mushrooms, minced
1 tablespoon butter
¼ pound smoked salmon,
  finely chopped
2 tablespoons minced parsley
2 tablespoons sour cream
Freshly ground white pepper
  to taste

½ pound fish fillets (trout is
  especially good)
1 tablespoon butter

1 egg yolk, beaten
1 tablespoon cold water

Dissolve the yeast in the warm water along with the sugar. Then stir in the 2 tablespoons of butter and the egg yolks, salt and milk, which has been heated to lukewarm. Mix in the flour to make a soft dough. Turn out onto a floured board and knead until smooth and elastic. Place the dough in a greased bowl and turn once to grease the top. Cover and let rise in a warm place until doubled in bulk, about 2 hours.

Meanwhile, prepare the filling. Sauté the fillets in 1 tablespoon of the butter until they are done. Sauté the minced mushrooms in the remaining tablespoon of butter for just a few minutes. Flake the fish into a bowl and stir in mushrooms, salmon, parsley and sour cream. Season.

When the dough has risen, punch it down and then turn it out onto a floured board. Roll it out very thinly and with a 3-inch cookie cutter, cut out 2 dozen rounds. In the center of each round of dough place a heaping tablespoon of the filling.

Now shape the rasstegai. Starting just to the left of center of one of the rounds, bring two edges together to meet. Overlap one edge over the other and seal the left side of the pie. Now bring the two edges of dough together just to the right of the center of the pie, overlapping one edge over the other to seal. The result is an enclosed pie with a hole 1½ inches in diameter in the top center. Flare the edges of dough around the hole slightly to make it look rounder. Shape all the pies in this manner.

Place the pies on a greased baking sheet. Cover and let rise until almost doubled in bulk, 45 minutes to 1 hour. Brush the pies with a mixture of egg yolk and cold water.

Preheat the oven to 350°F. Bake the pies for 15 minutes, until golden. Serve warm or at room temperature.

Yield: 2 dozen pies.

✲)✺(✲)✺(✲)✺(✲)✺(✲)✺(✲)✺(✲)✺(✲)✺(✲)✺(✲)✺(✲)✺(✲)✺(✲)✺(✲)✺(✲)✺(✲)✺(✲)✺(✲)✺(✲)✺(✲)

COULIBIAC OF SALMON
⚑ KULEBYAKA ⚑

Of all Russian pies, *kulebyaka* is the most glorious, the *pirog* (pie) *par excellence* of the Russian cuisine. When made in the classical manner, it is elaborate and time-consuming, but the results are well worth the effort involved. *Kulebyaka* differs from the more common *pirog* in that the filling is assembled in layers, rather than being mixed together, and its finished shape is narrow and high instead of wide and flat. Perhaps the best description of a perfect *kulebyaka* is given by the court stenographer in Chekhov's "The Siren": "The *kulebyaka* should be appetizing, shameless in its nakedness, a temptation to sin." Would that one could sin more often with this magnificent pie!

Start preparing the puff pastry for the *kulebyaka* a day ahead of time.

PUFF PASTRY

2 cups flour	*½ cup unsalted butter*
¾ teaspoon salt	
½ cup water	*1 egg, lightly beaten*

In a medium-sized bowl, mix together the flour and salt. Add enough water to make a fairly soft dough. Knead it lightly.

Place the butter in a large bowl of ice-cold water. Working quickly, knead it with your fingers and shape it into a 4-inch square. Do not let the butter get too soft.

Roll the dough out to a 12-inch square. Place the butter in the center of the dough, then fold the sides of the dough up around the butter. Wrap in waxed paper and refrigerate for 30 minutes.

Roll the dough out into a long rectangle. Fold it into thirds. Turn the dough so that the raw edges are facing you and roll it out once more into a long strip. Fold in thirds once more. You have just completed two "turns" of the dough. Wrap the dough in waxed paper and refrigerate for 30 minutes.

Roll the dough out for a third time into a long strip; fold it into thirds. This is the third "turn." Refrigerate for 30 minutes.

Roll out the dough a fourth time, fold it in thirds and refrigerate. At this point, the dough may be held overnight in the refrigerator—in fact, it is a good idea.

The next day, roll out the dough into a long strip and then fold it into thirds. This is the fifth "turn." Refrigerate for 30 minutes.

Roll out the dough into a long strip, fold in thirds and wrap in waxed paper again. You have just completed the sixth and final "turn." The dough is now ready to be used. Keep it wrapped in the refrigerator until you are about to assemble the *kulebyaka*.

The next step in preparing *kulebyaka* is to make *blinchiki* (thin pancakes). These also may be prepared a day ahead, but they should be kept at room temperature overnight.

BLINCHIKI

1 egg, separated	*Pinch of sugar*
1¼ cups milk	*Pinch of salt*
4 tablespoons butter, melted	
1 cup flour	*Butter for frying*

Beat the egg yolk with the milk. Add the melted butter. Stir in the flour, sugar and salt. Beat the egg white until stiff but not dry, then fold it into the batter.

Heat a crepe pan or frying pan and brush it with butter. Fry the *blinchiki* one at a time until all the batter has been used up. Use only about 1 tablespoon of batter for each pancake, which should be as thin as a crepe.

If you are preparing them ahead of time, lightly brush each pancake with melted butter and stack them one on top of the other. Cover with plastic wrap or aluminum foil.

When ready to use the *blinchiki,* trim them into rectangles.

Next, prepare the remaining ingredients for the filling.

FILLING

4 eggs, hard-boiled	6 tablespoons raw rice
	1 tablespoon snipped fresh dill
½ pound mushrooms, trimmed and sliced	(or ¾ teaspoon dried dill)
1 tablespoon freshly squeezed lemon juice	4 tablespoons butter
	1 onion, chopped
2 tablespoons butter	1 ounce vesiga* or Chinese bean threads
Salt, freshly ground white pepper to taste	
½ cup dry white wine	Melted butter
1½ pounds salmon fillets	

Cut the hard-boiled eggs into thin slices. Set aside.

Toss the sliced mushrooms with the lemon juice. In a large kettle melt the 2 tablespoons of butter and stir in the mushrooms. Add salt and pepper to taste. Pour the wine into the pot. Cover and steam the mushrooms for 5 minutes. Then place the salmon fillets on top of the mushrooms and poach them, covered, until done, about 10 minutes. Do not overcook.

With a slotted spoon remove the salmon and mushrooms from the pot and set them aside. Measure the liquid remaining in the pot. There should be ¾ cup. (If there is not, add enough wine to make ¾ cup.) Cook the rice in this liquid until it is done. Stir in the dill.

Sauté the onion in the 4 tablespoons of butter until golden.

Boil the Chinese bean threads in salted water until soft and transparent, about 20 minutes. Drain. Mince the bean threads and add to the onion.

ASSEMBLY

On a floured cloth, roll the dough out to a 12 x 18-inch rectangle. (Throughout this whole process, try to work as quickly as possible so that the dough does not soften too much.)

* *Vesiga* is the gelatinous dried backbone of the sturgeon. If available, it gives a unique flavor to the *kulebyaka*. To prepare *vesiga,* soak it for several hours in cold water, then rinse. Put it in a pot with clean water, bring to a boil and simmer until tender, about 2½ hours. Drain and mince. I find that the Chinese bean threads (vermicelli) are a good substitute, as do the Russians living in San Francisco, who shop at the Chinese markets.

Spread half of the *blinchiki* (which have been cut into rectangles) in a strip 5 inches wide down the center of the dough, leaving a good inch of dough at either end. On top of the *blinchiki* place half of the rice mixture.

On top of the rice place half of the onion–bean thread mixture, then half of the sliced hard-boiled eggs, then half of the mushrooms. On top of the mushrooms place all of the poached salmon fillets, pressing down gently with the palm of your hand.

Now reverse the order. Top the salmon with the rest of the mushrooms, then the egg slices, the onion–bean thread mixture and the rice. Top the rice with the remaining trimmed *blinchiki*. Press down gently on the filling to mold it together.

Bring the two short ends of the dough up over the filling to enclose it, then carefully bring the two long sides of the dough up over the filling to meet in the center. Seal the edges securely, using a little cold water, if necessary, to help them adhere. Very carefully invert the *kulebyaka* onto a large baking sheet, which has been brushed with cold water.

Cut three small holes in the top of the dough. Decorate the *kulebyaka* with leftover bits of dough, using some of the beaten egg from the pastry recipe to help them adhere. Brush the dough all over with beaten egg. Place the *kulebyaka* in the refrigerator and chill for 30 minutes.

Preheat the oven to 400°F. Bake the *kulebyaka* for 10 minutes at 400°F, then reduce the heat to 350°F and continue baking for 20 to 25 minutes, until puffed and brown.

Serve with plenty of melted butter. (If desired, some melted butter may be poured into the holes in the *kulebyaka* when it is removed from the oven, but be careful not to add too much, lest the dough become soggy.)

Yield: 8 to 10 servings.

VARIATIONS:

1. The cream cheese pastry from the Cranberry-Apple Roll may be substituted for the puff pastry. Use one and a half times the amount given.
2. Substitute thickly sliced smoked salmon for the fresh salmon.

RUSSIAN CHICKEN PIE
💥 *KURNIK* 💥

Kurnik, whose name derives from the Russian word for hen, *kuritsa,* is yet another sort of Russian pie enclosed in rich pastry top and bottom. It's a stunning dish and good party fare, since it may be made early in the day and reheated at the last minute.

PASTRY

1½ cups butter, at room temperature	*2 egg yolks*
12 ounces cream cheese, at room temperature	*3 cups flour*
	½ teaspoon salt
	2 teaspoons baking powder

Cream the butter and cream cheese together. Mix in the egg yolks. Stir in the flour, salt and baking powder until smooth.

Divide the dough into two balls. Wrap each ball in waxed paper and chill in the refrigerator for at least 30 minutes before using.

CHICKEN

1 4-pound stewing chicken, including giblets	*1 onion, quartered*
4 cups cold water	*1 bay leaf*
1 sprig parsley	*8 black peppercorns*
1 large carrot, scraped	*1 teaspoon salt*
	1 teaspoon tarragon

In a large stockpot bring all the above ingredients to a boil. Simmer, covered, for 1½ hours, or until the chicken is tender. Then strain, reserving the chicken stock.

Remove the skin from the chicken and discard it. Separate the meat from the bones and cut the meat into small pieces. Chop the giblets.

Reserve the carrot and cut it into ¼-inch slices.

✿◇

FILLING

3 cups reserved chicken stock	*1 pound mushrooms, trimmed*
¼ cup sour cream	*and sliced*
1 tablespoon snipped fresh dill	*4 tablespoons chopped parsley*
(or 1½ teaspoons dried dill)	
¾ teaspoon salt	*4 hard-boiled eggs, coarsely*
1 cup uncooked rice	*chopped*
¼ cup butter	*1 egg yolk*
2 onions, sliced	*2 teaspoons cold water*
2 tablespoons butter	

First, heat 1 cup of the reserved chicken stock. Stir in the sour cream and dill, mixing well. Stir in ¼ teaspoon of the salt. Pour the mixture over the chopped chicken pieces, stirring to coat them well. Set aside.

Cook the rice in 2 cups of the reserved chicken stock, along with the remaining ½ teaspoon of salt, just until the liquid is absorbed. Do not overcook. Set aside.

Sauté the sliced onions in the ¼ cup of butter until soft and golden; then stir in the remaining 2 tablespoons of butter and the mushrooms. Sauté for about 3 minutes, until the mushrooms are just barely cooked. Stir in the parsley and the reserved sliced carrot. Drain off excess liquid and set aside.

ASSEMBLY

Remove one ball of dough from the refrigerator. Roll it out on a floured board to a circle about 12 inches in diameter. Line a 9-inch springform pan with the dough. Preheat the oven to 400°F.

Taking one third of the rice, place a layer of it on the bottom of the pastry. Top the rice with half of the chicken, then half of the chopped hard-boiled eggs, then half of the vegetable mixture. Top the vegetables with half of the remaining rice in an even layer, and then repeat the layering with the remaining ingredients, ending with a layer of rice on the top. (There will be 3 layers of rice and 2 of the other ingredients.)

Roll out the second ball of dough and cover the pie with it, sealing the edges well. Cut a round hole 1½ inches in diameter in the center of the top crust to allow steam to escape. Decorate the top crust with cut-out scraps of dough in a fanciful pattern.

Beat the egg yolk with the 2 teaspoons of cold water. Brush the mixture over the dough. Bake the *kurnik* at 400°F for 20 minutes, then reduce the heat to 350°F and continue baking for 25 minutes longer, or until the crust is golden. Allow the *kurnik* to cool in the pan for 20 minutes, then remove the sides of the pan to serve.

Yield: 8 to 10 servings.

VARIATION: It is a little less complicated to bake the *kurnik* in a regular pie plate, although the result will not be as spectacular. Roll out half of the dough and fit it into a 10-inch pie plate. Proceed as directed above, covering the filling with the remaining dough and crimping the edges well to seal. Cut a hole in the top crust to allow the steam to escape and bake as directed above. This version of *kurnik* is served directly from the pie plate.

CHICKEN KIEV
☙ KIEVSKIE KOTLETY ☙

These rich rolls of chicken encasing lightly herbed butter are a symbol of Russian *haute cuisine*. No one knows exactly when they were created, but their origin can be traced to the Ukrainian city of Kiev. Long before Moscow became the Russian capital, Kiev served as the major center of trade and culture. It was the first seat of the medieval Russian empire, founded on three hills overlooking the Dnieper River. Stimulated by the fertile soils and abundant wild food of the region, the culinary art has been practiced for many centuries in the Ukraine, producing such gastronomic *tours de force* as *borshch, pampushki, galushki* and the rightly renowned Chicken Kiev.

When cutting into Chicken Kiev, beware! When properly prepared, the cutlets will release a spurt of hot, rich butter, sometimes catching the diner unawares.

2 large whole chicken breasts, split	*Salt and freshly ground pepper to taste*
¼ pound butter, slightly softened	*Dijon-style mustard*
Freshly chopped parsley, chives and tarragon to taste	*Flour*
1 teaspoon freshly squeezed lemon juice	*2 eggs, lightly beaten*
	Fine dry bread crumbs
	Vegetable oil for deep frying

Cream the butter with any combination of finely chopped herbs you desire. (I use about 1 teaspoon each snipped fresh chives and tarragon and a bit more parsley.) Blend in the lemon juice. Shape the butter into four rolls, long enough to be placed lengthwise on the chicken pieces without extending over the edge of the meat and leaving a 1-inch border. Place the rolls of butter in the refrigerator to chill until firm.

Meanwhile, skin and bone the split chicken breasts. Then, between two sheets of waxed paper, pound each half-breast with a mallet until thin and flat, about ⅛-inch thick, being careful not to tear the meat. Lightly salt and pepper the chicken, and set aside.

When the butter is firm, remove it from the refrigerator. Spread each chicken fillet with a thin layer of Dijon mustard. Place a roll of butter lengthwise along each piece. Tuck in the ends of the fillets and roll them up, making sure that the butter is completely enclosed within the chicken packet. Dredge each fillet in flour, dip in the beaten eggs and then in the dry bread crumbs, so that it is completely coated. Adjust the fillets into uniform ovals. Put the fillets in the refrigerator and leave to chill for at least one hour (they can be held for 3 to 4 hours).

Preheat the vegetable oil to 360°F in a deep-fat fryer. Remove the fillets from the refrigerator and immerse them, only one or two at a time (depending on the size of the fryer), in the hot oil. Do not crowd them. Fry the fillets for 5 to 8 minutes, or until golden. Serve immediately. (If they must be held until the remaining breasts are fried, place them in a warm oven for no more than 5 minutes.)

Chicken Kiev is traditionally served with fried potato baskets (Straw Potatoes) filled with young green peas.

Yield: 4 servings.

NOTE: If no deep-fat fryer is available, the dish also works well when the fillets are simply fried in a frying pan over medium-high heat in a mixture of 4 tablespoons butter and 1 tablespoon vegetable oil. Cook the fillets for about 5 minutes on each side.

A highly unorthodox but delicious variation of Chicken Kiev is made by replacing the herb butter with a flavored cream cheese, such as Boursin, that has been shaped into rolls. Proceed as directed above.

For traditional Chicken Kiev, the wing bone is left attached to the chicken breast. Bone the breast as described above, then cut off the tip of the wing so that only a short projection remains. At serving time this stump is usually outfitted with an aluminum or paper frill to look fancy; I myself prefer the sleeker look of the cutlets without the wing bone.

CHICKEN CUTLETS
🏹 POZHARSKIE KOTLETY 🏹

Like Chicken Kiev, these delicate cutlets are a classic of Russian cuisine, evoking the elegant meals of the days of the tsar. Unlike Chicken Kiev, their origin can be traced back to the nineteenth century and the small merchant town of Torzhok. Before the advent of the Moscow–St. Petersburg railway, well-heeled Russians traveled by coach between the two cities, stopping frequently at way stations to rest and refresh themselves. One such way station was at Torzhok, where the head chef was a culinary wizard named Pozharsky. These cutlets are his legacy to the Russian cuisine.

Pozharsky originally made his cutlets from the wild game he trapped in the surrounding woods, but today they are most often prepared from chicken or veal. And today the traveler, well-heeled or not, simply hops on the Red Arrow Express between Moscow and Leningrad, finding himself at his destination overnight and having feasted on nothing more substantial than a glass of hot tea and any sandwiches he was foresighted enough to bring along.

*2 large, whole chicken breasts,
    skinned and boned
½ cup light cream
3 large slices day-old French
    bread (preferably sourdough-
    style), trimmed of crusts and
    torn into pieces
1 egg yolk
⅓ cup butter, softened at room
    temperature and creamed*

*¾ teaspoon salt
¼ teaspoon freshly ground
    black pepper*

*Flour
4 tablespoons butter
1 tablespoon cooking oil*

Sliced mushrooms, sautéed

In a food processor or meat grinder, grind the raw chicken finely.

In a large bowl, pour the cream over the bread. Mix with a spoon until the bread has absorbed all the liquid.

Add the ground chicken to the bread mixture, along with the egg yolk, the ⅓ cup of butter, salt and pepper. Beat until smooth and well blended.

In a large heavy frying pan heat the 4 tablespoons of butter and the oil. Shape the chicken mixture into 8 oval patties, dredging each one well in flour so that it is not sticky. (It helps if your hands are also well floured.)

When the butter is hot, put the patties in the frying pan and cook them over medium-high heat until they are golden brown, about 5 minutes on each side. Be careful not to overcook them, as they must remain moist. Serve immediately, garnished with sautéed sliced mushrooms.

Yield: 4 servings.

VARIATION: Substitute 1 pound of veal for the chicken; proceed as directed above. Or use a combination of half veal and half chicken.

CHICKEN STUFFED WITH PARSLEY AND LEMON
🜨 KURITSA, FARSHIROVANNAYA PETRUSHKOI 🜨

A noteworthy combination.

1 5-pound roasting chicken	½ teaspoon sweet paprika
1 lemon, quartered	⅛ teaspoon cayenne pepper
Salt, pepper to taste	1 teaspoon crushed savory
	6 ounces parsley, stems
1 tablespoon butter	removed, finely chopped
2 tablespoons olive oil	Juice of 1 large lemon
3 medium onions, finely	8 tablespoons butter, cut into
chopped	bits
2 cloves garlic, crushed	
Salt, freshly ground pepper	8 tablespoons butter
to taste	⅓ cup chicken broth

Wipe the chicken and rub it inside and outside with the lemon quarters, squeezing as much juice as possible onto the chicken. Sprinkle with salt and pepper. Set aside.

In a large, heavy-bottomed frying pan melt the 1 tablespoon of butter and the olive oil. Stir in the onions and garlic and cook over medium heat until soft and translucent, but not brown. Season with the salt, pepper, paprika, cayenne and savory. Stir in the parsley. Pour the lemon juice over all. Stir in the 8 tablespoons of butter and cook, stirring constantly, until the butter melts. Leave the mixture to cool slightly, then stuff the chicken with this mixture. Close the cavity opening well.

Melt the remaining 8 tablespoons of butter in a Dutch oven large enough to hold the chicken. Brown the chicken in the butter, turning it to cook evenly on all sides. Be careful not to tear the skin. When the chicken is brown, add the chicken broth. Cover the pot tightly. Simmer until the chicken is tender, about 1½ hours. Check periodically to make sure there is enough liquid in the pot; add more if necessary. Transfer to a platter and serve.

Yield: 4 to 6 servings.

NOTE: This dish will be only as good and as tender as the chicken you use. Go to a reliable butcher; otherwise the result may be less than delectable.

SPRING CHICKEN WITH GOOSEBERRY SAUCE
TSYPLYONOK POD SOUSOM IZ KRIZHOVNIKA

In old Russia, so many spring chickens were sacrificed in the name of genteel dining that they were commonly called the "great martyrs" (*velikomuchenitsy*). Here, the young fowl graciously accepts a gilding of gooseberry sauce in this subtle and delicate dish.

2 2-pound spring chickens	1 tablespoon butter
¼ teaspoon salt	1 tablespoon flour
½ onion	2 egg yolks, lightly beaten
2 sprigs parsley	1½ tablespoons freshly
3 teaspoons dried tarragon	squeezed lemon juice
2 tablespoons butter	1 tablespoon sour cream
	Salt, freshly ground white
8 ounces fresh gooseberries*	pepper
½ cup chicken stock	Freshly ground nutmeg to taste

* If fresh gooseberries are not available, substitute 1 16-ounce can of gooseberries, drained. Press the berries through a sieve to make a puree, and then proceed as directed above.

Preheat the oven to 450°F. Salt the chickens inside and out. Place one-quarter onion, 1 sprig of parsley and 1½ teaspoons of tarragon in the cavity of each chicken. Place the chickens in a roasting dish and dot them with the 2 tablespoons of butter. (If desired, new potatoes and onions may be roasted along with the chickens.) Place the chickens in the oven and immediately reduce the heat to 350°F. Roast until tender, about 20 minutes to the pound, basting occasionally.

Meanwhile, prepare the sauce. Cook the gooseberries in the chicken stock until tender, 15 minutes. Drain them, reserving the stock. Press the berries through a fine sieve to make a puree; set aside.

Measure the reserved chicken stock, adding more if necessary to make ½ cup. In a saucepan melt the 1 tablespoon of butter; stir in the flour and cook for a minute. Gradually whisk in the reserved chicken stock, then add the gooseberry puree.

Carefully add a little of the hot sauce to the egg yolks, then whisk the yolks into the sauce. Stir in the lemon juice, sour cream, and salt and pepper to taste. If the berries are especially tart, add a little sugar to taste. Just before serving, grind some fresh nutmeg into the sauce.

Serve the sauce in a sauceboat with the roast chicken.

Yield: 4 servings.

TURKEY BREAST WITH APPLES
❦ FILE INDEIKI S YABLOKAMI ❦

A novel way to prepare turkey—and an excellent one.

2 pounds boned, rolled and tied
   breast of turkey
2 cups rich chicken stock
6 black peppercorns
1 sprig parsley
1 onion, quartered
1 carrot, scraped and cut in half

2 tablespoons butter
2 tablespoons flour
2 heaping tablespoons sour
   cream
Salt, freshly ground pepper
   to taste
¼ teaspoon crushed thyme

¼ cup butter
3 medium tart apples, peeled,
   cored and sliced

½ cup grated sharp Swiss-style
   cheese
Parsley

In a Dutch oven, braise the turkey breast in the stock, along with the peppercorns, parsley, onion and carrot for 45 minutes to 1 hour, or until tender. Cool slightly; remove the string from the turkey roll and cut the meat into 8 slices, about 1 inch thick. Reserve the stock.

Melt the ¼ cup of butter in a large frying pan. Add the apples and cook them over medium heat until just tender, about 5 minutes. Remove the apples with a slotted spoon and set aside. Put the turkey slices in the frying pan and cook them over medium heat, turning once, until they are lightly browned.

Grease an oven-proof casserole large enough to hold the turkey slices in a single layer. Place the slices in the casserole and top them with the apples.

To make the sauce, melt the 2 tablespoons of butter in a saucepan, then stir in the flour and cook for just a minute. Gradually whisk in ¾ cup of the stock the turkey was cooked in, stirring constantly until thickened. Then stir in the sour cream, salt, pepper and thyme.

Pour the sauce over the turkey and apples, and then sprinkle the cheese over all. Place the casserole under the grill, and grill until browned and bubbly. Garnish with parsley and serve at once.

Yield: 4 to 6 servings.

BRAISED RABBIT IN SOUR CREAM
🜚 KROLIK, TUSHONYI V SMETANE 🜚

An exciting dish, both wild and elegant.

1 3-pound rabbit cut into
  serving pieces
¼ cup flour
Salt, pepper

3 tablespoons butter
1 tablespoon vegetable oil
¾ teaspoon marjoram

1 medium onion, chopped
1 medium carrot, scraped and
  chopped

1 tablespoon butter
1 tablespoon flour
1 cup rich chicken stock
3 tablespoons red wine vinegar
1 cup sour cream
Salt, freshly ground pepper
  to taste

2 tablespoons flour
Splash of sherry

Dredge the rabbit pieces in the flour, which has been seasoned with salt and pepper, coating them well. Brown the rabbit in a large frying pan in the 3 tablespoons of butter and the vegetable oil. When the pieces have been browned, season them with the marjoram, then transfer them to a Dutch oven and keep warm.

In the same frying pan fry the onion and carrot for about 15 minutes, or until soft. Place the cooked vegetables in the Dutch oven with the rabbit.

In a medium-sized saucepan melt the 1 tablespoon of butter and then add the 1 tablespoon of flour, whisking until smooth. Gradually stir in the chicken stock, stirring until the sauce has thickened. Then add the vinegar and sour cream. Season with salt and pepper. Pour the sauce over the rabbit and vegetables. Cover, bring to a boil and simmer for 1 hour.

Place the 2 tablespoons of flour in a small bowl and add a little of the sauce to make a thin paste, then stir the paste back into the sauce and cook for a few minutes more, until the sauce has thickened. Add a splash of sherry before serving.

Yield: 4 to 6 servings.

HALIBUT STEAKS WITH CAVIAR
✠ PALTUS PO-ASTRAKHANSKI ✠

These halibut steaks topped with a delicate *mirepoix* are exquisite as they are, but the caviar garnish gilds the lily. The dish is named after the port city of Astrakhan on the Volga River, not far from the Caspian Sea, where much of the famed Russian caviar is processed.

1 small onion, finely chopped	6 peppercorns
2 ounces green beans, finely chopped	2 cloves garlic
	1 bay leaf
1 carrot, scraped and finely chopped	½ teaspoon marjoram
2 ounces mushrooms, finely chopped	3 tablespoons butter
	3 tablespoons flour
Salt, pepper to taste	⅓ cup heavy cream
2 tablespoons butter	4 teaspoons freshly squeezed lemon juice
	3 tablespoons black caviar
4 ½-pound halibut steaks	
1 cup dry white wine	2 teaspoons black caviar

Prepare a *mirepoix*. Mix together the onion, green beans, carrot, mushrooms, salt and pepper. Place the vegetables in an oven-proof dish and dot them with the 2 tablespoons of butter. Cover and bake at 350°F for 30 minutes.

Place the halibut steaks in a large, shallow oven-proof dish. Add the white wine, peppercorns, garlic, bay leaf and marjoram. Cover and poach in a preheated 350°F oven for 15 to 20 minutes, or until the fish is done.

Remove the halibut from the poaching liquid and keep it warm. Reserve the liquid.

In a medium-sized saucepan melt the 3 tablespoons of butter and stir in the 3 tablespoons of flour. Cook over low heat for just a minute. Then stir in the poaching liquid, whisking constantly, and cook until the sauce has thickened. Then stir in the cream, lemon juice and the 3 tablespoons of caviar.

Place the halibut steaks on a serving platter. Top each steak with some of the *mirepoix*, spreading it rather thickly over the top of each steak. Pour the sauce over the vegetables and fish, and garnish each steak with ½ teaspoon of black caviar. Serve immediately.

Yield: 4 generous servings.

STURGEON WITH CHERRY SAUCE
鱼 OSETRINA POD VISHNYOVYM SOUSOM 鱼

Early travelers to Russia had fantastic tales to tell of the abundant fish in the rivers and streams. More than one visitor to Siberia and the Ukraine wrote of fish so numerous they were forced out of the water by the sheer weight of their numbers. The fishermen had only to approach the shore and gather them up. Moreover, the fish were often so large that it took three or four men to carry a single one (or so the seventeenth-century journals claim). But by the nineteenth century the plentiful stocks had been so depleted that only the wealthy could afford to put sturgeon on their dinner table; yet it has remained a Russian favorite.

4 ½-pound sturgeon steaks	½ cup cherry juice from the
1 cup dry white wine (or	canned cherries
vermouth)	2 tablespoons (scant) freshly
6 peppercorns	squeezed lemon juice
1 bay leaf	2 teaspoons sugar
	Salt, white pepper to taste
3 tablespoons butter	3 tablespoons Madeira
3 tablespoons flour	1 tablespoon capers
1 cup sour cherries (from	
1-pound can)	

Place the sturgeon steaks in a large, shallow oven-proof dish. Add the white wine, peppercorns and bay leaf. Cover and poach in a 350°F oven for 15 to 20 minutes, or until the fish is done.

Remove the fish from the poaching liquid and keep it warm. Reserve the liquid.

In a medium-sized saucepan melt the butter and stir in the flour, cooking over low heat for just a minute. Then gradually stir in the poaching liquid, whisking constantly. Cook until the sauce has thickened.

Stir in the sour cherries and the cherry juice, lemon juice, sugar, salt and pepper to taste. Add the Madeira and capers.

Place the sturgeon steaks on a serving platter and pour the sauce over them. Serve immediately.

Yield: 4 servings.

COD WITH EGG AND BUTTER SAUCE
TRESKA S POL'SKIM SOUSOM

In Russia, this method of preparing cod is popularly known as Polish-style. It is a very rich dish, especially nice when presented in small, deep casseroles for individual servings.

2 pounds cod (or other fish), cut into 2-inch cubes	12 tablespoons butter (1½ sticks)
Salt, pepper to taste	6 tablespoons freshly squeezed lemon juice
¾ cup dry white wine	
¾ cup fish or chicken stock	3 hard-boiled eggs, coarsely chopped
6 black peppercorns	
1 sprig parsley	6 tablespoons minced parsley
½ teaspoon thyme	½ teaspoon salt
1 to 2 pounds new potatoes	

Preheat the oven to 350°F. Season the cubes of fish with salt and pepper. Place them in an oven-proof dish and add the wine, stock and seasonings. Bring to a simmer over medium heat, then transfer the dish to the preheated oven. Poach for 15 minutes, or until the fish is flaky but still holds its shape.

Meanwhile, boil the potatoes in salted water. They don't have to be peeled. Cut into quarters or halves.

Prepare the sauce. Melt the butter with lemon juice over low heat. Add the eggs to the butter mixture, along with the parsley and salt.

To serve, place the potatoes in the bottom of a serving dish or individual casseroles. Top with a layer of fish. Pour the sauce over all. Serve at once.

Yield: 4 servings.

BEEF STROGANOFF
♨ BEF-STROGANOV ♨

In the nineteenth century, Russians of gentle birth often spent the social season in Paris. Although they professed a reverence for all things French —to the extent of employing local cooks—the Russians secretly cherished a love for their own native cuisine. This led to the invention of many new dishes bearing the names of the Russian nobility: Veal Orloff, Salad Demidoff, Nesselrode Pie. Beef Stroganoff was born in a similar way, the brainstorm of the French chef to Count Pavel Stroganov, a popular society figure in Paris at the turn of the century. The Stroganovs were one of the oldest noble families in Russia; as far back as the sixteenth century, when they were still merchants, Tsar Ivan the Terrible had granted them the right to develop land in Siberia. As their enterprise grew, so did their wealth, and by Count Pavel's time the family had been flourishing for several generations.

In order to come up with a dish to please his benefactor, Count Stroganov's chef simply added some very Russian sour cream to a basic French mustard sauce and *voilà!* It was a success. He named the dish after his employer, and Beef Stroganoff soon became an international favorite. Unfortunately, it has suffered all too often from a liberal addition of tomato paste and even ketchup; but made according to the original recipe, it is a noteworthy dish.

1½ pounds tenderloin of beef, trimmed and cut into strips 2 inches long and ½ inch thick	*2 tablespoons butter*
	2 tablespoons flour
	1 teaspoon dry mustard
	1 cup rich beef bouillion*
2 tablespoons butter	*¼ cup sour cream*
1 small onion, sliced paper-thin	
Salt, freshly ground black pepper	*Parsley*

Cut the beef into strips and set aside.

In a heavy frying pan melt the 2 tablespoons of butter and sauté the onion until soft and just barely golden. Add the meat all at once and

---

* To make a rich bouillion, boil down 2 cups of basic bouillion to concentrate it, or else a commercial condensed broth may be used.

cook over high heat for just a few minutes, until it is cooked through. Season with salt and pepper to taste. Set aside, but keep warm.

In a small saucepan melt the remaining 2 tablespoons of butter. Mix together the flour and the dry mustard and whisk into the butter. Cook for a minute, then gradually add the bouillion, stirring constantly, until a fairly thick sauce has been formed. Stir in the sour cream, mixing well. Pour the sauce over the meat, check for seasoning and heat through, but do not boil.

Spoon the meat and sauce onto a large platter (not a bowl) and garnish with parsley. Serve with Straw Potatoes mounded decoratively on top of the meat.

Yield: 4 to 6 servings.

NOTE: Mushrooms may be added to Beef Stroganoff if desired, although they are not strictly authentic.

STRAW POTATOES
🎏 *KARTOFEL' SOLOMKOI* 🎏

4 baking potatoes (the Russet variety is good)

Vegetable oil for deep frying
Salt

Peel the potatoes and cut into julienne strips. (This is most easily done with the julienne disk of a food processor.)

Heat the vegetable oil to 365° in a deep-fat fryer. Drop the potato strip a few at a time into the pot. Do not crowd them. Fry the potatoes until they just begin to turn golden, then remove them from the fat and drain on paper towels.

Just before serving the potatoes, heat the oil a second time to 370°F. Add the half-cooked potatoes a few at a time. They should cook through in just a few seconds and should be crisp and brown.

Drain the potatoes on paper towels. Salt to taste.

Yield: 4 to 6 servings.

NOTE: Potato baskets, often filled with young peas as a traditional garnish for Chicken Kiev, may be made by placing the raw julienne strips of potato in a commercial basket mold and proceeding as directed above.

HUSSAR-STYLE BEEF
☫ MYASO PO-GUSARSKI ☫

Hussars were the elite of the tsars' cavalry. Decked out in their smart uniforms of bright blue and red, astride the finest horses in the Empire, they were known for their high-living, often dandified ways. Interestingly, many of the hussars were descended from cossacks, who joined the guard in 1756, bringing with them a tradition of colorful language and daredevil style.

It is hardly surprising, then, to find such a showy dish as Hussar-Style Beef named after these guards. While admitting certain similarities to Beef Wellington and Saddle of Veal Orloff, Hussar-Style Beef uses native Russian methods and ingredients to achieve its splendid results—splendid enough to serve at your best dinner party, yet hearty enough to feed a troop of hungry cossacks.

2 packages active dry yeast	3 tablespoons grated Swiss-style
¾ cup water	cheese
¾ cup rye flour	2 teaspoons sour cream
	Freshly ground black pepper
2 1½-pound pieces top round	
of beef, 1 inch thick	2 cups water
2 tablespoons butter	1 tablespoon salt
1 large onion, quartered	4 cups rye flour
1 cup rich beef stock	2 cups white flour
¾ pound mushrooms, trimmed	
3 tablespoons butter	2 tablespoons butter
1 cup plus 2 tablespoons finely	2 tablespoons flour
grated stale black bread	
crumbs	Minced parsley

First, prepare a sponge for the dough. Dissolve the yeast in the ¾ cup of water. Stir in the ¾ cup of rye flour until well mixed, then cover and let rise in a warm place for 1 hour.

Meanwhile, start preparing the beef. In a large Dutch oven brown the steak in the 2 tablespoons of butter. Then add the onion and stock. Cover the pot and simmer for 10 minutes, no more. Remove the meat to a board to cool. Reserve the stock.

Finely chop the quartered onion from the stockpot. Chop the mushrooms finely. Melt the 3 tablespoons of butter in a large frying pan. Sauté the onions until golden, then stir in the mushrooms and the bread crumbs and cook for 10 minutes more. Remove from the heat, then stir in the cheese and sour cream. Add freshly ground black pepper liberally. Set aside.

When the meat has cooled enough to handle, with a sharp knife cut each piece thinly on the diagonal, cutting all the way through, but keeping the shape of the steak intact by reassembling the pieces. The pieces should be ¼ to ½ inch thick.

By this time the sponge should be ready. Stir in the 2 cups of water, the salt, and the remaining flour. Turn out onto a board and knead until smooth and satiny. Place in a greased bowl, turning dough to grease the top, and let rise in a warm place until doubled in bulk, about 1½ hours.

Meanwhile, spread some of the cooled mushroom filling between the slices of beef, reassembling the steak as you go. I find this easiest to do by spreading one slice of beef with the filling and placing it flat on the board. Spread the next slice with filling and place it flat on top of the preceding piece, continuing in this manner until four spread slices are stacked together. Then place this group of slices upright again, and proceed to the next. Continue spreading the mixture on the slices until each steak has been completely reassembled again.

When the dough has risen, punch it down and knead for a minute. Then divide it in half. Working with one piece of dough at a time, divide each into two pieces, one slightly larger than the other. Roll out the slightly smaller piece to an oval ¼ inch thick. The oval should 1 to 2 inches larger than the reassembled steak on all sides.

Place this oval on a greased baking sheet. Using two spatulas, carefully transfer the stuffed steak onto the oval of dough, centering it. Then roll out the second piece of dough and fit it on top of the steak, sealing the edges well by joining them with the bottom piece of dough. It helps to turn the bottom piece of dough up over the top piece at the edges, forming a rim, so that it won't come unsealed during baking. Use a little cold water if necessary to help the dough adhere.

Repeat this same procedure with the remaining ball of dough and the second steak. Let the pies rise until doubled, about 45 minutes.

Preheat the oven to 375°F. Bake the pies for about 40 minutes, or until the crust sounds hollow when tapped. Brush with melted butter to make the crust glisten.

While the pie is baking, prepare a sauce. Melt the 2 tablespoons of butter in a small saucepan and add the 2 tablespoons of flour. Cook for a minute over medium heat, stirring constantly. Then pour in 1 cup of the reserved stock to make a gravy. Keep warm over low heat.

When the pie is done, with a very sharp knife cut a large oval lid in the top crust, leaving an edge of only about 2 inches on all sides. Drizzle some sauce over the neatly sliced meat that is revealed inside, and sprinkle some minced parsley for color. Bring to the table with the crust slightly ajar to reveal the meat. Pass the rest of the sauce separately.

Yield: 10 servings.

BEEF STEW WITH RUM
✠ TUSHONOYE MYASO S ROMOM ✠

Here is an unusual and colorful stew that my grandmother used to make. In Russia it was reserved for special occasions because rum, unlike the common vodka, was a luxury item.

1 large onion, sliced
2 cloves garlic, crushed
2 tablespoons vegetable oil
3 pounds lean stewing beef
Salt, freshly ground black
* pepper to taste*
1 tablespoon Worcestershire
* sauce*
1 large bay leaf, crumbled
1 teaspoon ground savory
1 handful of fresh parsley
1 cup water

1 carrot, scraped and cut into
* ½-inch rounds*
2 parsnips, peeled and cut into
* ½-inch rounds*

¼ pound mushrooms, trimmed
* and thickly sliced*
1 to 1½ pounds tiny new
* potatoes, scrubbed but not*
* peeled*

2 tablespoons flour
2 heaping tablespoons green
* olives, minced*
1 16-ounce jar whole spiced
* crab apples*
2 tablespoons juice from the
* apples*
¼ cup dark rum

Parsley

In a stewpot sauté the onion and garlic in the oil until golden. Add the beef and brown it on all sides over medium-high heat. Season to taste with salt and pepper. Add the Worcestershire sauce, bay leaf, savory and parsley and pour the water over all. Cover, bring to a boil and simmer for 1 hour.

After the stew has simmered for 1 hour, stir in the carrot, parsnips, mushrooms and potatoes. Continue to simmer, covered, until the meat and the vegetables are tender, about 45 minutes.

When the stew is ready, strain it, reserving the broth. Place the meat and vegetables in a deep serving dish and keep warm. Return the broth to a saucepan and add the flour, which has been made into a paste with a little of the broth. Cook over medium heat, stirring constantly, until the gravy has thickened.

Add the olives and the spiced apple juice. Stir to mix well; continue cooking for 1 minute. The gravy will turn a deep rose color from the spiced apple juice.

Remove the sauce from the heat and stir in the rum. Immediately pour the sauce over the reserved meat and vegetables, mixing well. Serve garnished with the whole spiced crab apples and parsley.

Yield: 4 hearty servings.

VEAL STEW WITH CHERRIES
TELYATINA, TUSHONAYA S VISHNEI I FASOL'YU

Anyone who has read Chekhov's *The Cherry Orchard* knows of the Russians' fondness for cherries. Especially prized are the tart *morelivki* (morello cherries), which flourish in the central heartlands of the Soviet Union. In this recipe, the cherries are combined with veal—a meat delicate enough to absorb their flavor—and the result is a stew of a beautiful wine-red color and a subtly sweet taste.

1 cup dried white beans

2 pounds stewing veal, cubed

2 tablespoons flour

4 tablespoons butter

4 large scallions, including the
green tops, chopped

2 cups canned morello cherries
(sour cherries)

1 cup juice from the cherries

½ cup Madeira or Port

1 teaspoon salt

Freshly ground white pepper
to taste

A few grindings of fresh
nutmeg

Soak the beans overnight in water, and then cook them until just tender. Drain and set aside.

Dredge the veal cubes in the flour, then brown them in the butter. Add the scallions, cherries, cherry juice, Madeira or Port, salt, pepper and nutmeg to the veal. Bring to a boil and simmer for 1½ hours. Fifteen minutes before serving, stir in the cooked beans.

Yield: 4 to 6 servings.

NOTE: This stew will taste even better if made a day ahead and allowed to chill overnight. Reheat to serve.

ROAST WHOLE CALF'S LIVER
🦬 ZHARENAYA PECHONKA 🦬

Many years ago, in the very first home I ever visited in the Soviet Union, I was offered some delicious baked liver, served cold in one large piece and sliced very thinly. I remember being struck not only by the delicious flavor, but by the realization that there is more to calf's liver than the precut slices one normally buys at the supermarket. Since that day I have served roast whole liver many times, and I think it tastes even better straight from the oven. The whole liver may be ordered from any butcher or grocery meat department.

1 whole calf's liver (2 to 2½ pounds)	Salt, freshly ground pepper to taste
½ pound bacon	2 bay leaves, crushed
2 large onions, sliced	1 teaspoon basil
½ cup olive oil	½ teaspoon mace
¼ cup dry red wine	¼ teaspoon ground cloves
¼ cup red wine vinegar	½ teaspoon ground coriander

In a large, shallow oven-proof dish place the liver, bacon and onions. Mix together the remaining ingredients and pour the mixture over the meat. Marinate, covered, at room temperature for 4 hours, turning occasionally.

When ready to cook, sprinkle the liver with more salt and pepper. Lift the liver up and place some of the onion slices under it, then place the remaining slices on top. Spread the bacon crosswise across the top of the liver, covering it completely (the onion will be between the liver and the bacon).

Preheat the oven to 400°F. Place the liver in the oven and immediately reduce the heat to 350°F. Bake for 1 hour, or until done.

To serve, remove the liver from the marinade and strew the onions and bacon over it. If the liver is to be served cold, discard the bacon.

Yield: 6 servings.

VARIATION: A delicious variation is to chill the liver and slice it thinly, then marinate for several hours in any leftover marinade from Marinated Mushrooms.

COLD STUFFED EGGPLANT
☙ BAKLAZHAN FARSHIROVANNYI ☙

This stuffed eggplant looks spectacular and tastes every bit as good. As the slices fall away, the inside is revealed to be ribboned layers of eggplant and vegetable puree.

¼ cup olive oil	2 eggs, beaten
1 pound carrots, scraped and finely chopped	½ cup fine dry bread crumbs
2 pounds tomatoes, peeled and finely chopped	¾ cup olive oil
½ cup flour	½ teaspoon salt
	1 cup Basic Tomato Sauce

1 large eggplant (2 pounds)

First, prepare the filling. Heat the ¼ cup of olive oil in a large frying pan. Add the carrots and tomatoes and cook, covered, over medium heat for ½ hour, until the carrots are just barely tender; then simmer uncovered for 30 minutes until all moisture has evaporated.

While the vegetables are cooking, prepare the eggplant. Slice it lengthwise, unpeeled, into ½-inch-thick slices (you will need a very sharp knife to do this). Dip each slice in the flour, then the egg, and finally the bread crumbs until well coated. Try to keep the slices in their natural succession, since you will want to reassemble the eggplant.

Heat about ¼ cup of the olive oil in a large frying pan. Fry the breaded slices on both sides until golden. (The 2 endpieces should be fried on one side only—the skinless side. Repeat this process until all the slices have been browned, adding more oil to the pan as necessary. Drain on paper towels.

When the carrots and tomatoes are ready, puree them in a blender or food processor until a coarse puree has been formed (do not make it fine and smooth—there should still be some lumps of carrot in it).

Reassemble the cooked eggplant slices until the vegetable looks whole again. Then, taking one slice at a time, salt individually and spread some of the vegetable puree on each slice. Tie a string around the reassembled eggplant to hold it together, and place it in a greased baking dish.

Preheat the oven to 350°F. Pour the tomato sauce over the eggplant.

Bake, uncovered, for 45 minutes, basting twice with the tomato sauce. Remove it from the oven and cool to room temperature, then chill, preferably overnight, before serving.

To serve, cut the eggplant into crosswise slices to reveal the ribboned layers of vegetable puree.

Yield: 6 servings.

MUSHROOMS IN SOUR CREAM
GRIBY V SMETANE

A fortuitous marriage of two Russian favorites.

1 pound mushrooms, sliced paper-thin	½ cup sour cream
1 quart boiling salted water	4 tablespoons grated onion
Juice of ½ lemon	Dash of cayenne pepper
	Freshly ground white pepper

Boil the mushrooms in the water with the lemon juice for 1 minute. Refresh them under cold running water and pat dry. Add the remaining ingredients, mixing well. Cover and chill for several hours in the refrigerator before serving.

Yield: 4 to 6 servings.

BUCKWHEAT GROATS WITH MUSHROOMS AND CREAM
DRAGOMIROVSKAYA KASHA

Here, homely buckwheat groats are embellished with mushrooms galore in a dish named for the nineteenth-century general Mikhail Dragomirov.

1 recipe Buckwheat Groats,
   which has been kept warm
2 pounds mushrooms, trimmed
   and minced
4 tablespoons butter
½ cup heavy cream

Salt, freshly ground black
   pepper to taste
4 tablespoons chopped parsley

Dried Mushroom Sauce
Cooked carrots

In a large frying pan cook the mushrooms in the butter until the pan juices have evaporated. Then stir in the cream, salt and pepper. Cook for 1 minute. Remove from the heat and stir in the parsley.

Grease a 1-quart mold. Place one third of the cooked groats in the mold, pressing down with the back of a spoon. Make sure they cover the entire bottom of the mold. Place half of the mushroom mixture on top of the groats, leaving about 1 inch on all sides along the edges. Top the mushrooms with half of the remaining groats, then add the rest of the mushrooms. The top layer will consist of the last third of the groats.

Press down firmly with the back of a spoon, then unmold onto a serving plate. Serve with the Dried Mushroom Sauce poured over it. Pass extra sauce in a gravy boat. Garnish with cooked carrots, which have been cut into fanciful shapes.

Yield: 8 to 10 servings.

SOUR CREAM AND JAM PIE
☙ SMETANNIK ☙

Smetannik, whose name derives from the Russian smetana, "sour cream," is a gloriously rich pie, its buttery crust holding copious amounts of sour cream, jam and nuts.

PASTRY

2 cups flour
Pinch of salt
Grated rind of 1 lemon

1 cup unsalted butter, cut into
   pieces
2 egg yolks
1 tablespoon ice water

FILLING

1½ cups pecans or walnuts, ground	¼ teaspoon almond extract
½ cup sour cream	1½ cups raspberry jam (preferably seedless)
1 egg yolk	
1 teaspoon cinnamon	1 teaspoon sugar

To make the pastry, mix together the flour, salt and lemon rind. With a pastry blender or your fingers, cut the butter into the flour mixture until it resembles coarse meal. Work in the 2 egg yolks and water until the dough holds together, adding more cold water if necessary. Shape the dough into two balls. Wrap each in waxed paper and chill in the refrigerator for 1 hour.

Meanwhile, prepare the filling. Grind the nuts. Stir in the sour cream, egg yolk, cinnamon and almond extract.

Remove one ball of dough from the refrigerator. Roll it out to fit into a 9-inch pie plate. Spread the raspberry jam evenly across the bottom of the pie crust. Top the jam with the pecan–sour cream mixture, spreading it with a spatula so that it covers the jam evenly.

Preheat the oven to 375°F. Roll out the remaining dough into a top crust and position it over the filling. Trim the crusts and crimp the edges together to seal. Prick the top of the crust with a fork in a decorative pattern, and then sprinkle it with the sugar. Bake the pie for 35 to 40 minutes, or until lightly browned. Cool on a rack before serving.

Yield: 8 to 10 servings.

EUGENIA TORTE
☙ TORT "EVGENIA" ☙

New culinary creations were traditionally named in honor of family members, and no doubt this delicate torte is a tribute to a long-forgotten Eugenia. I have adapted this recipe from a limited-edition cookbook published in the San Francisco Russian community in the 1930s.

4 eggs, separated
2 egg yolks
½ cup superfine sugar
Grated rind of 1 large orange
¾ cup sifted potato starch
1 rounded tablespoon ground
  unsalted *pistachios*

1 rounded tablespoon ground
  blanched almonds

¼ cup sliced blanched almonds
¼ cup thick apricot jam

FROSTING

½ cup finely chopped unsalted
  pistachios
1 cup sifted confectioners' sugar
1 teaspoon orange-flower
  water*

¼ cup heavy cream

2 tablespoons finely chopped
  unsalted *pistachios*

Separate the eggs. Beat the 6 yolks together with the superfine sugar until thick and lemon-colored. Stir in the orange rind, potato starch and ground nuts.

Beat the egg whites until stiff but not dry. Fold into the cake batter.

Preheat the oven to 350°F. Prepare two 8-inch round cake pans. Grease them lightly, then fit a round of waxed paper onto the bottom of each pan and grease the waxed paper.

Pour the batter into the prepared pans and bake the cakes for 20 minutes. Let them cool in the pans for 10 minutes, then turn them out onto racks. Peel off the waxed paper and leave the cakes to cool.

Meanwhile, toast the ¼ cup of almonds until just golden in a 300°F oven for about 10 minutes.

* Orange-flower water is available in specialty stores. Freshly squeezed orange juice may be substituted, but the flavor will not be as delicate.

When the cakes have cooled, sandwich the 2 layers together with the apricot jam, which has been sprinkled with the toasted almonds.

Prepare the frosting. Mix together the ½ cup of finely chopped pistachios and the confectioners' sugar, orange-flower water and cream. Spread the icing over the top and sides of the cake, working quickly before it hardens. Sprinkle the remaining pistachios over the top of the cake.

Yield: About 12 servings.

QUEEN CAKE
⚔ *KOROLEVSKII TORT* ⚔

Old Russian cookbooks list several variations for this rich meringue-topped cake, which is said to have been introduced by the Nordic Prince Rurik, who was invited to rule over ancient Russia in 862 A.D. Along with his retinue he brought the Scandinavian taste for meringue and fruit combinations.

DOUGH

5 eggs, separated
½ cup sugar
1 tablespoon dark rum

Grated rind of 1 lemon
2 cups flour

FILLING

2 pounds tart apples, pared,
* cored and finely chopped*
1 cup dry white wine
½ cup sugar (or less, to taste)
½ cup golden seedless raisins
⅓ cup black cherry preserves

½ cup coarsely chopped
* blanched almonds, toasted*
¼ teaspoon ground cardamom
* (optional)*
1 tablespoon flour

MERINGUE

5 egg whites
¾ cup sugar

Pinch of cream of tartar

Prepare the filling first. Simmer, uncovered, the apples and the wine, ½ cup of sugar and raisins for 20 minutes. Remove from the heat and stir in the preserves, toasted nuts, cardamom and the 1 tablespoon of flour. Set aside to cool.

While the filling is cooling, prepare the dough. Beat the egg yolks with the ½ cup of sugar until thick and lemon-colored. Stir in the rum, lemon rind and enough flour to make a fairly firm dough. With floured hands knead the dough until smooth.

Divide the dough in half. Roll out each round to 9 inches in diameter. Place one of the rounds in the bottom of a greased false-bottomed tart pan, spreading the dough with your fingers so that it comes up the sides of the pan.

Spread the cooled apple filling on the bottom round of dough in the pan. Cover the filling with the second round, sealing the edges of the crusts to keep the filling in. Prick the top in a few places.

Preheat the oven to 350°F. Bake the cake for 30 to 35 minutes, until golden. Allow the cake to cool on a rack.

Just a couple of hours before serving, prepare the meringue topping. Beat the egg whites with the sugar and cream of tartar until stiff but not dry. Spread the meringue over the top of the cake, covering the crust completely. Bake in a preheated 325°F oven for about 15 minutes, until golden. Cool the cake slightly, then remove the rim of the pan. Serve the cake at room temperature. (Do not prepare the meringue topping too much in advance because it does not hold well.)

Yield: 10 to 12 servings.

❖◆❖

BABA AU RHUM
⚘ ROMOVAYA BABA ⚘

Although *romovaya baba* has been adopted into the classical French cuisine, its roots are Slavic: it was created at the court of the deposed Polish king Stanisław Leszczyński. The word *baba* is a pejorative term for "old lady" (the original shape of the cake was said to resemble an old woman in skirts), but the dessert's whimsical moniker belies its true elegance.

1½ packages active dry yeast (1½ tablespoons)	¼ cup unsalted butter, at room temperature
¼ cup warm water	¼ teaspoon (scant) salt
	2 tablespoons sugar
3 eggs, well beaten, at room temperature	2¼ cups flour
	⅓ cup currants

SYRUP

1¼ cups sugar	Juice of ½ lemon
¾ cup water	¾ cup light rum

Dissolve the yeast in the warm water until bubbly. Then beat in the eggs, butter, salt, sugar and flour, mixing well. Stir in the currants. In the bowl, work the dough with your hands for 10 minutes. (The dough will be sticky.) Cover the bowl and let the dough rise for 1 hour.

Liberally grease 8 baba molds (2½ inches high). With a spoon, fill the molds about one-third full with the dough. Then place them in a warm spot and allow the dough to rise just to the tops of the molds.

Preheat the oven to 375°F. Bake the babas for 15 to 20 minutes, or until a cake tester comes out clean. Turn the cakes out onto a wire rack.

Next, prepare the syrup. Bring the sugar, water and lemon juice to a boil, stirring until the sugar dissolves. Boil for about 5 minutes, until a thin syrup is formed. Stir in the rum.

While the babas are still warm, place them in a large bowl. Spoon the hot syrup over them, turning them gently to soak on all sides. Keep spooning the syrup until it has all been absorbed. Then set the babas on a plate to dry slightly. Serve at room temperature. The babas should be served the same day they're prepared; otherwise they will be soggy.

Yield: 8 small cakes.

CHARLOTTES
🗲 SHARLOTKI 🗲

Here are two recipes for charlottes, one to be served hot, the other cold. Baked Apple Charlotte is an old dessert with variations in many national cuisines. The cold version is a more recent creation, the brainchild of the great French chef Carême, who dreamed up the luxurious Charlotte Russe, or Russian Charlotte, while cooking for Tsar Alexander I around the time of Waterloo. Carême's Charlotte Russe is made of ladyfingers filled with a thick Bavarian cream. The recipe became so popular that it crossed the Atlantic with the waves of immigrants to the New World, where it was hawked in the streets of New York at the turn of the century.

The cold charlotte I'm presenting here is even tastier than the original, I believe. It too bears a Russian sobriquet, Charlotte Malakoff, having probably been named to commemorate the French victory at Malakoff (Malakhov) Hill during the Crimean War. In this version, the basic Charlotte Russe is rendered lighter and more delicate by substituting whipped cream for the Bavarian cream.

· I ·
✿ BAKED APPLE CHARLOTTE
✿ SHARLOTKA YABLOCHNAYA ✿

1 1-pound loaf stale white
   home-style bread
¾ cup dark rum
⅓ cup sugar
6 tablespoons unsalted butter

4 pounds tart cooking apples,
   peeled, cored and coarsely
   chopped

Grated rind and juice of
   1 lemon
¼ cup sweet white wine
¼ cup sugar
2 tablespoons unsalted butter
1 teaspoon cinnamon

1¼ cups thick apricot jam

SAUCE

¾ cup heavy cream
¼ cup sifted confectioners'
   sugar
¾ cup sour cream

Grated rind of ½ lemon
¼ teaspoon almond extract
½ teaspoon vanilla extract

Trim the crusts from the bread. Slice the bread into ½-inch-thick slices. Cut each piece lengthwise into thirds. There will be about 2 dozen pieces.

Preheat the oven to 250°F. Dip each piece of bread lightly in the rum to moisten on both sides, and then into the sugar, coating it lightly. Place the bread fingers on a rack in the oven and bake for 10 minutes, or until just barely dry to the touch. Do not allow the bread to harden.

Melt the 6 tablespoons of butter in a heavy frying pan. Lightly fry the bread slices until golden, on one side only.

Butter a 2-quart charlotte mold and dust it lightly with sugar. Arrange a few of the bread slices to cover the bottom of the mold, fried side down. Then position the other bread fingers vertically around the sides of the mold, fried side out. The fingers should overlap slightly. Reserve a few for the top.

Next, prepare the filling. Place the apples in a large frying pan with the lemon rind, lemon juice, wine, sugar, butter and cinnamon. Cover; simmer until tender, about 20 minutes. Then stir in the apricot jam, mixing thoroughly, and continue to cook, uncovered, until the mixture resembles a thick puree (it will remain lumpy).

Preheat the oven to 375°F. Allow the apple mixture to cool slightly, then pack it into the bread-lined mold. Top with the reserved fingers of bread, fried side up. Cover the mold. Bake the charlotte for 45 minutes.

Remove the charlotte from the oven and let it cool in the mold for at least 30 minutes. Then invert it onto a plate and serve it warm with the sour cream sauce.

To prepare the sauce, beat the heavy cream until it holds soft peaks. Beat in the confectioners' sugar, then fold in the remaining ingredients. Chill until serving time.

Yield: 6 to 8 servings.

NOTE: The bread used *must* be sturdy in order to hold the filling (the bread fingers perform the function of ladyfingers in the more usual cold charlottes). If spongy bread is used, the charlotte will collapse.

· II ·

CHARLOTTE MALAKOFF
☸ *SHARLOTKA MALAKOVA* ☸

15 ladyfingers (approximately)
8 tablespoons unsalted butter
1 cup confectioners' sugar
4 ounces almonds
1 ounce semisweet chocolate
2 cups heavy cream
4 tablespoons framboise
  (raspberry brandy)

½ cup heavy cream
2 tablespoons confectioners'
  sugar

Raspberries

Lightly butter a 2-quart charlotte mold. Place a round of waxed paper on the bottom of the mold. Line the mold along the sides with lady-fingers. Set aside.

Cream the butter; beat in the confectioners' sugar and continue beating until light. Grind the almonds and grate the chocolate finely. Stir the almonds and chocolate into the butter mixture. Whip the 2 cups of heavy cream until it stands in firm peaks, beating in the framboise toward the end.

Gently fold the whipped cream into the butter mixture, making sure that it is well incorporated. Pour into the prepared mold. Cover and chill for at least 2 hours.

Just before serving, whip the ½ cup of heavy cream with the remaining confectioners' sugar until stiff. Unmold the charlotte onto a serving platter, and with the whipped cream decoratively pipe rosettes on top of the dessert.

Serve with fresh or frozen raspberries.

Yield: 6 to 8 servings.

GURIEV KASHA
⚜ GUR'EVSKAYA KASHA ⚜

This classic Russian dessert is as full of calories as it is of panache. It was named after Count Dmitri Guriev, Tsar Alexander II's Minister of Finance, well known for his high-living ways. Guriev Kasha may be served warm from the oven or chilled.

6¾ cups light cream (or half
  milk and half cream)*
¾ cup regular Cream of
  Wheat (farina)
Pinch of salt
¼ cup sugar
1½ teaspoons vanilla extract

½ pound walnuts, coarsely
  chopped

½ cup sugar
1 teaspoon freshly squeezed
  lemon juice

12 ounces brandied fruit,
  drained and coarsely chopped
2 teaspoons sugar

Bring the cream to a boil in a deep saucepan, and then slowly pour in the Cream of Wheat, stirring constantly. Add the pinch of salt. Cook over medium heat, uncovered, until thick. Then stir in the sugar and vanilla extract. Keep warm.

While the Cream of Wheat is cooking, caramelize the nuts. In a large frying pan place the sugar and the lemon juice. Carefully heat until the sugar begins to melt, stirring constantly. Continue to cook until the sugar turns golden brown and syrupy; do not let it burn. Immediately stir in the walnuts and coat them well. Keep warm.

* Traditionally, the layers of Guriev Kasha are separated by skins formed from cooked milk. To make these milk skins, use half light cream and half milk in the amount called for above. Pour the mixture into a large, shallow pan and bake at 400°F until a skin forms on top. Carefully transfer the skin to a buttered plate. Make five or six skins in this manner. Measure the remaining milk, adding more cream if necessary to bring it to 6¾ cups. Then cook the Cream of Wheat in it as directed above. When Guriev Kasha is made with milk skins, it is usually prepared in one large dish. The skins are layered with the Cream of Wheat, fruit and nuts.

Grease 4 8-ounce glass serving bowls. In the bottom of each bowl place a layer of the cooked Cream of Wheat, then top it with a layer of caramelized nuts. Top the nuts with some drained brandied fruit, and then repeat the layering. The top layer should be Cream of Wheat.

Decorate the tops of the desserts with extra nuts and fruits. Sprinkle each dish with ½ teaspoon of sugar and brown under the grill. For a more flamboyant touch, top the Guriev Kasha with Spun Sugar (see below).

Yield: 4 servings.

SPUN SUGAR

8 ounces cube sugar   *⅓ cup water*
⅛ teaspoon cream of tartar

Take a dowel or broomstick 1 inch in diameter and support it between two chairs, or between the kitchen counter and a chair. It should be at about waist height. Grease the dowel liberally with vegetable oil.

In a small, deep saucepan, place the sugar, cream of tartar and water. Bring to a boil, stirring. When the crystals have dissolved, wash down the sides of the saucepan with a small brush dipped in water, until no sugar crystals remain.

Boil the syrup rapidly until it reaches 312°F on a candy thermometer. (You must watch carefully because this happens rather quickly.) Just at this point remove the syrup from the heat and, working as quickly as possible, take a wire whisk and dip it into the syrup. Throw the thick sugar syrup across the dowel, letting it drip down and turn into strands of spun sugar. Continue throwing the hot sugar onto the dowel until it is all used up, heating the sugar gently if necessary.

Gather the spun sugar from the dowel and gently shape it into one or several mounds of caramel-colored strands. The sugar does not keep well, especially in damp weather, so it is best to prepare it no more than a few hours before serving time.

NOTE: For ease in cleaning up, it's best to spread newspaper on the floor underneath the dowel to catch any sugar syrup that drips onto it.

THE TSARINA'S CREAM
🦂 KREM TSARITSY 🦂

Even the Tsarina, Empress of All Russia, seems too lowly an eponym for this exquisite dessert. So divine is its flavor that some people call it *pishcha bogov,* "food of the gods." A perfect ending to a rich meal.

1 package unflavored gelatin
  (¼ ounce)
¼ cup water

2 cups heavy cream
½ cup plus 2 tablespoons
  confectioners' sugar
¼ teaspoon almond extract

1¼ teaspoons rose water
5 tablespoons Maraschino
  liqueur
½ cup unsalted pistachios,
  chopped, or ½ cup lightly
  toasted blanched sliced
  almonds
Green food coloring

Soak the gelatin in the ¼ cup of water, then heat gently until the gelatin dissolves.

Whip the cream just until it begins to form soft peaks. Then beat in the dissolved gelatin, which has cooled somewhat, and the confectioners' sugar, almond extract, rose water and Maraschino liqueur. Fold in the nuts. Then add 2 to 3 drops of green food coloring, to tint the mixture pale green. If, with all the beating and folding, the cream is still not in stiff peaks, give it a few more turns with the whisk.

Turn the mixture into a 1-quart mold or into 6 individual molds. Sprinkle some chopped pistachios on the top.

Chill for several hours before serving.

Yield: 6 servings.

BERRIES AND CREAM
☙ *YAGODY* ☙

The Russians have a penchant for berries, the glorious fruits of a summer season all too brief in the northern climate. During the summer they flock to the countryside for wild strawberries, raspberries, blackberries, cloudberries, lingonberries and other berries too numerous to name. Perhaps the best way to enjoy berries is straight from the bush, but a favored Russian combination is berries and cream. Here are two variations on that theme.

In the first recipe, sour cream gives the berries a Slavic twist. The second recipe, Strawberries Romanov, is now an international favorite. The dessert was no doubt dubbed Romanov—the name of the tsarist dynasty that ruled over Russia for several centuries—because of its spendthrift use of rich ingredients. But don't expect to find Strawberries Romanov in the Soviet Union today: Romanov is no longer a name to be commemorated there, even in a dessert.

· I ·

BERRIES WITH SOUR CREAM
⚙ *YAGODY SO VZBITOI SMETANOI* ⚙

1 cup sour cream
2 tablespoons sugar

¼ teaspoon vanilla extract

Mix together the sour cream, sugar and vanilla extract in a medium-sized bowl, and beat with an electric mixer for 10 to 15 minutes, until the cream has doubled in bulk. Spoon the beaten cream over berries, and serve.

NOTE: In order for the cream to attain the greatest volume, both the bowl and the beaters should be well chilled before the whipping begins.

❀◈❀

• II •
STRAWBERRIES ROMANOV

1 pint strawberries, hulled
2 tablespoons sugar
¼ cup Cointreau or Triple Sec
2 tablespoons freshly squeezed
    orange juice

2 egg whites

⅛ teaspoon cream of tartar
½ cup sugar

½ cup heavy cream
1 tablespoon confectioners'
    sugar

Place the strawberries in a bowl and toss them with the 2 tablespoons of sugar. Mix together the Cointreau or Triple Sec and orange juice, pour over the berries, and leave to macerate for 2 hours at room temperature.

Beat the egg whites with the cream of tartar until they begin to hold soft peaks. Gradually beat in the ½ cup of sugar, beating until a thick meringue has been formed.

Preheat the oven to 275°F. Line a baking sheet with aluminum foil and grease the foil. With a spoon make 8 rounds of meringue on the foil, flattening the centers slightly with the bowl of the spoon. Bake the meringues for 1 hour, or until lightly browned. Remove to a rack to cool.

To serve the dessert, whip the cream with the confectioners' sugar. Place a generous portion of macerated strawberries on top of each meringue round. Top with the whipped cream.

Yield: 4 servings.

RHUBARB MOUSSE
🌿 *MUSS IZ REVENYA* 🌿

Improbable as it sounds, rhubarb belongs to the same family as buckwheat, that perennial Russian favorite. Prepared here with a judicious amount of sugar and cream, it makes an exquisite dessert.

2 to 3 large stalks of rhubarb, cubed (4 cups)	*1 tablespoon cornstarch*
1½ cups sugar	*1 cup heavy cream*
½ teaspoon cinnamon	*¼ teaspoon almond extract*
	½ teaspoon vanilla extract

Place the rhubarb cubes in a heavy saucepan along with the sugar and cinnamon; stir to mix well. Cover and simmer over low heat until the rhubarb is just tender, about 5 minutes. Strain the juice from the cooked rhubarb into a measuring cup. There should be about 1¼ cups. Reserve the cooked rhubarb.

Rinse out the saucepan and return the rhubarb juice to it. Mix the cornstarch with a small amount of the juice in a bowl, then add it to the saucepan. Cook the mixture over medium heat for about 15 minutes, or until the mixture has thickened and is reduced to ¾ cup.

Stir the thickened juice into the reserved rhubarb. Set aside to cool to room temperature.

Beat the cream until stiff, beating in the almond and vanilla extracts. Fold in the cooled rhubarb carefully, until it is well blended with the cream. Chill until serving time.

Yield: 4 to 6 servings.

FROSTED CRANBERRIES
❧ KLYUKVA S SAKHAROM ❧

In many Soviet restaurants these beautiful frosted berries may be ordered for dessert. They arrive at the table mounded high in a footed glass bowl, sparkling and festive. Try them as a perfect highlight for your next holiday buffet.

1 pound cranberries   *1½ cups sugar*
1 egg white

Beat the egg white until foamy but not stiff. Pour the cranberries into the foamy egg white, stirring gently until the berries are completely coated.

Put the sugar in a large bowl and add the cranberries. Toss until the berries are completely coated with sugar.

Preheat the oven to 150°F. Spread the cranberries in a shallow pan (about 12 x 18 inches) in a single layer. Place in the oven for about 12 minutes, or until the sugar has melted.

Turn the berries out onto a large sheet of waxed paper (about 2 feet long) and separate them so that the frosting can harden. Leave the berries to dry overnight at room temperature. Store in an airtight container. The cranberries will keep in the refrigerator for about two weeks.

Yield: 4 to 6 servings.

☗ · III · ☗

HOLIDAY CELEBRATIONS

ussians are a celebratory people, always eager for an excuse to make merry—and the merrymaking usually revolves around food. When Russians celebrate, it's a lavish affair; there's no stinting on ingredients or proportions. A holiday feast is not just for family, it's a *pir na ves' mir,* a "feast for all the world." (Russians are as given to hyperbole as they are to extravagance.) Under the old Russian Orthodox calendar, there were plenty of holidays, each an excuse to celebrate. And around these excuses developed traditional meals, accruing ritual as the years went by.

Russian holidays evolved from the pagan pantheistic festivals of the ancient Slavic tribes, coinciding with the natural change of seasons and the harvest cycle. After Grand Prince Vladimir accepted Christianity for Russia in 988 A.D., the pagan rites were gradually assimilated by the clergy, until the springtime merrymaking celebrating the start of a new planting season came to glorify the Orthodox Easter, and the winter festivities, once celebrating the rebirth of light into the world after the winter solstice, became Christmas.

The Russian Orthodox calendar was based on a succession of feasts and fasts, with the presence or lack of food playing a central role in worship. Everyone took part in the feasting, of course, but except for the major fasts, like Lent, most Russians just went right on eating. After the fall of the Romanovs in 1917, the traditional Russian religious holidays were either abolished or reformed to become secular occasions. What had been the elaborate Christmas festival became the New Year's celebration; Easter was superseded by International Workers' Day on May 1. The other holidays are observed only rarely in the Soviet Union today, although émigré communities continue to celebrate them.

All of the old Orthodox feast days were associated with special dishes, often made from foods unavailable at other times of the year. Russians love to regale one another with delicacies. But the newer Soviet holidays have yet to produce ritual dishes. Consequently, the holidays described in this chapter are those celebrated by the Russian Orthodox Church, in which the role of food bears greater significance.

☼ EASTER (PASKHA) ☼

By far the most important holiday in the Russian Orthodox Church is Easter, a time of great feasting and rejoicing, falling as it does after the six-week Lenten fast, when no meat or dairy products are allowed—a considerable deprivation in a climate where vegetables are often scarce. During the week preceding Easter, known as Passion Week (*strastnaya nedelya*), the foods for the feast are prepared. One can only imagine the extremes of temptation these holiday cooks are subjected to, preparing delicacies from the finest available ingredients after six long weeks of denial. Finally, on Easter Eve, the table is set with an abundant spread, featuring the traditional *paskha, kulich* and decorated eggs. This custom of decorating eggs can be traced back to the pagan spring festivals, when eggs were painted with bright colors to symbolize the blossoming of the plant world. Today egg painting is considered an art form, especially in the Ukraine, where the intricate designs are applied by a complex process of dipping in beeswax and dye baths. These spectacular Ukrainian eggs are known as *pisanki*.

Once the table has been set with the ritual foods, the Russians throng to the cathedral, where a midnight Mass is celebrated. (This Mass is so meaningful that even today, in the provincial cities of the Soviet Union, the populace makes an effort to attend.) When I was in Rostov-on-Don, the police were called out to control the large crowd trying to make its way into the cathedral. The police would allow only the *babushki*—women over sixty, for the most part—to go in, but the crowd continued to mill around the square outside, hoping for a glimpse of the procession of the cross. The same crowds are attracted halfway around the world in San Francisco. The entire block around the Orthodox cathedral is closed to traffic on Easter Eve. Even that enormous cathedral cannot accommodate everyone, and people spill off the cathedral steps, crowding into the street. Traditionally, the women arrive at the cathedral carrying baskets filled with Easter foods to be blessed—*kulich, paskha* and dyed eggs. The church itself is redolent with the heavy scent of incense wafting from ornate censers. The crowd presses close together as the midnight service begins. Soon it is time for the most dramatic part of the service, the *krestnyi khod,* "procession of the cross." As the cathedral doors are swung open, the priest intones several times *Khristos voskrese,* the congregation responding with *Voistine voskrese:* "Christ is risen; truly He is risen," words from the Church Slavonic that are still spoken in Easter greeting today among the older generation. Holding the cross high, the priest, followed by altar boys and much of the congregation, proceeds through the main doors of the church and circles the building three times.

After the service, people return to their homes, where the Easter breakfast—in its most literal sense—is enjoyed. The table has been set like a *zakuska* table, only on a grander scale, decorated with flowers and greenery to celebrate the arrival of spring. In the center of the table there is usually a *barashek iz masla* (lamb molded out of butter), its body textured by having been rubbed with cheescloth to resemble fleece. The lamb holds a sprig of greenery in its mouth, and sometimes its neck is adorned with a parsley collar. Flanking the butter lamb are the two most symbolic Easter dishes, the *paskha* and the *kulich. Paskha* is perhaps the most glorious version of cheesecake to be found in any national cuisine. It evolved from the ancient Slavic custom of eating cottage cheese (*tvorog*) with honey at the onset of spring, but nowadays the cheese is sweetened with sugar. Traditionally the *paskha* is molded in a pyramid-shaped form indented with the Cyrillic letters *XB,* which stand for "Christ is risen." If the form does not already bear these letters, they are applied by careful decoration with currants or glacéed fruits.

The *paskha* is sliced and spread on its companion, *kulich,* a tall, stunning loaf of saffron-scented bread, topped with a mushrooming crown. The crown is first cut off from the top, and then the loaf is sliced horizontally. (The crown is always replaced after serving so that the bread will retain its moistness as well as its visual appeal.) Around the table other sweets and confections also proclaim *XB.* Typical Russian Easter desserts include *mazurki* (rich cookies), *krendel'ki* (boiled pretzel-shaped cookies), and *babki* (sweet yeast-raised cakes, which often exceed the *kulich* in height, attaining up to 19 inches, but not decorated as elaborately as *kulich*). More substantial fare is provided by roast ham or suckling pig. And, of course, the table is laden with baskets of brightly dyed and decorated eggs displayed on beds of green leaves or grass.

The Easter table in all its glory remains set for at least a week, with replacement delicacies constantly coming in from the kitchen to welcome hungry guests. The visiting begins on Easter Sunday. On this first day only the men go out visiting, while the women stay at home to receive guests and regale them with the abundance of their table. After the first day the women go visiting, too, and guests roam from house to house, bringing greetings to all with "Christ is risen," accompanied by three kisses on alternate cheeks. The usual meal hours are suspended, as people eat whenever guests arrive or they themselves go visiting. Easter is the height of the religious year, a time when the best foods are offered and enjoyed, the occasion for much indulgence.

In fact, the Russian Easter is such an occasion that it became the object of irreverent satire from the pen of Teffi in 1912. In her "Easter Advice to Young Homemakers," a spoof on the leading cookbook of the time, Teffi makes fun of all the ritual Easter foods in turn, finally reaching the chicken:

> Besides what's been mentioned above, you must put either a turkey or a chicken on the Easter table, depending on what terms you and your grocer are on. But no matter what kind of bird it is, you are bound to dress its stumps with pantaloons of frilled paper if you have any couth at all. This will immediately raise the bird in the esteem of your guests. . . .
>
> Under one of the bird's wings you must tuck its own liver; under the other—its kidney. A chicken decked out this way will look as if it's about to rise into the air and take off on a long journey with all its essentials in hand, having forgotten only its head.

❀ BUTTER FESTIVAL (MASLENITSA) ❀

Perhaps the closest rival to the Easter feast is found in the gorging that precedes the great Lenten fast. This revelry is known as the Butter Festival, and since it offers the last chance to eat dairy products for a long six weeks, the Russians make the most of it. *Maslenitsa* (from the word *maslo,* "butter") is a carnival time akin to the Western Mardi Gras. Young people used to build ice hills and send burning effigies of winter crashing down their slopes; they constructed large bonfires (fire signified the pagan worship of the sun); they hired troikas for gay rides in the country.

But the favorite pastime, providing the best entertainment of all, was (and still is) the eating of *blini*. *Blini* are thin pancakes traditionally made with buckwheat flour and leavened with yeast. They are round, as the ancient Slavs made them in the image of the sun, and are served with a wide choice of condiments: they can be spread thickly with butter and topped with red or black caviar, smoked sturgeon, salmon or herring; or they can be served sweet, spread with sour cream and jam. The Russians eat large numbers of these light pancakes—at one time in anticipation of the rigorous fast ahead, but now simply out of pleasure. Even though *maslenitsa* is no longer officially recognized, Russians are always on the lookout for an excuse to eat *blini*. The pancakes are so popular that they have even worked their way into speech: an expression meaning "to live high off the hog" has come down in contemporary language as "This isn't everyday life, it's Butter Festival!" And of flatterers it is said, "He tries to slip like a buttery *blin* into your mouth."

☼ ARRIVAL OF SPRING (ZHAVORONKI) ☼

The only other springtime festival worthy of note is by custom celebrated on March 9, the day the skylarks, or *zhavoronki,* are said to return from their winter migration. Young girls used to go out into the fields to toss bread crumbs to the birds, wishing them welcome as the harbingers of spring. Bake shops were full of sweet rolls molded in the form of larks, and even today these confection larks are prepared in early March, although their significance has been lost.

☼ CHRISTMAS (ROZHDESTVO) ☼

Just as the spring solstice is greeted with celebration, so winter, too, brings festivities. Like Easter, the Russian Orthodox Christmas ends a period of fasting, which is broken on Christmas Eve; and like Easter, Christmas has elaborate customs. Before sitting down to the ritual meal, the head of the household goes out into the street, seeking any wayfarers who might not have a home for Christmas and inviting them inside to share in the breaking of the fast. On Christmas morning the young girls bring boughs of cherry blossoms to the church to place before the icons. The boughs are cut on St. Catherine's Day (December 7) and kept in water so they will bloom at Christmas. Other gifts are offered as well, such as homemade *ledentsy,* fruit-flavored hard candies wrapped in brightly colored paper. Amusements include *kolyadovanie,* when groups of young people go from house to house singing in exchange for small gifts. Another favorite custom is mummery (wonderfully described in Volume 2 of Tolstoy's *War and Peace*), for which the young people dress in exotic costumes and travel by sleigh from house to house, spreading mirth and good cheer.

Christmas means feasting in all lands; in Russia the holiday fare features *kut'ya,* a dish of steamed, sweetened wheat with fruit and raisins, and *vzvar,* stewed dried fruits. In the Ukraine a fancy braided loaf, known as *kolach,* is served, sometimes adorned with candles. Other foods that might enhance the Christmas Eve meal include hot soups, especially rich with fats for the occasion; *pirozhki,* filled with meat or cabbage or mushrooms; fish, usually carp, served hot or sometimes cold in aspic; and roast goose stuffed with fruit. Most homes are decorated with a Christmas tree, introduced by Tsar Peter the Great, Russia's first Westernizer. In tsarist Russia, among the gentry, it was often a matter of great pride to have the largest and most ornate tree. Today, in the Soviet Union, the custom of having a holiday tree still prevails, only now it is considered a New Year's tree.

✿ THE NEW YEAR (NOVYI GOD) ✿

Strictly speaking, the New Year is a Soviet holiday, a time of partying and drinking, but since the occasion has taken on folkloric aspects, it deserves mention here. Some of the Russian New Year's customs are similar to Western tradition: the tree is put up and decorated with tinsel and ornaments, and *Ded Moroz,* or Grandfather Frost, makes a holiday appearance. *Ded Moroz* is a character out of old Russian folklore, a tall, bearded figure encrusted in snow and ice who lives in an ice cave and chats with the creatures of the forest. Resurrected to play a refreshingly whimsical role in contemporary socialist life, *Ded Moroz* can be ordered by telephone to pay a visit to the children on New Year's Day. He is accompanied on his rounds by another folk figure, *Snegurochka,* the Snow Maiden, a princess dressed in white and shades of blue, sparkling with snowflakes. She and Grandfather Frost distribute sweet cookies called *pryaniki,* which symbolize a sweet new year for the children. Since the Soviet New Year is a family holiday, a large meal featuring roast goose or chicken is usually prepared. This meal is eaten only after midnight, when the first vodka toasts to the New Year have been made.

✿ *NAME DAY (IMENINY)* ✿

Finally, food plays a significant role in the Russian Name Day festivities. The Name Day was celebrated in old Russia more often than the actual birthday. Before the Revolution, only the names of saints recognized by the Russian Orthodox Church were deemed suitable for a newborn child. Each day on the Orthodox calendar was named for a saint, as was each child, and the Name Day was celebrated according to the saint's day on which it fell. The Name Day celebrant customarily hosted a party, inviting friends and family to share in the traditional treat of *krendel'*, a large, rich pretzel-shaped loaf of sweet bread. Along with the *krendel'* there might be *khvorost,* thin, deep-fried cookie twists sprinkled with powdered sugar. These sweets were often washed down with thick hot chocolate fortified with beaten egg yolks.

Although all of the recipes in this chapter are closely associated with specific holidays, they can be made at any time. *Blini* are wonderfully appropriate for a fancy brunch. *Krendel'* and *kulich* are excellent breads to serve at teatime. *Kut'ya* should please one's vegetarian friends. And it's a shame to eat *paskha* only once a year!

RUSSIAN EASTER CHEESECAKE
✠ *PASKHA* ✠

Here are recipes for three different kinds of *paskha*—evidence of my own weakness for this rich cheesecake. *Paskha* may be boiled or unboiled. The boiled version requires more effort, but it stays fresh longer, which was an important consideration in the days before refrigeration. My own favorite is the unboiled *paskha* in the first recipe, lighter than the others since whipped sweet cream is used in place of sour cream. The recipe was given to me by Maria Nikolaevna, a Russian émigré of the first wave who still loves to cook in the traditional style. The other two recipes have been adapted from Elena Molokhovets's renowned nineteenth-century cookbook.

· I ·
MARIA NIKOLAEVNA'S *PASKHA*

2½ cups sugar (preferably vanilla sugar)*
5 large egg yolks
1 pound unsalted butter

3 pounds Russian Cottage Cheese (tvorog) *or farmer cheese*
1 whole vanilla bean
1 pint heavy cream

Beat the sugar and egg yolks together until light and thick. In a separate bowl, cream the butter until smooth, then add the beaten sugar and egg yolks, mixing well.

Press the *tvorog* through a fine sieve, then mix it in well with the butter mixture, beating until the mixture is completely smooth. Slit the vanilla bean lengthwise and scrape the seeds out into the mixture. Stir in the cream.

Line a 3-quart *paskha* mold or large clay flowerpot with cheesecloth. Pour the cheese mixture into the mold, folding the cheesecloth over the top. Set the mold in a bowl in the refrigerator. Place a saucer on top of the

---

* Vanilla sugar is made by placing a whole vanilla bean in a container of sugar and leaving it there to flavor the sugar. Before using for the first time, the sugar should be allowed to sit for 1 week. Replace the vanilla bean every 3 months or so.

mold, and set several heavy cans on it to weight the cheese mixture down and force the liquid out through the drainage hole in the bottom of the mold or flowerpot.

Let the *paskha* drip overnight in the refrigerator, until all excess liquid has dripped out. Unmold.

Decorate the sides of the *paskha* with the letters *XB* in currants or nuts. Serve with Russian Easter Loaf (*kulich*).

Yield: 1 *paskha*.

VARIATIONS:

1. Add 1 cup finely chopped *unsalted* pistachios to the cheese mixture.
2. Add 1¾ cups dark seedless raisins, 2½ tablespoons finely chopped blanched almonds, and finely chopped mixed peel to taste to the cheese mixture.

NOTE: In all of these *paskha* recipes, *unsalted* butter *must* be used.

Always make sure that the *tvorog* is well sieved and thoroughly blended with the butter and other ingredients; otherwise the *paskha* will turn out lumpy and unstable.

After scraping the inside of the vanilla bean, some cooks then chop the bean itself finely and add it as well.

· II ·
ROYAL *PASKHA*
✿ *PASKHA TSARSKAYA* ✿

3 pounds Russian Cottage Cheese (tvorog) *or farmer cheese*	*2 cups superfine sugar*
5 whole eggs, lightly beaten	*1 vanilla bean, scraped*
½ pound unsalted butter	*½ cup finely chopped blanched almonds*
2 cups sour cream	*½ cup currants*

In a large frying pan stir together the *tvorog,* eggs, butter and sour cream. Heat the mixture just to the boiling point, stirring until smooth and creamy. *Do not allow to boil.* When the mixture is completely smooth, remove from the heat and set the frying pan over ice to stop the cooking. Stir the mixture until it cools to lukewarm.

Stir in the remaining ingredients. (The vanilla bean is slit lengthwise and the seeds are scraped into the mixture). Then chill the mixture in a bowl in the refrigerator until it has slightly thickened.

Line a 3-quart *paskha* mold or a flowerpot with muslin. Pour the cheese mixture into it. Proceed as in the above recipe, weighting the cheese mixture down from above and allowing it to drip overnight.

Yield: 1 *paskha*.

· III ·
PINK *PASKHA*
❁ *ROZOVAYA PASKHA* ❁

¼ *pound unsalted butter*
¾ *cup superfine sugar*
3 *whole eggs*
2 *pounds* Russian Cottage
   Cheese (tvorog) *or farmer*
   cheese

2 *cups sour cream*
1 8-*ounce jar seedless raspberry*
   jam

Cream the butter and sugar until light and fluffy, then beat in the eggs.

Put the *tvorog* through a fine sieve, then mix it with the butter mixture, beating until completely smooth. Stir in the sour cream, then the jam.

Line a 2-quart *paskha* mold or flowerpot with cheesecloth. Pour the cheese mixture into it and proceed as directed above.

Yield: 1 *paskha*.

NOTE: This pink *paskha* should always be served alongside the more traditional white one.

RUSSIAN EASTER LOAF
✠ KULICH ✠

Many Russian families still treasure an heirloom recipe for *kulich*. The traditional loaf is saffron-flavored and somewhat dry in texture, but it may also be made rich in butter and cake-like, as in the second recipe below. Old-fashioned cooks still treat their *kulichi* very gently upon removal from the oven. They turn the bread out onto a large down-filled pillow and carefully roll it from side to side until it is completely cool, so that the loaf does not lose its shape. *Kulich* may be decorated with silver or varicolored dragées or, for a dramatic effect, crowned with a large red rose.

· I ·
TRADITIONAL *KULICH*

1 package active dry yeast
¼ cup lukewarm water
¼ cup sugar
½ cup milk
1 cup flour

8 tablespoons unsalted butter,
at room temperature
½ cup sugar
8 egg yolks
1 vanilla bean, scraped

½ teaspoon saffron threads,
crumbled
1 tablespoon rum
Pinch of salt
3½ cups flour
¼ cup candied orange rind
⅓ cup currants
¼ cup sliced blanched almonds
2 egg whites

ICING

1½ cups confectioners' sugar,
sifted

¼ teaspoon almond extract
2 to 3 tablespoons hot water

Dissolve the yeast in the warm water. Stir in the ¼ cup of sugar and the milk, which has been heated to lukewarm. Then stir in the 1 cup of flour. Cover and let rise in a warm place for 1 hour. This is the sponge mixture.
 Cream the 8 tablespoons of butter with the ½ cup of sugar and then

beat in the egg yolks. Stir the sponge mixture in, then add the scraped seeds from the vanilla pod.*

Dissolve the saffron in the rum; let infuse for 10 minutes and then add it to the mixture. Stir in the salt and enough flour to make a soft dough. Add the candied orange rind, currants and almonds.

Beat the egg whites until stiff but not dry, then carefully fold them into the dough. Turn the dough out onto a lightly floured board and knead gently until pliant. Place in a greased bowl, turning dough to grease the top. Cover and let rise until doubled in bulk, 1½ to 2 hours.

Grease a tall 2½-quart mold. If no mold is available, then use a 2-pound coffee can. Grease the can and line it with brown paper, turning the edges of the paper out over the top of the can. Grease the paper so that the *kulich* will not stick.

Punch down the dough and knead lightly, then place it in the prepared mold or can. Let rise until it comes just to the top of the mold or can, no more. (The unrisen dough should come no farther than two-thirds of the way up the sides of the mold; otherwise you will have to use 2 cans.)

Preheat the oven to 400°F. Bake the loaf at 400°F for 10 minutes, then reduce the heat to 350°F and continue baking for 35–40 minutes.

While the loaf is baking, prepare the icing. Sift the confectioners' sugar, then stir in the almond extract and enough hot water to make a pourable icing that is not too thin.

Turn the loaf out of the mold or can, and while it is still slightly warm, glaze with the icing.

Decorate the iced loaf as desired.

Yield: 1 large loaf.

NOTE: To serve the *kulich,* cut off the mushroom crown and set it aside. Then slice the *kulich* horizontally, replacing the crown after serving to keep the bread moist and its symmetry intact.

---

* To scrape a vanilla bean, slit it lengthwise along one edge. Then, with a fine, sharp knife, scrape out the moist insides of the pod and add them to the dough. Some cooks then chop the pod itself finely and add it as well.

‎❦❦❦❦❦❦❦❦❦❦❦❦❦❦❦❦❦❦❦❦❦❦❦❦❦❦❦❦❦❦❦❦❦❦❦

· II ·
CAKE-LIKE *KULICH*

An easy, no-knead loaf that will not, however, mushroom like the previous one.

¾ cup heavy cream	6 tablespoons sugar
1 package active dry yeast	4 egg yolks
2 tablespoons sugar	½ teaspoon salt
1 cup flour	½ teaspoon vanilla extract
	2 cups flour
10 tablespoons unsalted butter,	¼ cup raisins
at room temperature	¼ cup sliced blanched almonds

Heat the cream to lukewarm, then stir in the yeast, the 2 tablespoons of sugar and the 1 cup of flour, mixing well. Cover the bowl and let rise in a warm place for 45 minutes to 1 hour. This is the sponge mixture.

Cream the butter with the 6 tablespoons of sugar. Then beat in the egg yolks, salt and vanilla extract. Stir in the sponge mixture, then add enough flour to make a soft dough. Stir in the raisins and almonds. Place in a greased bowl, turning dough to grease the top, and let rise, covered, until doubled in bulk, 1½ to 2 hours.

Punch down the dough. Prepare a 2½-quart mold or 2-pound coffee can as described in the above recipe for Traditional *Kulich*. Place the dough in the mold or can and let rise until it just reaches the top of the mold or can.

Preheat the oven to 375°F. Bake the loaf for about 1 hour and 15 minutes, or until it sounds hollow when tapped. If necessary, cover the top with aluminum foil to prevent excessive browning. When done, turn out of the mold and glaze with icing, as described above.

Yield: 1 large loaf.

FRESH HAM COOKED WITH HAY
❦ *BUZHENINA* ❦

Hay may be obtained from local stables or farms, but if it is not available, then simply skip the first step, though the boiled meat will lose a certain subtlety of flavor. A "must" for the Easter table!

1 fresh ham (12 to 14 pounds)	*1 large carrot, scraped and cut*
4 large handfuls of hay	*into chunks*
2 dozen black peppercorns	*2 onions, quartered*
16 allspice berries	*1 parsley root, peeled and*
4 teaspoons crushed dried	*coarsely chopped*
thyme	*1 gallon* Black Bread Kvass *or*
2 bay leaves	*dark beer*

GLAZE

¼ cup dark brown sugar	*1½ tablespoons* Russian-Style Mustard

Rinse the meat. Place it in a very large stockpot with the hay and enough cold water to fill the pot. Bring the water to a rolling boil, then remove the pot from the heat and let stand for 15 minutes. Return the pot to the heat and bring to a new boil, then let stand off the heat for 15 minutes more.

Repeat this procedure one more time, bringing the water to a boil a third time. This time simmer the ham for 10 minutes. Then drain and rinse the ham.

Place the ham in a clean pot with the remaining ingredients, adding enough kvass or beer to cover it. Bring to a boil and skim the foam from the surface. Then simmer, covered, until done, about 20 minutes to the pound, or until the ham reaches an internal temperature of 150° to 160°F.

Remove the ham from the pot, then score the fat on it. Combine the brown sugar and mustard, then rub the mixture over the ham.

Preheat the oven to 425°F. Bake the ham until glazed, about 8 minutes. Serve hot or cold, with Chestnut Puree (see below). Garnish with Spiced Pickled Cherries or other pickled fruits.

Yield: About 20 servings.

CHESTNUT PUREE

1 pound roasted whole
 chestnuts (available at
 specialty stores)
2 cups chicken stock
2 tablespoons butter

2 tablespoons sour cream
Salt, freshly ground white
 pepper to taste
Freshly grated nutmeg

Simmer the chestnuts in the chicken stock for 30 minutes, then put them through a vegetable mill. Stir the remaining ingredients into the puree, mixing well. If the puree seems too thick, whisk in a little more stock. Serve hot.

RUSSIAN PANCAKES
❦ BLINI ❦

Now an international favorite, *blini* are one of the oldest Slavic foods, dating back to the heathen tribes that worshipped the sun and created pancakes in its image. These earliest pancakes were called *mlini*, from the verb *molot'* ("to grind"), and the word is still preserved in the Ukrainian, Serbian and Croatian tongues. Light and porous, *blini* are designed to soak up lots of butter.

Traditionally, one is expected to gorge oneself on *blini*. Literary and actual precedents are numerous in Russian life: Gogol's Chichikov of *Dead Souls* finishes off nearly fifteen of the pancakes while visiting the widow Korobochka, dipping them repeatedly in melted butter and gobbling them down three at a time, while the downfall of the nineteenth-century gourmand Lyapin was in the two dozen *blini* he once consumed before dinner.

To ensure perfect *blini*, Russian cooks use a special pan. Once seasoned, this pan is never washed, just wiped out with salt. The old-fashioned *blini* pan was clever indeed: four to six small indented pans were joined by a long central body with a handle, so that mounds of *blini* could be turned out very quickly. But a good cast-iron frying pan will work just as well. Simply be sure to add more butter to the pan after each *blin* so that the next one won't stick. (Russian cooks use an onion half or a raw potato or a stale crust of bread to daub on the butter.) If, however, the first *blin* you make turns out badly, don't despair. The Russians have a saying for this (as for every) eventuality: *"Pervyi blin komom"*—"The first *blin*'s a lump." I myself like to consider this first *blin* the cook's prerogative and pop it right into my mouth.

1 package active dry yeast	3 eggs, separated
2 cups milk	¼ cup sour cream
1 teaspoon sugar	¾ teaspoon salt
¾ cup buckwheat flour	1½ cups white flour
	½ cup heavy cream
2 tablespoons butter	

Dissolve the yeast in ¼ cup of the milk, heated to lukewarm. Then stir in the sugar and 1¼ cups more of the milk. Add the buckwheat flour and stir briskly to mix. There should not be any lumps. Cover the sponge mixture and let rise in a warm place for 1 hour.

Melt the butter and mix it with the egg yolks and the sour cream. Add this mixture to the sponge, along with the remaining ½ cup of milk, the salt, and the white flour. Cover the bowl and let rise in a warm place for 2 hours. (Make sure you have beaten the flour in well; there should not be any lumps.)

Beat the cream until stiff. Beat the egg whites until stiff but not dry and fold them into the cream. Fold this mixture into the batter. Then let the batter rest for 30 minutes more.*

Heat one or several cast-iron pans. Brush with butter (and a little vegetable oil, if desired); when the butter is hot, the pans are ready.

Use 2 tablespoons of the batter for each *blin,* taking it from the top of the batter each time so that the rest doesn't fall. Pour it onto the prepared pan and swirl the pan to make a pancake about 5 inches in diameter.

Cook the *blin* for just a few minutes, until bubbles appear on the surface, then turn and cook the other side until faintly browned. The *blini* are best served hot from the pan, but if they must be held, pile them in a deep dish, brushing each one with butter, and cover the top of the dish with a linen towel.

---

* If the batter seems too thick at this point, a little warmed milk may be carefully added.

۞∤۞∤۞∤۞∤۞∤۞∤۞∤۞∤۞∤۞∤۞∤۞∤۞∤۞∤۞∤۞∤۞∤۞∤۞∤

Serve the *blini* with a choice of the following garnishes:

Melted butter
Sour cream
Black caviar
Red caviar
Chopped pickled herring
Chopped onion
Chopped hard-boiled egg
Smoked salmon
Jam

Yield: About 6 servings.

NOTE: Should there be any *blini* left over, they may be used to make *blinchiki:* Spread the cooked *blini* with any desired filling (cottage cheese, ground meat, creamed mushrooms, jam) and fold the pancake around the filling like an envelope. Fry in butter until browned on all sides.

LARK-SHAPED BUNS
🐦 *ZHAVORONKI* 🐦

In old Russia larks were seen as the harbingers of spring, and sweet buns (*zhavoronki*) were baked in their image to welcome in the new planting season and the prosperity people hoped it would bring. In Ivan Goncharov's novel *Oblomov,* the hero Oblomov has a famous dream in which scenes of his childhood are replayed. He recalls the flurry of springtime activity as the lark buns are baked in the kitchen. Each year his mother supervised their preparation, asserting she'd have to renounce spring entirely if she didn't prepare *zhavoronki* for her darling boy. The buns, symbolic of spring, become symbolic of a golden childhood for Oblomov.

Prepare sweet raised *pirozhki* (Variation 1 to Basic Raised *Pirozhki* Dough) as directed in Chapter 2.

Punch down the risen dough and divide it into 24 pieces. Out of each piece fashion a lark-shaped bun as follows:

Separate each ball of dough into thirds. With one third of the dough make an oval body for the lark. With a sharp knife make a diagonal slash part way through the dough, extending from the bottom of the oval about two thirrds of the way up. This will represent a wing.

Flatten the second piece of dough slightly. Cut it into a broad triangle. Attach the triangle to the under side of the oval on the right-hand side, so that the point of the triangle is hidden. These are the tail feathers. With a sharp knife make a few horizontal cuts in the tail part way through the dough.

Take the last third of dough and shape it into a circle that is elongated at one end. This is the head. Attach it to the upper left-hand side of the oval body, with the elongated part sloping downward. Place a currant in the head for an eye.

Transfer the "lark" to a greased baking sheet. Repeat the process with the remaining 23 pieces of dough.

Let the buns rise, covered, for about 20 minutes, or until doubled in bulk.

Brush the buns with beaten egg yolk; decorate them with pearl (crystal) sugar and sliced blanched almonds.

Bake in a preheated 350°F oven for 20 minutes, or until golden. Transfer to a rack to cool.

Yield: 24 buns.

NOTE: If the pieces of dough do not adhere well, brush them with a little cold water to make them stick.

COMPOTE OF DRIED FRUITS
☙ VZVAR ☙

This compote of dried fruits is a specialty of southern Russia and the Ukraine (where it is known as *uzvar*). In Ukrainian families, the compote is always served alongside *kut'ya* at the yearly Christmas dinner celebrating the breaking of the fast. Preparations for *vzvar* are begun months in advance, in late summer, when fresh fruits are gathered and hung to dry in large bunches in pantries, in storerooms or along the wattle fences of rural homesteads—a picturesque sight.

3 cups boiling water	3 ounces dried pears
¾ cup honey	3 ounces dried apple slices
2 whole allspice berries (or	3 ounces prunes
⅛ teaspoon mixed spice)	3 ounces dried peaches
1 stick cinnamon	3 ounces dried apricots
½ small lemon, sliced	3 tablespoons brandy

In a saucepan combine the water and honey, stirring until the mixture is smooth. Add the allspice, cinnamon stick and lemon. Add the dried pears and apples. Bring to a boil, cover and simmer for 10 minutes.

Then stir in the prunes and dried peaches. Bring to a boil again, cover and simmer for 10 minutes more.

Finally, add the apricots, bring to a new boil, cover and simmer the fruits until tender, about 15 minutes.

Remove the compote from the heat. Discard the cinnamon stick and allspice berries. Stir in the brandy. Cover the pan and allow the fruit to steep until lukewarm. Then refrigerate if desired.

The compote may be served warm or chilled. Spoon the fruits along with some of the liquid into glass serving bowls so the colorful orange, yellow and brown of the mixture can be seen.

Yield: 4 to 6 servings.

NOTE: The fruits in the compote should be cooked only until tender and not overcooked to a pulp.

WHEAT BERRIES WITH HONEY AND NUTS
☙ KUT'YA ☙

Kut'ya is strongly associated with ritual. An ancient dish, it was served at funerals to send off the dead. In some areas of Russia, people ate the grain right at the grave site, tossing a handful onto the coffin, where it might "moisten the dry lips of the dead." This funereal connotation appears in Fyodor Sologub's novel *The Petty Demon*. Sologub's hero is the provincial schoolteacher Peredonov, one of whose essential traits is paranoia. Peredonov imagines the threat of poisoning everywhere. He's equally afraid to take a wife and to drink his evening coffee. When Pavlushka, an old acquaintance, comes for a visit, the conversation quite naturally turns to food, specifically *erly,* a wheat and honey dish from Pavlushka's village. Because Peredonov has never tasted *erly,* Pavlushka explains that it's like the funeral porridge *kut'ya.* At the mere mention of *kut'ya,* Peredonov becomes suspicious. "Funeral fare," he thought. "Pavlushka wants to send me to my grave."

But this dish of wheat and nuts has more pleasant associations as well, since it is traditionally served on Christmas Eve to help in breaking the fast. Some families arrange the *kut'ya* on a bed of hay in remembrance of Christ's birth in a manger; others toss a spoonful of the honey-soaked grain up to the ceiling. If it sticks, the bees will swarm and the harvest will be bountiful. If not . . .

Kut'ya is delicious and bound to delight vegetarian friends. For the sake of tradition, serve it with *vzvar* as an accompaniment to roasted meat.

1 cup wheat berries	*¼ cup poppy seeds*
¼ pound almonds	*½ cup chopped almonds*
2 cups water	*2 tablespoons honey*
½ teaspoon salt	

Soak the wheat berries overnight in ample water to cover.

The next day, make almond milk. Place the almonds in a saucepan with the water. Bring to a boil, then remove the pan from the heat and let the almonds steep until the water comes to room temperature.

Drain the wheat. Drain the almonds, reserving the milk.

Pour the almond milk over the wheat and stir in the salt. Bring to a boil, then simmer slowly until the wheat is tender, about 2 hours.

Meanwhile, soak the poppy seeds in water for 30 minutes to soften. Then grind them.

Toast the chopped almonds at 325°F for 10 minutes, until golden brown.

When the wheat is tender, stir in the poppy seeds. Add the honey, mixing well. Transfer the wheat to a serving dish and sprinkle it with the toasted almonds.

Yield: 8 servings.

ROAST GOOSE WITH APPLES
☙ GUS' ZHARENYI S YABLOKAMI ☙

As this Russian-style goose roasts, the apples in the stuffing are transformed into a thick sauce: meat and condiment in one. This makes an excellent holiday meal when served with baked sugared apples and buckwheat groats.

1 6-pound goose	Olive oil
Salt	½ cup chicken or beef stock
Thyme	
3 to 4 large tart apples, peeled, cored and chopped	Tart apples
	Sugar

Rub the inside of the goose with salt and thyme. Let sit for ½ hour.

Preheat the oven to 450°F. Stuff the goose with the chopped apples and rub the skin lightly with olive oil. Place the goose on a rack in a roasting pan, breast side up.

Roast the goose at 450°F for 15 minutes. Then reduce the heat to 325°F and pour the stock into the roasting pan. Prick the skin of the goose, then roast for about 2½ hours more, or until done (it should take about 25 minutes per pound). Baste the goose every ½ hour or so.

About 1 hour before the goose is done, prepare the baked apples. Slice each apple into eighths, and place the slices in a greased shallow baking dish. Sprinkle the apples lightly with sugar and baste them with some of the goose fat from the pan. Cover and bake at 325°F for 50 minutes.

Serve the roast goose with the sugared baked apples and Buckwheat Groats.

Yield: 4 to 6 servings.

DEEP-FRIED "TWIGS"
🐾 KHVOROST 🐾

Khvorost are a popular Christmas treat. These cookies came to Russia by way of Scandinavia, where similar treats, *klenäter,* are still prepared for the Swedish Christmas board. In Russian, *khvorost* means "twigs," and the gnarled shape and crisp texture of the cookies do seem to recall small branches. When they are sprinkled with a goodly amount of confectioners' sugar and piled high on a plate, one can easily imagine forest twigs covered with snow.

While *khvorost* are usually made from a sweet noodle dough, rolled out thinly and cut into intricate shapes, some cooks pour a liquid batter into the hot fat, and the cookies assume free-form shapes. Even more spectacular are the Tatar-style *khvorost.* The dough is deep fried in a single large piece to form an elaborate edible rose.

2½ cups flour	Pinch of salt
2 egg yolks	
1 whole egg	
2 tablespoons rum	Vegetable oil for deep frying
½ teaspoon vanilla extract	
¼ cup light cream	½ cup confectioners' sugar,
¼ cup confectioners' sugar,	sifted
sifted	1 heaping teaspoon cinnamon

Place the flour in a mixing bowl and make a well in the center. Into the well pour the egg yolks, whole egg, rum, vanilla extract and cream. Using a fork or your hands, mix well. Then stir in the ¼ cup of confectioners' sugar and the salt. Knead the dough lightly until it holds together, then place it under an overturned bowl and let stand for 30 minutes.

On a floured surface, roll out the dough at least ¹⁄₁₆ inch thick. Then, with a fluted pastry cutter, cut out strips 1 inch wide and 5 inches long. With a sharp knife make a slit in the center of each strip.

Preheat the oil in a deep-fat fryer to 365°F. Working with one strip of dough at a time, slip one end of the strip through the slit in the center, forming a half-bowknot.

Drop the cookies into the hot fat, a few at a time, and cook until golden all over, turning once. Remove from the fat with a slotted spoon and drain on paper towels.

Mix the ½ cup of confectioners' sugar with the cinnamon. Sprinkle the *khvorost* liberally with the sugar mixture and mound them onto a serving platter.

Yield: About 4 dozen cookies.

VARIATION: To make four stunning Tatar "roses," roll out the dough into a long rectangle. Along both long sides of the rectangle, make alternating diagonal slashes radiating out from the center of the rectangle (a knife may be used, but a fluted pastry cutter is nicer). After the rectangle has been slashed, make three or four 1-inch-long slits along the edge of each strip. Take a rolling pin, and starting at a narrow end, carefully roll the rectangle of dough onto the pin. Immerse the dough (still on the rolling pin) into the hot fat, spinning the rolling pin constantly so the flaps of dough created by the slashing will open up like a rose. Drain on paper towels and sprinkle with confectioners' sugar mixed with cinnamon before serving.

RUSSIAN GINGERBREAD
☙ *PRYANIKI* ☙

Pryaniki are the oldest Russian sweet, older than Christianity itself in Russia. The earliest ones were rather coarse, heavily spiced and baked without any leavening at all, but over the ages their texture and flavor have been refined. Many different varieties of *pryaniki* can be found, according to region and local method, but the most classic of all are those resembling a chewy, spicy gingerbread, cake-like instead of crisp. Such *pryaniki* are still baked in the city of Tula, south of Moscow, a city renowned as well for its beautifully crafted samovars.

Pryaniki are either molded free-form in whimsical shapes (*siluetnye*) or pressed with a wooden stamp to imprint a design on the surface (*pechatnye*). They are often frosted or filled with thick jam, as in the recipe below. The cookies keep well; in fact, some of the most beautiful examples, in the shapes of reindeer, horses and cocks, are still preserved in the Ethnographic Museum in Leningrad.

2 tablespoons butter	cardamom, ginger, mace
½ cup honey	and cinnamon
1 egg	2 tablespoons crushed blanched
1¾ to 2 cups flour	almonds
¼ teaspoon baking soda	½ cup thick jam (plum is
¼ teaspoon each ground	especially good)

GLAZE

½ cup confectioners' sugar	2 tablespoons freshly squeezed
	lemon juice

Cream the butter and honey, then beat in the egg. Stir in the baking soda, spices and almonds, mixing well. Add enough flour to make a soft dough. Wrap the dough in waxed paper and chill in the refrigerator for 1 hour.

Preheat the oven to 350°F. On a floured board roll the dough out ⅛ inch thick. Cut out the rounds with a 2½-inch cookie cutter. Spread a generous teaspoon of jam on half of the rounds. Top each jam-covered round with a plain round, sealing the edges with your fingers, then crimping them decoratively. Place on a greased baking sheet.

Bake for 10 minutes at 350°F, then reduce the heat to 325°F and continue baking for 8 to 10 minutes more. Cool on a rack.

To prepare the glaze, mix together the confectioners' sugar and lemon juice. Pour over the cooled cookies.

Yield: 18 cookies.

MINT COOKIES
⚜ MYATNYE PRYANIKI ⚜

In Leningrad on the Nevsky Prospect there's a bakery and coffee shop that used to be known as Filippov's. The walls are paneled in mahogany, the ceiling is mirrored, the floors are marble. Entering the shop is almost like entering another era. An enticing array of cookies and cakes beckons from behind large glass-enclosed cases. The specialty of the house is these mint cookies, sold by the gram and offered to the buyer in paper cones. They're so light and refreshing, they're hard to resist.

1¼ cups sugar
½ cup water
3 cups flour
½ teaspoon baking soda

¼ teaspoon (generous)
  peppermint extract
1 egg, beaten

In a small saucepan bring the sugar and water to a boil. Bring the syrup to just below the soft ball stage (to about 230°F on a candy thermometer), to the point where it will spin a thick thread. Immediately remove the syrup from the heat and cool to lukewarm.

Meanwhile, combine the flour and baking soda. (The cookies will be even lighter if the flour is sifted first.) Stir in the cooled syrup, the peppermint extract and the egg.

With your hands, knead the dough until it is a uniform mass that holds together. This will take several minutes. The dough will be sticky.

Preheat the oven to 350°F. Lightly grease two baking sheets.

Pinch off pieces of dough the size of walnuts, roll them into balls between your palms, and place them on the baking sheets. Then, with a glass or a decorative stamp, lightly flatten the balls.

Bake for 10 to 12 minutes, or until the cookies are just faintly golden. They should not brown. Remove to wire racks to cool.

Yield: 30 cookies.

NAME DAY LOAF
❄ *KRENDEL'* ❄

Krendel' is a pretzel-shaped loaf of sweet bread. Both the name and the shape of the loaf originated with the German bakers who were numerous in Russia from the late thirteenth century on, especially in the merchant town of Novgorod. *Krendel'* is a corruption of the German *Kringel,* a round cookie. The pretzel shape inspired the guild signs that were symbolic of the baker's art. *Krendel'* dough is similar to the dough used for *kulich,* and in fact some cooks use the same recipe interchangeably, altering only the shape of the final loaf.

1 package active dry yeast	¾ teaspoon ground cardamom
½ cup milk, lukewarm	½ teaspoon nutmeg
½ cup sugar	¼ teaspoon ground anise
1 cup flour	3½ cups flour
	⅓ cup sliced blanched almonds
8 tablespoons unsalted butter, at room temperature, cut into bits	⅓ cup golden raisins
3 whole eggs	1 egg yolk
½ teaspoon salt	1 tablespoon cold water
	Pearl (crystal) sugar

Make a sponge by dissolving the yeast in the milk. Add the ½ cup of sugar and 1 cup of flour. Cover and let rise in a warm place for 1 hour.

Gradually stir in the butter and eggs, beating well after each addition. Add the salt and spices, then stir in enough flour to make a soft dough. Stir in the almonds and raisins.

Turn the dough out onto a floured board and knead until smooth and elastic. Place in a greased bowl, turning dough to grease the top. Cover and let rise for 1½ to 2 hours, until doubled in bulk.

Grease a large baking sheet. Punch down the risen dough. Knead it for 1 or 2 minutes on the floured board. Then shape it into a long roll, about 3½ feet long, which tapers at the ends.

Bring the tapered ends of the roll up and around to the center of the roll, overlapping them to form a large pretzel shape. (This is easiest to do once the roll is already on the baking sheet so that it doesn't have to be transferred.) Cover the *krendel'.* Let rise for 30 to 40 minutes.

Preheat the oven to 375°F. Brush the loaf with a glaze made from the egg yolk beaten with the cold water. Sprinkle generously with pearl sugar. Bake for 30 to 35 minutes, until the loaf is nicely browned and sounds hollow when tapped.

Yield: 1 large loaf.

DOUGHNUTS
🐲 *PONCHIKI* 🐲

Doughnuts are a great favorite in the Soviet Union, especially in Moscow, where they are rarely prepared at home since it's so easy to run to the nearest doughnut stand and get them piping hot from a large vat of fat, over which an equally large woman usually presides. Russian doughnuts are traditionally fried in oil and lard, with a few tablespoons of vodka added to keep them from absorbing too much grease. Here I've opted for pure vegetable oil. These *ponchiki* may well be the lightest doughnuts you've ever tasted.

1 package active dry yeast	*¼ teaspoon cinnamon*
½ cup plus 3 tablespoons milk	*1 2-inch piece of vanilla bean,*
3 tablespoons sugar	*split and scraped*
2 egg yolks	*2 cups flour*
3 tablespoons butter, at room	
temperature	*Vegetable oil for deep frying*
¼ teaspoon salt	
1 tablespoon dark rum	*Confectioners' sugar, sifted*

Dissolve the yeast in the 3 tablespoons of milk, which has been heated to lukewarm. Then add the remaining milk, sugar, egg yolks and butter. Stir in the salt, rum, cinnamon and vanilla seeds, which have been scraped from the beans. Stir in the flour. The dough will be very soft and sticky. Leave it in the bowl to rise, covered, in a warm place until doubled in bulk, 1½ to 2 hours.

Generously coat your hands with flour and turn out the dough onto a well-floured board. Since the dough is so sticky, it will be necessary to coat its surface with flour in order to roll it out, but be careful not to use more than is necessary, or else the doughnuts will not be light.

With a floured rolling pin, roll out the dough to ½-inch thickness. Cut out rounds with a doughnut cutter. Set them aside to rise again, covered, for 20 to 25 minutes, or until doubled in bulk.

Preheat the vegetable oil in a deep-fat fryer to 365°F. Drop in the risen doughnuts, not more than 2 or 3 at a time, and cook them until golden brown, turning only once. The cooking time will be about 5 minutes.

Remove the doughnuts from the fat and place on paper towels to drain. Sprinkle with confectioners' sugar and serve warm.

Yield: About 1 dozen doughnuts.

BLUEBERRY ICE CREAM
❊ MOROZHENOYE S CHERNIKOI ❊

Legend has it that ice cream was introduced to Russia in the sixteenth century by the Italian workmen who came to Moscow at Ivan the Terrible's behest. He wanted them to build a cathedral the likes of which the world had never seen. Alas, the world was not to see anything similar again. Once they had finished their work, Ivan blinded the Italians to prevent them from duplicating their feat. But they left behind two great legacies for the Russian people, which are beloved to this day: the spectacular St. Basil's Cathedral on Red Square, and ice cream. Russian ice cream is excellent, and it is eaten year-round. Commercially prepared ice cream is mainly vanilla, but at home it is often flavored with fruit, as in the recipe below.

1 pint fresh blueberries	Pinch of salt
1 cup sugar	4 egg yolks
1 tablespoon vodka	2 cups scalded milk
2 teaspoons freshly squeezed	1 cup sour cream
lemon juice	1 cup heavy cream

In a large bowl crush the blueberries. Add ½ cup of the sugar, the vodka and the lemon juice. Set aside.

In the top part of a double boiler put the remaining sugar, the salt and the egg yolks. Beat until light and fluffy. Gradually add the scalded milk, mixing well. Cook until just thickened, about 5 minutes (do not cook any longer or the mixture will curdle). Set aside to cool.

Meanwhile, in the large bowl of an electric mixer beat the sour cream at high speed for about 10 minutes, until nearly doubled in volume. Whip the heavy cream until stiff.

Carefully fold the beaten sour cream and heavy cream into the cooled custard mixture. Then stir in the sweetened blueberries. Pour into an ice-cream freezer and freeze according to manufacturer's instructions.

Yield: About 3 pints.

RUSSIAN HOT CHOCOLATE
⚔ *KAKAO S YAICHNYM ZHELTKOM* ⚔

Russian-style hot chocolate is so rich that it has come to symbolize the good life—at least for the great Soviet satirist Mikhail Zoshchenko. In his story "The Lilacs Are Blooming," Zoshchenko targets the social climber Volodin, whose only aspiration in life is to better his position. Accordingly, Volodin marries for status, not for love, and he is thrilled to find that weekly hot chocolate is part of the bargain: "Now he could eat all kinds of respectable foods: soups, meat, tomatoes, meatballs, and the like. In addition, once a week he drank cocoa with the whole family; he was amazed and delighted at this rich drink, the taste of which he'd forgotten over the eight or nine years of his bleak camp life."

This is the perfect drink to serve after a winter outing.

2 cups milk
2 tablespoons unsweetened
cocoa powder
¼ cup superfine sugar

1 egg yolk

Sweetened whipped cream
(optional)

In a saucepan heat the milk and cocoa powder, stirring with a whisk until the cocoa has dissolved.

In a small bowl combine the sugar and egg yolk.

When the milk is hot, whisk a small amount of it into the sugar and egg yolk mixture, stirring rapidly so that the yolk doesn't cook. Then pour the yolk mixture back into the milk, stirring constantly.

Heat the hot chocolate, but do not boil. Serve immediately, with sweetened whipped cream, if desired.

Yield: 2 servings.

WINE BOWL
KRYUSHON

In *Pnin,* Vladimir Nabokov's classic portrait of a Russian émigré living in America, one of the few things Professor Pnin manages to do right is make this aromatic punch, which he serves at a faculty party. Were one to follow Pnin's prescription exactly, the punch should be served from an aquamarine crystal bowl, and the sauterne should be Château d'Yquem. But since few of us have aquamarine crystal bowls at hand, and since the precious Château d'Yquem sells for something more than $100 a bottle, I have found it economical and not at all detrimental to substitute a lesser vintage, as well as a lesser bowl. This is a sensational punch.

> 1 bottle sauterne, well chilled   ½ cup Maraschino liqueur
> 5 tablespoons freshly squeezed
>   grapefruit juice

Combine the above ingredients and serve over ice in a crystal bowl.

Yield: 10 to 12 servings.

NOTE: As the sweetness of the sauterne varies with each bottle, the punch may take more or less of the other ingredients for a perfect balance.

⚶ · *IV* · ⚶

❖◈❖

AT THE DACHA: RUSSIAN HOME COOKING

❖❱

*T*he October Revolution of 1917 caused an upheaval in Russian life and society. One thing that did not change, however, was the Russians' deep love for their countryside. In the old days the gentry would migrate each summer to their country estates, escaping the heat of the cities. These large estates were composed of a manor house, vast meadows, fields, woods and a village for the peasants who lived there year-round and worked the estate for the mostly absentee owners. A few landowners chose to dwell on their property, but more often than not they were considered provincial for doing so. Today, of course, the large estates no longer exist, but a yearly summer exodus from the cities still takes place. And the scale is even larger now that the bulk of the Russian population is urban.

Every summer the Russians flock to the country to be renewed by the lush rural life after their winter's confinement, and they remember it fondly throughout the ensuing year. Each time they serve wild strawberries, or pickled field mushrooms, or salted forest mushrooms, or tart lingonberries and currants in whose dusky flavor the scent of late summer still lingers, the host is likely to proclaim, "We picked these ourselves at the dacha last summer!" This is followed by a sigh and a silence, as all those present indulge in nostalgic reverie of the halcyon summer days.

Dacha means "summer house" in Russian, but the term has come to be more loosely applied to just being in the country, even for a picnic. The dachas of old were large, comfortable wooden houses, often gaily colored and adorned with intricate wood carvings on shutters and gables. Sometimes they were fairly isolated; in other instances whole villages were made up of summer homes. One such picturesque village is Repino, named after Ilya Repin, the great Russian painter of the *peredvizhniki* ("Itinerants") school, famous for his landscapes and historical portraits. Repino is· just north of Leningrad, in what was formerly Finnish Karelia. Its streets are narrow and winding, lined on both sides with charming two-story wooden houses. The village borders on a small pine and birch forest, which yields abundant wild berries and mushrooms in the summer and early fall and provides wonderful cross-country ski trails in the winter. Now the houses are neglected and in need of repair, but the village still retains its storybook charm.

Today ordinary Russians rarely own their own dachas; more often they rent a room or a floor of one of the large old houses to use as a summer base. Frequently there is no indoor plumbing, but the accommodations are not meant to be luxurious. Simplicity contributes to the charm of the dacha and the sense of closeness to nature. Gazing out onto a birch wood or frolicking in the tall meadowgrass or catching the scent of a wood stove in the chilly late summer air—these are the moments Russians wax nostalgic about when they think of time spent at the dacha.

Not only are the accommodations rudimentary, the pace of life is slowed down. Food preparation is simplified, too. The recipes offered in this chapter are typical of Russian fare that might he enjoyed at a dacha. There are no complicated preparations, no time-consuming labors, no pretension to elegance or expense, just the simple food of the Russian people, what they ate a hundred years ago and are still eating today; the "meat and potatoes" of the Russian cuisine.

A meal in a peasant home could hardly have differed more from the banquets served to the gentry and nobility. The first, most obvious limitation was the peasant cottage itself, whose only implements consisted of a few pots and pans and the huge Russian stove—a stove, however, perfectly geared to the long slow cooking that produces the best soups and stews and porridges, the mainstays of the peasant diet. Instead of a stunning parade of dishes, the peasants sat down to a single course: soup, *kasha* and bread. Yet this was no mean meal: the bread was rye, the loaves coarse and heavy but full of such nutrition and flavor that the peasants rightly believed that "a table with bread is an altar; without it, a plank." The variety of rye breads was great, each loaf taking its name from the region or village where it originated. White bread (*bulka,* from the French *boule*) was not known to the peasantry, since it was available only through the French and German bakers in the cities.

The peasant family's table usually stood in the icon corner of the cottage, and at mealtime a large bowl of steaming soup was placed in the center. Each member of the family had his own personal spoon—often ornately carved or lacquered with the bright yellow, red and black flourishes of the Russian *khokhloma* style—and everyone simply dug into the communal pot together. This practice saved both the expense of separate plates and the labor of washing them. Even today an expression used to convey grief or strong experience shared in common is *my s odnoi miski khlebovali,* "we have shared food from the same bowl." A guest was honored to be asked to partake of the communal meal.

In Russian fairy tales, peasant food makes frequent appearances, often as the key motivation for the story. One of the first tales Russian children read concerns a round loaf of rye bread, *kolobok,* the flour for which an old *babushka* barely manages to scrape together from the corners and cracks in her flour bin. She mixes the flour with sour cream, shapes the loaf, lovingly cooks it and set it on the window sill to cool. After hopping off the sill, *kolobok*'s further adventures rival the Gingerbread Man's, until *kolobok* is eaten up by a wily (and hungry) fox. In other folktales, no matter how brave the exploits of a handsome prince or how bitter the tribulations of a fair maiden, the characters always take the time to eat something—whether a simple repast in the forest hut of the witch *Baba yaga* or a royal feast at the tsar's palace. The tales tell, too, of the wondrous *skatert'-samobranka,* a tablecloth that not only spreads itself but causes the table under it to groan from the weight of so much food.

The Russians are both a superstitious and a thankful people, by nature still close to their pagan ancestors, who worshipped the sun. They do not forget the source of their daily bread: they love the soil and the rain and the summer sun, which nurture the grain and promise a rich harvest. Nor do they neglect the stove that transforms the grain into breads and porridges. In Vasily Shukshin's "In Profile and Full Face," written in the Soviet period, a young boy decides to leave his village to seek his fortune in the world, but before he leaves, his mother admonishes him, as she has in the past, to say farewell to the large Russian stove in the corner. The boy kisses the stove three times (the magical number) and intones: "Mother Stove, bless me on my long journey as you have blessed me with food and drink." When the boy leaves, his mother feels relieved to know that her son is traveling with the blessing of the stove, the symbol of home and warmth and family.

For city dwellers, summers at the dacha are long and languorous, with entire days spent wandering through the woods and fields picking berries and mushrooms. The variety is extensive. In berries, the Russians favor the tiny sweet wild strawberries, the red and black currants that overrun the kitchen gardens, the tart lingonberries and cranberries in the swamps of the lowlands, the ink-black bilberries and the golden cloudberries. Mushrooms, too, are ubiquitous and just as colorful as the berries, ranging in hue from the saffron *ryzhik* to more exotic shades of lilac and green. All are delicious when expertly chosen and prepared, and many if not most Russians still possess this expertise. All lands except army training grounds are open to gatherers. Throughout the summer the native riches of the Russian land are enjoyed to their fullest. Fresh fruits, greatly lacking during the long winter months, are plentiful, and the general feeling is one of abundance, even excess. The bounty is a source of pride to those who dwell on the land. In Fyodor Sologub's novel *The Petty Demon,* an argument starts as to whose farmyard produces the most eggs. The boasting goes on until finally one maid silences her neighbors by claiming that not only does her chicken lay two eggs a day, but a spoonful of butter besides! The boasting is not pure vanity; by custom the plenty is meant to be shared. The wealthy peasants of the Volga region used to host lavish fetes for their less fortunate compatriots, thereby showing off their own well-being, as well as trying to ingratiate themselves to the poorer peasants.

On the country estates of the gentry, too, while the food may have been more simply prepared than in the city, it was still a source of pride to serve food in endless quantities and transformations. One such country estate preoccupied with food is Oblomovka in Ivan Goncharov's novel *Oblomov.* The main character, Oblomov, sees Oblomovka in his famous dream, when he fondly recalls his idyllic childhood there, the pampering and the food:

The first and foremost vital concern at Oblomovka was food. What calves were fattened there for the holidays! What fowl were raised! How many subtle considerations, how many pursuits and worries there were in taking care of them! The turkeys and chickens intended for name-days and other celebrations were fed on nuts; the geese were deprived of any exercise at all and hung motionless in a sack for several days before the holiday, so they would swim in their own fat. What stores of jams and pickles and cookies there were! What honeys! What kvasses were brewed, and what pies were baked at Oblomovka!

The pies baked at Oblomovka were indeed wonderful. Baked on Sunday, they were large enough to last throughout the week, until Friday, when the last stale crumbs were given to beggars as charity.

In this chapter you will find recipes for the most basic foods of the Russian cuisine, some of which the Slavic peoples have been preparing (with ever greater refinement) for nearly a thousand years. You will find hearty soups, such as *borshch* (beet soup) and *shchi* (cabbage soup); grains cooked into *kasha* or robust rye bread; stews that are guaranteed to stick to your ribs; desserts as simple and sweet as baked apples with jam. You may even be surprised to find yourself exclaiming, in true Russian fashion, "I can't take another bite—but I will have a pie!"

CABBAGE SOUP
𝔅 *SHCHI* 𝔅

In Gogol's *Dead Souls* the scoundrel Chichikov is invited to dine with the landowner Manilov. As they sit down to the table, Manilov says, "Excuse us for not serving a dinner like they would in the elegant salons of the capital. Here we simply have *shchi,* in the Russian tradition—but it's straight from the heart. Please help yourself."

Shchi is the most Russian of soups, and coupled with *kasha,* it represents basic Russian fare, straightforward in both preparation and spirit. Russian folk wisdom advises, "If the *shchi*'s good, you don't need anything else." And it's true that a bowl of this hearty soup is enormously satisfying, needing only a chunk of black bread with garlic to round out the meal.

There are several different kinds of *shchi.* The original soup was made exclusively from fermented cabbage (sauerkraut), hence the name *kislye shchi* (sour cabbage soup). *Kislye shchi* is still very popular in the Soviet Union. It is a wintertime soup, harkening back to the days before mass production, when the soup could not be prepared until the sauerkraut, put up in the early fall, had fermented. At some point an inventive cook decided to make cabbage soup in the summer as well, and resorted to using fresh cabbage. Thus *lenivye shchi* ("lazy" cabbage soup) was born: the cook was able to avoid the laborious process of souring the cabbage before turning it into soup.

The *shchi* offered here is slightly unorthodox: it combines both the summer and winter variations, but the small dose of sauerkraut adds a nice tang without making the soup overly heavy. And this version of *shchi* can be served year-round with equanimity.

2 tablespoons butter	*(¾ pound), coarsely*
1 medium onion, coarsely	*shredded*
chopped	*½ cup sauerkraut*
1 small leek, white part only,	*1 tomato, peeled and cut into*
thinly sliced	*chunks*
1 small carrot, scraped and	*Salt, freshly ground black*
thinly sliced	*pepper to taste*
5 cups rich beef stock	*Sour cream*
1 small head of white cabbage	*Fresh dill (optional)*

Melt the butter in a stockpot. Add the onion, leek and carrot and sauté until they just begin to soften. Pour in the stock and bring to a boil. Stir in the cabbage, sauerkraut and tomato.

Simmer, covered, for about 50 minutes, or until the cabbage is tender. Check for seasoning. To serve, top each portion with a dollop of sour cream and a sprinkling of fresh dill, if desired.

Yield: 4 to 6 servings.

NOTE: As with most Russian soups, the *shchi* tastes best when prepared a day ahead and refrigerated overnight before serving.

UKRAINIAN-STYLE BEET SOUP
☙ BORSHCH UKRAINSKII ☙

Native to the Ukraine, *borshch* is one of the great soups of the world. Well over a hundred varieties of the soup exist—rather a startling total when one considers the relatively small size of the Ukraine. Although as many as twenty different ingredients may go into a well-flavored *borshch*, the common component is beets, lending the soup its characteristic flavor and color. (The sole exception to this rule is the so-called "green" *borshch*, flavored with spinach and sorrel.) Each region of the Ukraine boasts its own preparation of *borshch*, and the best of these have transcended local boundaries. One finds Kiev-style *borshch* made with lamb and mushrooms, *borshch* from Poltava with poultry and dumplings. The Galician-style soup is heavy with potatoes, while Chernigov cooks add yellow squash to the broth. Lvov has a version with small, mild frankfurters, but in Konotop three different meats make up the soup. Other varieties of *borshch* appear throughout Russia: Moscow-style, rich with tomatoes; "navy" *borshch*, made with bacon; and the ever-popular "soldiers'" *borshch*, designed to assuage grumblings both verbal and borborygmal.

As a general rule, the farther west one goes, the more beets are added to the soup. But even here the possibilities are numerous: they may be added raw in cubes or in julienne strips, or they may be baked first or boiled. Some cooks add raw beets to water and make a strong broth, then set it aside for a few days to ripen. Others add beets along with kvass, as in the recipe below. Or a sour tang can be had from soused apples, sauerkraut, even prunes. It all depends on the resources and imagination of the cook.

Ukrainians often eat *borshch* with *ushki*, tiny ear-shaped dumplings, while Muscovites prefer unsweetened *vatrushki* or *pirozhki*. But I find that a thick slice of black bread tastes best of all. Make this soup a day ahead for best results.

12 cups water
3 cups Beet Kvass
4 pounds beef shin or beef
  chuck with bone
¼ cup dried beans, soaked
  overnight
2 large beets, peeled and cut
  into julienne strips
3 tablespoons red wine vinegar
½ pound smoked pork butt

2 tablespoons butter
1 carrot, scraped and diced
1 onion, chopped
½ celery root, peeled and diced

¾ pound potatoes, peeled and
  cubed
1 small head of white cabbage,
  shredded
1 small tart apple, peeled,
  cored and diced

3 tablespoons tomato paste
1½ tablespoons salt
Freshly ground black pepper
  to taste

1 ounce salt pork
4 tablespoons minced parsley
1 bay leaf

In a large stockpot place the water and kvass. Add the beef. Bring to a boil, skimming the foam from the surface of the soup. Simmer for 1 hour.

Meanwhile, cook the dried beans in salted water until almost tender. Keep warm.

Sprinkle the raw beets with 2 tablespoons of the vinegar. Then add them to the soup, along with the pork butt. Cook for 10 minutes.

Sauté the onion, carrot and celery root in the 2 tablespoons of butter until softened, then add to the soup. Stir in the potatoes, cabbage and apple.

Drain the beans and add them to the soup, along with the tomato paste, salt, pepper, and remaining vinegar. Cook the soup for 20 minutes more.

Grind the salt pork together with the parsley, then carefully stir into the soup, mixing well. Stir in the bay leaf. Boil for 15 minutes longer. Let cool to room temperature, then refrigerate overnight before serving. Reheat the soup to serve.

Yield: 4 quarts.

MOSCOW-STYLE BEET SOUP
✥ BORSHCH MOSKOVSKII ✥

Here is *borshch* as prepared by a born-and-bred Muscovite, Klara Lei-vovna. Easy to prepare and rich in flavor, it is unexcelled for family dining.

2 pounds beef shin or beef
  chuck with bone
9 cups water

3 medium beets, peeled and
  cut in half
1½ tablespoons salt (or less, to
  taste)

2 medium potatoes, peeled and
  cubed
1 small carrot, scraped and
  grated

½ medium head of white
  cabbage (¾ pound),
  shredded
1 ripe tomato, coarsely chopped
6 tablespoons tomato paste
4 black peppercorns
Freshly ground black pepper
  to taste
2 tablespoons wine vinegar
1 teaspoon sugar
1 bay leaf

Sour cream

Simmer the meat in the water for 30 minutes. Then add the beets and salt. Boil for 10 minutes more.

Remove the beets from the broth and grate coarsely. Then return to the pot and add the remaining ingredients except the bay leaf and sour cream.

Simmer the soup until done, about 1½ hours. Remove from the heat and add the bay leaf. Let the soup cool to room temperature, then chill overnight. Next day, skim off the fat and reheat. Put a slice of meat and a dollop of sour cream in each bowl.

Yield: 3 quarts.

MIXED MEAT SOUP
🜪 SOLYANKA SBORNAYA MYASNAYA 🜪

Yet another of Russia's slightly sour soups.

2½ pounds beef shin or beef
    chuck with bones
6 cups water

1 veal kidney, sliced
Flour
2 tablespoons butter
2 medium onions, chopped

¼ pound cooked ham, chopped
¼ pound frankfurters, chopped

2 medium dill pickles, cut into
    julienne strips
1 tablespoon capers
½ cup olives, sliced
2 tomatoes, peeled, seeded and
    chopped
1 teaspoon tomato paste
4 ounces marinated mushrooms
1 teaspoon salt
Freshly ground black pepper
    to taste
1 bay leaf
2 1-inch-thick lemon slices

Cook the beef in the water for 1½ hours to make a rich broth (or substitute 6 cups prepared beef stock).

Dredge the kidney slices in flour and brown in 1 tablespoon of the butter. Brown the onions in the remaining butter. Stir the ham, frankfurters, kidney and onions into the beef stock. Cook for 15 minutes.

Then add the remaining ingredients and cook 10 minutes more.

This soup tastes best when made a day ahead and allowed to season overnight.

Yield: 2 quarts.

NOTE: As with most Russian soups, a dollop of sour cream tastes good in *solyanka*, too.

MUSHROOM AND BARLEY SOUP
❧ POKHLYOBKA ❧

Pokhylobka is a typical hearty peasant soup. In true rustic style, it is usually eaten with black bread generously rubbed with raw garlic. Real garlic lovers simply eat the garlic straight: take a whole peeled clove of garlic and dip it in salt before biting into it. This kind of garlic eating is best done among friends, however. It wasn't until I got to know my Russian hosts well that we dared eat the pungent cloves together.

2 tablespoons butter	1 tablespoon snipped fresh dill
2 onions, chopped	(or ½ teaspoon dried dill)
2 cloves garlic, crushed	½ cup raw pearl barley
6 cups rich beef stock	
1 large potato, coarsely	4 tablespoons butter
chopped	1 pound mushrooms, trimmed
2 carrots, scraped and sliced	and sliced
2 bay leaves	
1 teaspoon salt	1 tablespoon freshly squeezed
Freshly ground black pepper	lemon juice
to taste	Sour cream (optional)

In a stockpot or Dutch oven sauté the onions and garlic in the 2 tablespoons of butter until soft.

Pour in the stock, stirring well, then add the potato, carrots, bay leaves, salt, pepper, dill and barley. Bring the soup to a boil and simmer, covered, for about 1 hour, or until the barley is tender.

Sauté the mushrooms in the remaining 4 tablespoons of butter for 3 minutes. Stir them into the soup. Simmer for 10 minutes.

Just before serving, stir in the lemon juice. Test for seasoning. Pour the soup into bowls and garnish with a dollop of sour cream, if desired.

Yield: 6 to 8 servings.

VARIATION: For a more strongly flavored soup, 1½ ounces dried mushrooms may be substituted for the fresh mushrooms. Soak them in water to cover for 20 minutes, then drain and slice. Add to the beef stock along with the potato, carrots and barley.

TWO SUMMER SOUPS
🏂 *SVEKOL'NIK* and *KHLODNIK* 🏂

These two cold soups revitalize even as they nourish—perfect refreshment for a languid summer day. The first is a standard cold beet soup; the second, a flavorful import from Poland. Serve both soups well chilled.

· I ·
COLD BEET SOUP
✿ *SVEKOL'NIK* ✿

5 cups rich chicken stock
1 small onion, cut into
  julienne strips
½ large carrot, scraped and
  cut into julienne strips
1 small parsnip, peeled and
  cut into julienne strips
½ pound beets, peeled and
  cut into julienne strips
2 cloves garlic, crushed

Salt, freshly ground pepper
  to taste

2 tablespoons tomato paste
4 teaspoons sugar

2 tablespoons freshly squeezed
  lemon juice
Sour cream
Minced parsley

In a large stockpot bring the stock to a boil with the vegetables and garlic, salt and pepper. Simmer for 10 to 15 minutes. Then stir in the tomato paste and sugar. Continue cooking for 30 minutes more.

Let the soup cool to room temperature, then stir in the lemon juice. Taste for seasoning. Chill the soup in the refrigerator for several hours or overnight before serving.

This soup it best served in a glass bowl so that its ruby color is shown to advantage. Garnish with minced parsley and dollops of sour cream.

Yield: 4 to 6 servings.

· II ·
✿ KHLODNIK ✿

½ pound fresh beet greens

3 cups rich chicken stock
1½ cups Black Bread Kvass
½ cup sour cream

2 tablespoons snipped fresh dill
  (or 1 teaspoon dried dill)
1 tablespoon chives
½ pound cooked veal, cubed
2 large radishes, sliced

1 small dill pickle, diced
1 small cucumber, diced
1 small beet, cooked, peeled
  and diced
Salt, freshly ground pepper
  to taste
2 teaspoons sugar

Ice cubes
2 hard-boiled eggs, chopped

Cook the beet greens in boiling salted water for 25 minutes. Drain, squeezing out any excess liquid, and chop.

In a large bowl combine the stock, kvass and sour cream. Stir in the cooked beet greens. Then add the dill, chives, cooked veal, radishes, pickle, cucumber and beet. Season with salt and pepper to taste. Stir in the sugar. Mix all the ingredients together well.

Cover the soup and chill for at least 4 hours in the refrigerator.

To serve, place 1 or 2 ice cubes in each soup bowl and pour the soup over. Garnish each portion with chopped hard-boiled egg.

Yield: 6 to 8 servings.

COLD MEAT AND VEGETABLE SOUP
𝕏 OKROSHKA 𝕏

Okroshka is Russia's most popular cold soup and one of the easiest to prepare. The basic recipe calls only for chopped meats and vegetables doused with a liberal amount of kvass. But since such a sour taste is not always to Western liking, I have opted instead for a version of *okroshka* as prepared by the Russians living in Central Asia. There, a mixture of kefir and water is substituted for the kvass, making an attractive, refreshing soup.

2 hard-boiled eggs
1 teaspoon prepared mustard
¾ cup (generous) sour cream
1 tablespoon sugar
¼ teaspoon salt

2¼ cups plain Homemade
    Kefir
1¾ cups cold water

1½ cups mixed cooked meats,
    in julienne strips (beef,
    chicken, tongue, turkey, etc.)
2 scallions, chopped
6 red radishes, thinly sliced
1 small cucumber, finely
    chopped (do not peel unless
    waxed)
2 tablespoons snipped fresh dill
    (or 1 teaspoon dried dill)

Mash the egg yolks and mix with the mustard. Then stir in the sour cream, sugar and salt until well blended. Gradually beat in the kefir and then the water, until the mixture is well blended and frothy.

Stir in the meats and prepared vegetables. Chill the soup well before serving.

Yield: 8 servings.

VARIATION: A more authentic *okroshka* is made with kvass: for the kefir and water mixture substitute 4 cups of Black Bread Kvass. Just before serving, stir in 2 cups of sparkling water. Place an ice cube in each plate before ladling out the soup.

COLD FRUIT SOUP WITH DUMPLINGS
🎇 *KHOLODETS IZ VISHEN, GRUSH I SLIV* 🎇

Unlike the usual clear fruit soups thickened with cornstarch, *kholodets* is a well-textured puree. Served with light apple dumplings, it makes a stellar first course for hot-weather dining.

1 pound each apples, pears and plums	*½ cup soft fresh bread crumbs*
2 cups cold water	*¼ cup seedless raspberry jam*
1 tablespoon freshly squeezed lemon juice	*½ cup sugar*
Grated rind of 1 lemon	*¾ cup sweet white wine*
½ teaspoon cinnamon	*1 cup cranberry juice*

Peel and core the apples and pears. Pit the plums but do not peel. Place the prepared fruit in a large saucepan. Add the water, lemon juice, lemon rind, cinnamon and bread crumbs. Bring to a boil and simmer for 20 minutes, until the fruit is soft. Then put through a vegetable mill to puree.

Stir in the remaining ingredients. Chill well before serving, garnished with apple dumplings.

Yield: 6 to 8 servings.

APPLE DUMPLINGS
✹ *KLETSKI* ✹

2 medium apples, peeled, cored and finely chopped	*¼ cup sugar*
Juice and rind of 1 lemon	*1 whole egg, lightly beaten*
	¾ cup fine dry bread crumbs

Pour the lemon juice over the apples to keep them from turning brown. Then gently squeeze them dry. Mix the apples with the lemon rind, sugar, egg and bread crumbs. Chill in the refrigerator for 20 minutes.

Form the mixture into walnut-sized balls. Bring a large kettle of lightly salted water to a boil. Drop the dumplings into the water and boil them until they rise to the surface, about 5 minutes. Remove with a slotted spoon.

Cool to room temperature before serving in the soup.

Yield: 2 dozen dumplings.

BUCKWHEAT GROATS
※ GRECHNEVAYA KASHA ※

Besides cabbage soup, no food is more Russian than *kasha*. As one favorite saying goes, "Cabbage soup and *kasha*—that's our fare." And this statement is made with affection rather than irony or scorn. (While in English the word "kasha" refers to the cooked groats of buckwheat so closely associated with Russian cuisine, *kasha* in Russian applies to any grain cooked to porridge consistency.)

The eating of *kasha* goes back many centuries. The early Slavic tribes used to boil their porridge with so much liquid it resembled soup. This practice gradually died out, and by the twelfth century the preparation of *kasha* had become so refined that it was considered fitting provender for feasts. In fact, the word *kasha* was used synonymously with the word "feast" for a good two hundred years. Later, when the vast expanses of Siberia were first opened up for exploration in the sixteenth century, adventurers and traders carried with them huge sacks of buckwheat, since this hearty grain is easily prepared even under the most primitive conditions. At about the same time, the peasants began cooking *kasha* at home in their large Russian stoves, whose constantly falling temperatures ensured a perfect *kasha,* one that never burned, even when baked for long hours. Today the cooking process has been greatly simplified, and more often than not *kasha* is boiled on top of the range like rice. But it still tastes best when made in the traditional manner, baked in an earthenware pot in a moderate oven.

1 cup coarse-cut buckwheat groats	*2 cups boiling water*
½ teaspoon salt	*2 tablespoons butter, cut into bits*

In a large frying pan stir the groats over medium-high heat for about 5 minutes, until each grain begins to brown.

Preheat the oven to 350°F. Grease a 1½-quart earthenware casserole with cover.

Place the groats in the greased casserole and add the salt. Pour the boiling water over all. Dot with the butter. Cover the casserole and bake for 45 minutes.

Yield: 4 to 6 servings.

NOTE: Buckwheat groats are available in fine, medium and coarse grades. For the best flavor and texture, always choose the coarse variety.

VARIATIONS:

1. Place the grains in a large frying pan and crack 1 large egg over them, stirring well to coat each grain. Cook the groats over medium-high heat for about 5 minutes, or until all the moisture from the egg has evaporated. Then proceed as above.

2. Replace the boiling water with 2 cups broth in which dried mushrooms have been soaked. Add the soaked dried mushrooms (or fresh ones, sautéed in a little butter) to the groats before baking.

3. For a creamy consistency, boil 1 cup groats in 2 cups of water over high heat, uncovered, until the water is absorbed. Then stir in 2 cups of milk and cook the groats slowly, covered, over low heat until done, about 20 minutes. This is often served as a breakfast porridge.

4. Add 1 tablespoon snipped fresh dill to the boiling water before pouring it over the groats.

5. Add a little chopped onion that has been sautéed in butter to the groats before baking.

6. A good use for leftover groats is to make croutons (*grenki*). Spread leftover groats in a greased pan, leveling the top with a knife dipped in cold water. Place in the refrigerator and chill until firm. Then cut the groats into cubes. Dredge the cubes in flour, egg yolks and bread crumbs. Fry in plenty of butter until crisp and brown. These croutons taste quite good with Cabbage Soup (*shchi*).

RUSSIAN BLACK BREAD
🦌 *CHORNYI KHLEB* 🦌

In prerevolutionary days, the best black bread in Russia was baked at Filippov's bakery on Moscow's Tverskaya Boulevard, now Gorky Street. Filippov claimed that his secret lay in the flour he used. He shipped his grains in from Tambov Province, then ground them in his own mills before sieving to eliminate all the chaff. Filippov's loaves were so good that a shipment was sent daily to the royal court in St. Petersburg—and this before the advent of railways!

Today, in a less extravagant era, there is still great bread in Moscow. To my way of thinking the best is Borodinsky, made of rye and wheat flours and scented with coriander. Although it's impossible to re-create this bread exactly outside of Moscow, the recipe given here makes a valiant attempt, yielding a dark, full-flavored loaf with a good sour tang.

1 cup dark rye flour	*2½ cups dark rye flour*
1 cup flat beer	*1½ cups bran flakes**
	1½ tablespoons salt
2 packages active dry yeast	*2 teaspoons crushed coriander*
2 cups flat beer	*seed*
1 tablespoon butter	*2½ to 3½ cups unbleached*
2 tablespoons honey	*white flour*
1 tablespoon instant coffee	
1 square (1 ounce) unsweet-	*Cornmeal*
ened chocolate	

GLAZE

1 teaspoon cornstarch	*¼ cup plus 1 tablespoon water*

Five days before bread-making, prepare the starter by mixing the 1 cup of rye flour with the 1 cup of beer. Stir well. Let stand, covered, at room temperature for 5 days, stirring once a day.

On bread-making day, dissolve the yeast in 4 tablespoons of the beer,

* Bran flakes are available at health-food stores; do not use bran cereal.

which has been heated to lukewarm. Let stand for 5 minutes to soften the yeast.

Meanwhile, heat the butter, honey, coffee and chocolate together in a small saucepan, just until the chocolate melts. Set aside to cool to lukewarm.

Stir the starter mixture into the softened yeast. Then stir in the remaining beer, the 2½ cups of rye flour, and the bran flakes, salt and coriander, beating well.

Gradually beat in 2½ cups of the white flour, mixing well to form a soft dough, which will be slightly sticky.

Turn the dough out onto a floured board and knead until smooth and elastic, adding up to 1 cup more of the white flour. Shape into a ball and place in a deep, greased bowl, turning dough to grease the top. Cover and let rise in a warm spot until doubled in bulk, about 1½ hours.

Punch down the dough and knead briefly on a floured board. Divide in half and shape into 2 round free-form loaves. Place the loaves on a baking sheet, which has been sprinkled with cornmeal.

Cover the loaves and let rise until doubled in bulk, about ½ hour.

Preheat the oven to 400°F. Bake the loaves at 400°F for 10 minutes, then reduce the heat to 350°F and continue to bake for 50 minutes more, until the loaves are browned and sound hollow when tapped.

To make the glaze, dissolve the cornstarch in 1 tablespoon of the water. Place the remaining ¼ cup water in a saucepan and stir in the dissolved cornstarch. Bring to a boil, stirring constantly. Boil for 1 minute, until thickened.

Brush the baked loaves with the glaze, covering them evenly on all sides. Return to the oven for 3 to 4 minutes, until the glaze is set.

Cool on racks before serving.

Yield: 2 loaves.

RYE BREAD
⚓ RZHANOI KHLEB ⚓

The Soviet Union still boasts the cheapest bread in the world, with a standard loaf costing 20 kopeks, or about 25¢. The Russians love their bread, and the government encourages its consumption by keeping prices low. No wonder the average Russian eats a pound of bread a day! Although bread comes in many varieties, the favorite remains the basic rye loaf. Here is another recipe for rye bread, this one faintly sweet and aromatic.

2 cups boiling water	2 tablespoons dark brown sugar
2 rounded tablespoons black tea leaves, preferably fruit-scented, such as black currant or peach	1 cup day-old black bread crumbs
	1 tablespoon salt
	3 cups dark rye flour
	1½ to 2 cups white flour
½ cup sugar	
¼ cup boiling water	Cornmeal
2 packages active dry yeast	1 egg white
¼ cup warm water	1 tablespoon cold water

Pour the 2 cups of boiling water over the tea leaves and let steep until lukewarm (2 cups of cooled leftover tea may be used instead, but the tea should be strong). Strain.

Meanwhile, make the caramel coloring. In a large frying pan melt the sugar, stirring constantly until it turns a deep golden brown. Gradually pour in the ¼ cup of boiling water (it *must* be boiling) and stir until well mixed. Cool to lukewarm.

Dissolve the yeast in the ¼ cup of warm water. Stir in the cooled, strained tea and the cooled caramel coloring. Then add the brown sugar, bread crumbs, salt and rye flour, mixing well. Gradually stir in enough white flour to make a firm dough.

Turn the dough out onto a floured board and knead until smooth and elastic. Place in a greased bowl and turn to grease the top. Cover; let rise in a warm spot for 2 hours, or until doubled in bulk. Punch down the dough and shape into 2 free-form loaves.

Sprinkle a baking sheet with cornmeal and place the loaves on it. Cover and let rise until doubled in bulk, about 45 minutes.

Preheat the oven to 375°F. In a small bowl lightly beat the egg white; mix in the cold water. Brush the loaves with this mixture, then place in the oven and bake for 30 to 35 minutes, until nicely browned.

Yield: 2 loaves.

SOURDOUGH WHITE BREAD
❧ KHLEB IZ PSHENICHNOI MUKI ❧

The earliest leavened bread baked by the Slavs was a type of sourdough. A lump of dough was reserved from each bread-baking and allowed to ferment, then used as the starter for the next batch. Even today classic recipes for yeast-raised dough begin with an *opara,* or starter, to add that faint taste of sour the Russians so love. This bread is especially aromatic as it bakes, reminding one of early accounts of St. Petersburg, where the stirring odor of freshly baked bread drifted down the Nevsky Prospect at dawn.

2 cups unbleached white flour	*2 teaspoons salt*
1 cup water	*1 tablespoon caraway seed*
1 cup milk	*(preferably Russian black caraway)*
2 teaspoons active dry yeast	*4 cups unbleached white flour*
¼ cup warm water	
1 teaspoon sugar	*Cornmeal*

Five days before bread-making, prepare the sponge by mixing the 2 cups of flour, the 1 cup of water and the milk. Let stand, covered, at room temperature for about 5 days. The sponge will give off a strong, sour smell.

Once the sponge is ready, prepare the bread. Dissolve the yeast in the warm water along with the sugar. Stir the sponge, which will have separated, and add it to the dissolved yeast. Stir in the salt, caraway seed and flour, adding the flour gradually until a fairly firm dough has been formed.

Turn the dough out onto a floured board and knead until smooth and elastic, about 10 minutes. Place in a greased bowl, turning dough to grease the top. Cover and let rise until doubled in bulk, about 1½ to 2 hours.

Punch down the dough and knead again for a minute or two. Sprinkle a large baking sheet with cornmeal. Shape the dough into one large round loaf and place on the baking sheet.

Cover the loaf and let rise until doubled in bulk, about 45 minutes.

Preheat the oven to 400°F. With a sharp knife slash an X in the top of the loaf. Brush it with cold water and bake for 45 minutes, until the loaf is nicely browned and sounds hollow when tapped.

Yield: 1 large loaf.

NOTE: If you can get the dark, aromatic Russian black caraway, by all means use it. It will impart a special flavor to this bread.

BEEF STEW WITH HORSERADISH SAUCE
☙ TUSHONOYE MYASO S PODLIVKOI IZ KHRENA ☙

Don't be alarmed at the large amount of horseradish called for in this recipe. Over a low fire it marries well with the beef to produce a rich, hearty one-dish meal, which tastes equally good served cold.

3 pounds stewing beef	*2 tablespoons butter*
¼ cup butter	*3 tablespoons flour*
2 large onions, finely chopped	*½ cup prepared horseradish*
4 cloves garlic, crushed	*(or more, to taste)*
2 medium carrots, scraped	*2 tablespoons prepared mustard*
and finely chopped	*¼ cup sour cream*
2 cups beef broth	*Salt, freshly ground black*
2 cups dry white wine	*pepper to taste*
2 bay leaves	*Minced parsley*

Brown the stewing beef in the ¼ cup of butter, then remove from the pan and keep warm. Cook the onions, garlic and carrots in the pan for 15 minutes over medium-low heat. Then smooth the vegetables into an even layer over the bottom of the pan and place the browned meat on top of them. Pour the beef broth and wine over the meat; add the bay leaves. Cover and simmer for 1½ hours, until the meat is tender.

Strain the broth, reserving the meat and vegetables. Return the broth to the saucepan and reduce it by half, to 2 cups.

In a medium-sized saucepan make a roux of the butter and flour. Stir in the reduced beef broth. Stir until thickened, then add the horseradish and mustard. Gradually stir in the sour cream; do not allow the sauce to boil. Check for seasoning. Pour the sauce over the meat and vegetables and warm through.

Serve garnished with minced parsley.

Yield: 4 to 6 servings.

RUSSIAN-STYLE HAMBURGERS
🗡 BITKI 🗡

For a lively variation on the hamburger motif, try adding beets and caraway seed to ground beef. These patties are best served rare, and never in buns.

1 pound ground beef (preferably top round)	1 teaspoon caraway seed
1 medium beet	1 tablespoon butter
6 scallions, including 3 inches of the green tops	1 tablespoon oil
1 teaspoon salt	Tiny new peas

Boil the beet in salted water until tender. Slip off the skin and mince the beet.

Mince the scallions and combine with the beet and beef, along with the salt and caraway seed. Shape into 6 oval patties.

In a large frying pan heat together the butter and oil. Fry the patties over medium-high heat until they are just done, about 6 to 8 minutes. Serve garnished with tiny new peas.

Yield: 3 servings.

NOTE: These patties are also nice when topped with Dried Mushroom Sauce.

BAKED FISH WITH HORSERADISH
✮ PECHONAYA RYBA S KHRENOM ✮

Three Russian favorites—fish, horseradish and sour cream—are combined here in an excellent dish that's easy to prepare. Use horseradish flavored with beets for a rosy glow under the cream.

8 fish fillets, such as flounder or halibut (2 pounds)	½ teaspoon thyme
½ teaspoon salt	½ cup prepared horseradish
Freshly ground black pepper to taste	2 tablespoons butter
	½ cup sour cream

Preheat the oven to 375°F. Grease an oven-proof dish. Season the fish fillets with the salt, pepper and thyme.

Place four of the fillets in the baking dish. Spread half of the horseradish over them. Dot with half of the butter. Spread on half of the sour cream.

Place the remaining four fillets on top and repeat the procedure, spreading on the remaining horseradish, butter and sour cream.

Cover the dish and bake for 30 minutes. Remove the cover and continue baking for 15 minutes more, or until the fish is flaky.

Yield: 4 generous servings.

VARIATION: Place a layer of sliced sour apples between the two layers of fish fillets. Bake as directed.

POTATO AND HERRING BAKE
❊ KARTOFEL' S SELYODKOI ❊

The Baltic Sea has been so thoroughly fished over that herring is growing scarce, and this wonderful fish, once considered plebeian, is now a delicacy in the Soviet Union. Here, a single herring is economically stretched into a filling meal for four in a dish that is common to both northern Russia and Estonia.

1 salt herring (about ¾ pound)	Freshly ground black pepper
Milk	1 large onion, sliced
4 slices of bacon	Butter
4 medium potatoes	½ cup grated Parmesan cheese

Rinse the herring and soak it overnight in milk. Discard the milk. Skin the herring, then split it and remove the backbone. Cut the herring into 1-inch pieces.

Grease an 8-inch oven-proof casserole. Fry the bacon until just barely crisp, reserving the bacon grease. Allow to cool, then crumble. Peel the potatoes and slice thinly.

Preheat the oven to 375°F. Place one third of the potatoes in a layer in the bottom of the casserole. Pour half of the bacon grease over the potatoes, then sprinkle on half of the crumbled bacon, half of the sliced onion and half of the herring. Pepper liberally. Top with half of the remaining potatoes, then cover the potatoes with the rest of the bacon grease, bacon, onion and herring. Again pepper liberally and make a top layer with the remaining potatoes.

Dot the potatoes with butter and sprinkle them with the grated Parmesan cheese. Bake uncovered for 30 minutes, then cover the dish and bake for 30 minutes more. Serve hot.

Yield: 4 servings.

STUFFED CABBAGE LEAVES
❧ GOLUBTSY ❧

Stuffing cabbage leaves is an art in the Soviet Union, where each region and ethnic group claims its own expertise. One finds Central Asian cabbage stuffed with lamb, Baltic cabbage layered with bacon and a delightful sweet-and-sour cabbage attributed to Russian Jewish cookery. When cabbage leaves are stuffed and rolled into packets they are called *golubtsy*, "little doves," as the rolls resemble the small birds at rest with wings folded under. Sometimes, though, the head of cabbage is left whole, as in the second recipe below, a typically Russian preparation, and a splendid one.

· I ·
STUFFED CABBAGE LEAVES
(JEWISH SWEET-AND-SOUR STYLE)
✸ GOLUBTSY ✸

1 head of white cabbage
(about 2 pounds)

2 large onions, coarsely
chopped
3 tablespoons olive oil

¾ pound ground beef (or half
ground beef and half ground
veal)
3 tablespoons raw rice
1 large carrot, scraped and
grated
1 large clove garlic, crushed

¼ teaspoon crushed fennel
seed
2 tablespoons minced parsley
1 teaspoon salt
Freshly ground black pepper
to taste (use it liberally)
1 large egg, beaten

2 pounds ripe tomatoes, peeled
and cut into chunks (or 1
28-ounce can, drained)
⅓ cup fresh lemon juice
½ cup dark brown sugar
¼ teaspoon salt

Core the cabbage. Blanch it in boiling water for about 5 minutes. Remove from the pot and gently peel off the outer leaves. If the inner leaves are still too stiff to be removed, return the cabbage to the boiling water for another minute or so. Continue until all the leaves have been removed.

Use the small inner leaves or any damaged ones to line the bottom and sides of a 3-quart Dutch oven. Reserve the cooking liquid.

To prepare the onions, mix the onions with the olive oil in a heavy-bottomed frying pan. Pour over enough of the hot water from the cabbage pot to just cover the onions. Bring to a boil and simmer slowly, uncovered, for 45 minutes to 1 hour, or until the water has evaporated and the onions are golden. Stir occasionally to make sure the onions don't stick to the pan.

While the onions are simmering, prepare the filling. In a large bowl thoroughly mix together the ground beef, raw rice, carrot, garlic, fennel, parsley, salt, and pepper. Stir in the egg, blending well.

Now, starting with the largest leaves, take a cabbage leaf and place a mound of the filling along the center. Tuck up the bottom edge of the leaf first, then roll and tuck until the filling is completely enclosed in the leaf. Continue until all the filling has been used. There will be about 12 rolls.

Place half of the rolls in the cabbage-lined pot in a single layer. Cover with half of the prepared onions, then top with the remaining cabbage rolls and the rest of the onions.

In a medium-sized saucepan heat the tomatoes, pressing with the back of a spoon until they begin to give off juice. Stir in the lemon juice, sugar and salt. Bring to a boil. Pour over the cabbage rolls. The chunks of tomato will form a layer on top.

Cover the pot and simmer for 1½ to 2 hours.

Yield: 4 servings.

NOTE: These cabbage rolls are even better reheated the second day.

• II •
STUFFED WHOLE CABBAGE
❁ *KAPUSTA FARSHIROVANNAYA* ❁

*1 head of white cabbage
(about 2¼ pounds)*

*4 slices stale white bread,
crusts removed*
½ cup milk
1 pound ground beef
1½ teaspoons salt
*Freshly ground black pepper
to taste*

*½ teaspoon crushed hot dried
pepper*
¼ teaspoon caraway seed
*1 tablespoon snipped fresh dill
(or ½ teaspoon dried dill)*
4 tablespoons butter, melted
1 cup rich beef broth
1 cup sour cream

Core the cabbage. Place the cabbage in a large pot with a tightly fitting lid. Add some boiling salted water and steam the cabbage until just barely tender, about 25 minutes. Remove from the water and drain; set aside to cool.

Soak the stale bread in the milk. Squeeze out the excess milk and then mix the bread with the ground beef, salt, pepper, hot pepper, caraway seed and dill, blending well.

When the cabbage is cool enough to handle, carefully pull back each of the leaves, one at a time, being careful not to tear them from the base of the cabbage. Continue pulling back the leaves until only the tiny inner leaves remain in a point. Starting from the inside, brush some melted butter on each leaf as you work with it, then sprinkle it with salt. Place some filling on each leaf, and then carefully reposition the leaf as if you were putting the head back together again. Continue until all the leaves have been filled. Pour any extra butter over the cabbage.

Place the cabbage in a round 9-inch oven-proof dish. The dish should be just large enough to hold the cabbage comfortably and allow it to retain its shape. Preheat the oven to 350°F.

Pour the beef broth around the edges of the cabbage and place the dish in the oven. Bake, uncovered, for 40 minutes, basting occasionally with the broth if the cabbage looks dry on top. After 40 minutes, spread the top of the cabbage with the sour cream, masking it completely. Return to the oven and continue baking for 20 minutes more.

Serve the cabbage by cutting it into thick wedges and ladling the pan juices over it.

Yield: 4 hearty servings.

CABBAGE WITH NOODLES AND POPPY SEEDS
KAPUSTA S LAPSHOI I MAKOM

Since advertisements are rare in the Soviet press, I was surprised to see in a recent edition of the Leningrad *Pravda* a half-page spread for none other than cabbage. "Dear housewives," it exhorted, "there are 137 different and delicious ways to prepare cabbage! Try them all . . . cabbage is not only tasty, it's good for you." I don't know who determined the 137 variations, but this recipe for cabbage with noodles and poppy seeds is no doubt one of them. And just as the advertisement claims, it's both tasty and nutritious.

6 tablespoons butter
1 small head of white cabbage (1 to 1½ pounds), coarsely chopped
1 onion, coarsely chopped
2 small tart apples, peeled, cored and coarsely chopped

Salt, freshly ground black pepper to taste

3 ounces fettucine noodles
2 tablespoons butter
2 tablespoons poppy seeds

In a large frying pan melt the 6 tablespoons of butter. Stir in the vegetables and apples, coating them well with the butter. Add salt and freshly ground pepper to taste. Cover the pan; simmer for about 20 minutes, or until the vegetables are soft, adding a tiny bit of water if necessary to keep them from burning.

Cook the noodles in boiling salted water until barely tender. Drain. Stir in the remaining butter and coat the noodles well. Stir the cooked vegetables and apples into the noodles. Add the poppy seeds, and check for seasoning.

Yield: 6 servings.

NOTE: This dish improves after standing and tastes best when made ahead of time, refrigerated, and then reheated to serve.

CASSEROLE OF MASHED POTATOES
☙ KARTOFEL'NAYA ZAPEKANKA ☙

Potatoes are so much a part of the Russian diet that they are fondly called the *vtoroi khleb*, "second bread," of the people. But they were not always so popular. When the potato was first introduced in Russia in the early eighteenth century, the Russians were reluctant to cultivate this strange tuber. Under Catherine the Great attempts were made to popularize it, but people still felt suspicious of it, as Europeans did of the tomato at first. The government's determination to impose the potato on the popu-lace led to conflict in the first half of the nineteenth century, when there were numerous "potato rebellions," culminating in the so-called Potato Mutiny of 1842. This rebellion, a downright refusal by the peasants to plant potatoes, was the largest popular uprising of the nineteenth century in Russia. It was only after Tsar Nicholas I issued a harsh edict enforcing cultivation that the peasants submitted to his will, and by 1844 prizes were being offered for the best potato cultivation.

Of course, life in Russia today is unthinkable without the potato, and a favorite way of preparing this "second bread" is in *zapekanka*. This Russian version of mashed potatoes is often made livelier with a sauce of dried mushrooms, but if the pungent flavor of wild mushrooms is not to your liking, the casserole may be served plain or with a milder cham-pignon-based sauce.

2 pounds potatoes	3 large onions, thinly sliced
3 tablespoons butter, melted	2 tablespoons butter
1 cup milk	2 tablespoons vegetable oil
1 teaspoon salt	½ cup sour cream
2 eggs, lightly beaten	

Boil the potatoes in salted water until tender; peel and mash them. Stir in the 3 tablespoons of melted butter, the milk and the salt. Beat in the eggs.

While the potatoes are boiling, fry the onions until golden in the 2 tablespoons of butter mixed with the 2 tablespoons of oil.

Grease a 2-quart casserole. Place half of the mashed potatoes into it; smooth the top. Spread the onions in an even layer over the potatoes, and top the onions with the remaining potatoes. Spread the sour cream over the top.

Bake the casserole in a preheated 350°F oven for 30 minutes, or until lightly browned on top.

Yield: 4 to 6 servings.

DRIED MUSHROOM SAUCE
✹ GRIBNOI SOUS ✹

2 ounces dried black mushrooms	2 tablespoons butter
2¼ cups water	2 tablespoons chopped scallions
1 tablespoon butter	¼ teaspoon salt
1 tablespoon flour	Freshly ground black pepper to taste

Soak the dried mushrooms in the water for 1 hour. Drain, reserving the liquid.

In a saucepan melt the 1 tablespoon of butter. Stir in the flour and cook for a minute or two, until the flour begins to turn golden. Gradually stir in 2 cups of the reserved mushroom liquid. Bring to a boil; cook over medium heat for 15 minutes, or until the liquid is reduced by almost half.

Meanwhile, melt the 2 tablespoons of butter in a frying pan. Sauté the scallions and drained mushrooms, which have been finely chopped.

Add the scallions and chopped mushrooms to the sauce, along with the salt and pepper to taste.

Serve over the Casserole of Mashed Potatoes (see above) or Russian-Style Hamburgers.

Yield: 1 cup.

SAUERKRAUT WITH MUSHROOMS AND SOUR CREAM
KISLAYA KAPUSTA S GRIBAMI I SMETANOI

Should any sauerkraut be left at the bottom of the barrel, put it to good use in this flavorful accompaniment to pot-roasted meat.

¼ pound mushrooms
⅓ cup water
1 pound sauerkraut (about 2 cups), slightly drained

1 small tomato, coarsely chopped
½ cup sour cream
Freshly ground black pepper to taste

Chop the mushrooms finely. Place them in a saucepan with the water and bring to a boil.

Add the sauerkraut (do not squeeze it dry) and the tomato. Simmer for 5 minutes.

Stir in the sour cream. Season to taste, and serve at once.

Yield: 4 servings.

UKRAINIAN-STYLE COTTAGE CHEESE
MACHANKA

In the Ukraine, *tvorog* is often dressed up with rich cream and scallions. I like to serve this cheese spread thickly on black bread or as part of a mixed salad plate.

½ pound dry Russian Cottage Cheese (tvorog)
1 cup heavy cream

¼ cup chopped scallions
1 tablespoon snipped fresh dill
Salt to taste

Mix together all the ingredients. Use right away or chill.

Yield: 6 servings (or more as a sandwich spread).

CUCUMBERS IN SOUR CREAM
☙ OGURTSY V SMETANE ☙

Because there were no other green vegetables to be had the summer I spent in Leningrad, I virtually lived on this salad. But it's so good that I never grew tired of it and still find myself making these creamy cucumbers quite often—even when other vegetables are at hand.

2 cucumbers
1 cup sour cream
2 to 3 tablespoons cider vinegar
4 tablespoons snipped fresh
* chives*
2 tablespoons snipped fresh dill
* (or 2 teaspoons dried dill)*
Freshly ground white pepper
* to taste*
2 teaspoons salt

If the cucumbers have been waxed, peel them; otherwise, wash them well but leave the peel on. Slice the cucumbers very thin and pat them dry with paper towels. Mix together the remaining ingredients, adding vinegar to taste. Stir in the cucumbers. Let stand at room temperature for 30 minutes before refrigerating. Serve well chilled.

    Yield: 4 to 6 servings; more as a *zakuska*.

VARIATION: Add freshly grated horseradish to the sour cream mixture before stirring in the cucumbers. Use 1 to 2 tablespoons of the peeled root, to taste.

BEET SALAD
🗶 *SVEKOL'NYI SALAT* 🗶

A delectable salad, good on the *zakuska* table or as a complement to roasted meat.

1 pound beets	*¼ cup chopped moist prunes*
3 large cloves garlic, minced	*(or more, to taste)*
¼ cup chopped walnuts	*3 tablespoons mayonnaise*
(or more, to taste)	*Salt*

Scrub the beets and remove the green tops. Place the beets in a baking dish and bake at 375°F for 1 to 1½ hours, until soft.

When the beets are cool enough to handle, slip off the skins and shred the beets coarsely.

Add the garlic to the beets, along with the walnuts and prunes. Stir in the mayonnaise and mix well. Season to taste. Chill well before serving.

Yield: 6 servings.

CARROT SALAD
❦ SALAT "ZDOROV'YE" ❦

This combination of carrots, garlic and mayonnaise is known as Health Salad in the Soviet Union, for Russians believe that carrots thicken the blood—an asset in their harsh northern climate. This is a nice change from the usual sweet carrot salad with fruit.

½ pound carrots, scraped
1 teaspoon freshly squeezed
*   lemon juice*
4 cloves garlic, minced

3 tablespoons mayonnaise
Salt to taste

Parsley

Grate the carrots. Pour the lemon juice over them, mixing well. Add the garlic to the carrots. Stir in the mayonnaise and salt to taste. Chill for several hours before serving, garnished with parsley.

Yield: 4 servings.

RADISHES IN SOUR CREAM
❦ REDISKA V SMETANE ❦

Radishes are all too often relegated to the salad bowl. For a delicious change, try preparing them as a side dish, blanched and then mixed with sour cream and scallions.

1 pound red radishes
2 cups water
Salt

1 tablespoon sour cream
2 tablespoons chopped scallions

Wash and trim the radishes. Bring the water to a boil with salt and cook the radishes for about 4 minutes, until tender but still firm. Drain. Stir in the sour cream, chopped scallions and salt to taste, mixing well. Serve immediately.

Yield: 4 servings.

CELERIAC SALAD
☙ *VINEGRET IZ SEL'DEREINOGO KORNYA* ☙

This salad is cousin to the more familiar potato salad, but with a haunting flavor of celery.

1 celeriac (about 1¼ pounds)	*¼ cup white wine vinegar*
6 black peppercorns	*1 teaspoon* Russian-Style
1 small onion, quartered	Mustard
2 chicken bouillon cubes	*1 tablespoon minced parsley*
1 bay leaf	*Salt, freshly ground black*
	pepper to taste
¼ cup olive oil	

Trim the ends of the celeriac and peel it. Boil it until tender in salted water to which the peppercorns, onion quarters, bouillon cubes and bay leaf have been added. This will take about 45 minutes.

Drain the celeriac and cut it into cubes. While still hot, pour over it a dressing made from the remaining ingredients, which have been well blended. Let the salad stand at room temperature for 1 hour, and then chill. Serve cold.

Yield: 4 servings.

BAKED APPLES
☙ *PECHONYE YABLOKI* ☙

Russians are known to wax poetic at the mere mention of apples, of which they have many indigenous varieties. By consensus the favorite is the *antonovka,* a winter apple and the theme of Ivan Bunin's story "Antonov Apples." His narrative opens on a hot September day, when the air is heavy with the fragrance of Antonov apples ripening for the harvest. Throughout the story this particular autumnal smell evokes memories of bygone days on the estates of the Russian landed gentry, when the country houses were imbued with the smell of Antonov apples, a smell greeting the visitor as soon as he crossed the threshold. Those who knew and loved the country life maintained that "if the apples are good, the year will be, too." Here are two simple recipes for baked apples, both catering to the Russian sweet tooth.

· I ·

BAKED APPLES WITH JAM
❂ PECHONYE YABLOKI S VAREN'EM ❂

Rome Beauty apples (or other Seedless raspberry jam
 large, sweet cooking apples) Butter

Use one apple per person.

Preheat the oven to 375°F. Peel each apple 1 inch down the sides. Remove the core, leaving a generous hollow, to within ½ inch of the bottom, being careful not to pierce the bottom of the apple.

Fill each cavity with seedless raspberry jam. Dot the top of each apple with butter.

Place the apples in a baking dish. Pour in 1 inch of boiling water. Cover with foil. Bake for 30 minutes, or until tender but still intact.

Serve warm with sweet cream.

• II •
SOUFFLÉED BAKED APPLES
❀ YABLOKI SO SMETANOI ❀

2 pounds tart apples, peeled,
    cored and sliced
2 cups cold water
2 tablespoons freshly squeezed
    lemon juice

4 eggs, separated
¼ teaspoon almond extract
¼ teaspoon ground cardamom
1 tablespoon flour
½ cup (heaping) sugar

½ cup seedless raspberry jam
1½ cups sour cream

2 tablespoons sugar

In a saucepan combine the water and lemon juice. As each apple is peeled, cored and sliced, drop the slices into the water. Then bring the water to a boil and simmer the apples for 3 to 5 minutes, until tender. Drain.

Preheat the oven to 325°F. Grease a 9 x 13-inch glass baking dish. Mix together the poached apples and the jam, coating each slice. Spread the apples in an even layer in the dish.

In a small bowl combine the sour cream, egg yolks and flavorings. Stir in the flour and the ½ cup of sugar.

Beat the egg whites until stiff but not dry and gently fold them into the sour cream mixture. Spread over the apples. Sprinkle with the 2 tablespoons of sugar. Bake the apples for about 30 minutes, or until puffed and golden. Let the dessert stand for 10 minutes before serving so that it can be cut easily into squares.

Yield: 4 to 6 servings.

APPLE FRITTERS
🗲 OLAD'I 🗲

These apple fritters are made by the old Russian sponge method, yielding light and puffy pancakes suitable for brunch or dessert.

½ package active dry yeast
1 cup milk, lukewarm
2 tablespoons sugar
Pinch of salt
1 cup flour

2 eggs, separated
2 tablespoons butter, softened
1 cup flour

3 apples, peeled, cored and chopped
¼ cup sugar
2 tablespoons rum

Vegetable oil for frying

Confectioners' sugar

Dissolve the yeast in 2 tablespoons of the milk, then stir in the remaining milk, the sugar, the salt and the 1 cup of flour. This is the sponge. Cover it and let rise in a warm place for 1 hour.

Then stir in the egg yolks, butter and the remaining 1 cup of flour. Cover and let rise for 1½ hours.

Meanwhile, mix the apples with the sugar and rum. Let stand for 1 hour. When the batter has risen, stir in the apple mixture, including the liquid from the apples and rum.

Beat the egg whites until stiff but not dry and fold them into the batter.

In a large frying pan heat the vegetable oil. It should be 1 inch deep in the pan. Drop the batter by tablespoonsful into the hot oil and cook over medium-high heat until puffed and brown, turning once. Each fritter takes only about 4 minutes to cook.

Dust with confectioners' sugar and serve immediately.

Yield: 1½ to 2 dozen fritters.

RUSSIAN FRUIT PUDDING
KISEL'

Kisel' is the traditional Russian fruit pudding. Its name is derived from the word *kislyi,* "sour," since the pudding has a delightfully tart taste. *Kisel'* is also one of the oldest Russian foods. As early as the tenth century, Slavic tribes were making primitive puddings, but these precursors of *kisel'* were made from grains instead of fruit.

Controversy rages as to the perfect consistency for *kisel'*. It can be as thin as soup or as thick as molded jelly. I think the best consistency is somewhere in between: a slightly thickened pudding that can still be poured, as in the recipes below.

· I ·
STRAWBERRY *KISEL'*

1 pint fresh strawberries, hulled
1 cup water
½ cup superfine sugar

2 teaspoons potato starch
1 tablespoon freshly squeezed
  lemon juice
Drop of almond extract

In a heavy saucepan simmer the strawberries, uncovered, in the water for 15 minutes. Put through a vegetable mill, then stir in the sugar and the potato starch, which has been dissolved in the lemon juice.

Rinse out the saucepan and return the puree to it. Cook for just 2 to 3 minutes, until thickened. Stir in the almond extract, then pour into a bowl and let chill in the refrigerator. Serve well chilled in a deep glass bowl with fresh cream.

Yield: 4 to 6 servings.

· II ·
BLUEBERRY *KISEL'*

Substitute 1 pint of blueberries for the strawberries. Proceed as above.

· III ·
CRANBERRY *KISEL'*

½ *pound cranberries*	2 *teaspoons potato starch*
¾ *cup sugar*	1 *tablespoon freshly squeezed*
1 *cup water*	*orange juice*

Proceed as in the recipe for strawberry *kisel'*, substituting the cranberries and using ¾ cup sugar. After the cranberries have been put through the vegetable mill, force the puree through a fine sieve to remove all seeds. Then continue as directed above.

Yield: 4 to 6 servings.

NOTE: If a *kisel'* thick enough to mold is desired, substitute 1 tablespoon potato starch for the 2 teaspoons starch called for in the recipes.

RUSSIAN CHEESE PANCAKES
🌣 *SYRNIKI* 🌣

The name *syrniki* derives from the Russian word *syr,* "cheese." These delightful cheese pancakes provide a pleasant diversion from the usual griddle cakes for a Sunday-morning brunch or a late-evening supper.

2 *pounds* Russian Cottage Cheese (tvorog) *or farmer* cheese	1 *tablespoon sugar* ¾ *cup flour*
2 *egg yolks*	*Butter for frying*
1 *whole egg*	*Sour cream*
¼ *teaspoon salt*	*Sugar (optional)*

If the *tvorog* is wet, place it under a press until it loses all excess moisture. Then mix in the egg yolks, egg, salt, sugar and flour, blending well. Form the cheese mass into 2 sausage-shaped rolls. Chill for 30 minutes (or up to a couple of days).

When ready to serve the pancakes, cut the rolls into 1-inch-thick rounds, gently shaping the cheese mass into patties with your hands. Fry them in plenty of butter over medium-high heat until browned, turning once. Serve hot with sour cream and, if desired, sugar.

Yield: 4 to 6 servings.

VARIATIONS:

1. To make *tvorozhniki* (sweetened *syrniki*), to the basic recipe above add the grated rind of ½ lemon and 1 teaspoon vanilla extract, and substitute 4 tablespoons sugar for the 1 tablespoon called for. Proceed as directed above.

2. To make *lenivye vareniki* ("lazy" dumplings), shape the chilled cheese mixture into walnut-sized balls. Bring a large kettle of salted water to a boil, and gently boil the cheese balls until they rise to the surface, about 3 minutes. Serve with plenty of melted butter and sour cream.

RUSSIAN COTTAGE PUDDING
🌿 *DROCHONA* 🌿

Drochona, one of the oldest Russian foods, is a simple batter pudding, often spiked with grated potatoes, fruits, caviar. But even in its plain state, *drochona* is still satisfying: its name stems from the archaic verb *drochit'*, "to pamper" or "to coddle."

4 tablespoons unsalted butter	¼ cup milk
¼ cup sugar	1 cup cranberries, chopped
4 eggs	
1 cup flour	Jam
Pinch of salt	Cream

Cream the butter and sugar. Add the eggs one at a time, beating well after each addition. Gradually add the flour, then stir in the salt and milk. Beat on the high speed of an electric mixer for 5 minutes, or by hand, until the mixture is light and frothy. Then stir in the cranberries.

Preheat the oven to 350°F. Grease an 8-inch deep-dish pie plate well, then dust with flour. Pour the batter into the prepared plate, and bake the pudding for 40 minutes, until lightly browned.

Serve warm with jam and cream.

Yield: 4 servings.

EGG TODDY
🎏 *GOGOL'-MOGOL'* 🎏

The word *gogol-'mogol'* sounds as funny in Russian as it does in English. It's a whimsical name thought up to entice children to drink this nourishing egg-rich custard as fortification against colds and other ailments— but many children need no enticement at all. This recipe has been handed down through my mother's family under the name of "guggle-muggle," an even stranger appellation.

4 egg yolks
¼ cup light brown sugar
¼ cup hot milk

2 tablespoons rum
Nutmeg

Beat the egg yolks until light. Gradually add the sugar and continue beating until the mixture is fluffy. Slowly stir in the hot milk and the rum. Continue beating for 5 minutes more, then pour into glasses and serve. If desired, grate a little fresh nutmeg on the top.

Yield: 2 servings.

☙ · V · ☙

‡◊

FROM THE PANTRY

◊‡

The Russian pantry of old was a wonderland of sights and smells. In the cool air the pungent odor of smoked meats and pickled vegetables blended with the nutty scent of milled grains and the sweet fragrance of dried apricots and apples and pears. Shimmering jars of fruit preserves and brandies reflected all manner of conserves displayed on shelves along the facing wall. In a rear corner stood large oaken tubs brimming with *mochonye yabloki* (apples soaked in brine) and sauerkraut put up with caraway and other spices. Deep vats held cucumbers and mushrooms in various guises: salted heavily or lightly; pickled in vinegar; marinated in aromatic oils. Wild field mushrooms were strung on ropes and hung to dry in orderly profusion, accompanied by garlands of dried cherries and plums and other summer fruits. Coarse, heavy sacks of salt and wheat flour were in easy reach by the door, as were sparkling cones of crystal sugar. There were bins of buckwheat groats for *kasha* and hulled wheat for *kut'ya;* bins of buckwheat flour for *blini* and rye meal for black bread. Bags of dried beans were clustered in one section of the room. Butter was stored in a glazed tub in the "dairy corner," along with a variety of homemade cheeses, both hard and soft. The cottage cheese, *tvorog,* was hung in muslin bags to solidify over drip pans. Sides of ham and home-cured bacon were suspended from the rafters, as were sausages in fanciful shapes—links, rounds and tubes. Ropes of garlic and onions dangled in the air. Sometimes whole salted watermelons were piled high on the floor. Root vegetables, such as turnips and horseradish, lay buried in sand in a long, low box to remain fresh throughout the winter. A special area was set aside for the preparations of fish, especially sturgeon: *balyk,* the cured fillet; and *vesiga,* the gelatinous backbone, necessary for the perfect *kulebyaka.* Sturdy wooden shelves lined the room, and row upon row of fruit preserves, jams and jellies greeted the eye, each jar beckoning, promising delight. There were strawberries from the field and from the garden, simmered over a slow fire to rich thickness or suspended in brandy. Golden peaches floated in their own syrup or in a compote with other fruits. Bright tomatoes and peppers kept company in jars of *baklazhannaya ikra* (eggplant caviar). There were sweet, viscous syrups to use in baking and fruit drinks; glistening garnet and amber homemade brandies and liqueurs; vinegars and mustards steeped with wild herbs. This well-stocked larder was integral to every household in the days when a party of twenty or more might unexpectedly drop in for a refreshing meal.

The stores were replenished yearly. Once the fruits and vegetables were harvested, each household set itself to the arduous task of gathering, sorting and preserving newly picked produce. If their own harvest was lean, the landowners flocked to the district *yarmarka,* "fair," where goods could be bought, traded or sold. The country *yarmarka* was a festive event. The roads for miles around were jammed with all sorts of conveyances transporting people and their wares: rickety horse-drawn wooden carts piled high with produce, handcarts dragged by peasants in gaily colored shirts and skirts and bast sandals; sturdy carriages peopled with the well-to-do. Masses of villagers made their way to the fair on foot, carrying baskets of birch bark or bast filled to overflowing with the berries and mushrooms they had gathered with the early morning dew still on them. The more enterprising made the rougher journey to city centers, such as Moscow or Kiev, where their fresh country produce commanded high prices among urbanites eager for fruits and vegetables to put up for the winter. At the *yarmarka* the din of clattering cart wheels was rivaled only by the squawking of chickens, the honking of geese and the comical songs of hawkers peddling their goods. Mounds of orchard fruits sparkled in the midday sun; the sweet heavy scent of honey in combs and in jars pervaded the air, as did the buzzing of the bees hovering around; barrels of tiny, knobby cucumbers stood awaiting the pickling brine; boxes upon boxes of humble root vegetables begged not to be overlooked. And what apples there were! Tales of record harvests circulated from season to season, and there was hardly a landowner who didn't boast of apples the size of a dinner plate or watermelons as big as a beer barrel.

At summer's end, each household was caught up in frenetic activity—carting, chopping, stoking, stirring—to ensure a plentiful and tasty winter season. Other chores and duties were temporarily suspended as the frantic pace gathered momentum: the produce had to be processed quickly to taste its best, and the more that was processed the better. Most of the activity took place out of doors. To make jam, a large fire was built under heavy copper kettles hung from tripods. Another fire burned almost continuously under odd-looking retorts that distilled vodka and fruit brandies. For several weeks the yard had the appearance of a mad alchemist's laboratory. But the transformation of raw fruits into jams, confections and syrups, and of vegetables into preserves, was carried out in an orderly way. Nothing was allowed to go to waste. (Even the strong brine from pickles was—and is—commonly used as a cure for morning hangover, second only to another swig of vodka in its effectiveness.) Fruits were washed, but not peeled. Not all fruits were pitted, but any available pits were used to flavor vodka. Mushroom scraps were cooked into mushroom caviar. Odd bits of vegetables were turned into delicious summer soups. In the Golovlev family in Mikhail Saltykov-Shchedrin's novel *The Golovlevs,* such thriftiness turned into miserliness. The family matriarch, Arina Petrovna, had endless storerooms at her disposal, and each year she made her servants put up far more preserves than the family could eat because she could not bear to waste a thing:

With renewed zeal Arina Petrovna turned to her interrupted household duties. The summer preserving was drawing to a close. As the clatter of cooks' knives in the kitchen died down, activity in the office, barns, pantries and cellars redoubled. The preserving, salting, and stocking up were in full swing. Stores for the winter were gathered from all over; from all of Arina Petrovna's family estates dried mushrooms, berries, eggs, vegetables and the like were brought in by the cartload. All of these were measured, processed and added to the stores from previous years. It wasn't for naught that a whole series of cellars, pantries and barns had been built for Arina Petrovna, the lady of the estate; they all were filled to bursting and in spite of the servants' frequent pilferings, contained quite a lot of spoiled material, which one didn't dare approach because of the rotten smell. Spoiled and unspoiled were separated at the end of the summer. Whatever seemed unreliable was given to the servants.

"These pickles are still good, they're just a little slimy on top, and they smell a bit off. I'm sure the servants will enjoy them," said Arina Petrovna as she ordered this or that tub left untouched, whether for her own use or to go rotten later on.

Summer preserving was anticipated by all as a time of pleasure as well as of labor. Massive wooden tables were set up in the shade of leafy poplar and linden trees. Here the cleaning and sorting and chopping of the produce took place. The servants shredded endless heads of cabbage for sauerkraut and snapped bushels of beans. They chopped yellow squash and eggplant for "poor man's caviar," and pickled sunflower seeds from the flower's dried head. If rain threatened, the tables were moved inside into the summer kitchen, a pleasant, well-scrubbed structure separate from the main house. (During the summer all of the cooking was carried on in this kitchen so as not to overheat the living areas.) The interest in preserving was shared by servant and mistress alike. Many of the gentry prided themselves not only on their excellent produce but also on the special recipes and methods they applied. In Tolstoy's *Anna Karenina,* the princesses make sure to supervise the cook's jam-making, lest she fail to conform to their new method of boiling the fruit without any water at all.

Jam-making was of particular importance because a truly well-laid tea table offered several varieties of jam, each shimmering translucently against the stark white backdrop of a linen tablecloth. In Ivan Bunin's "Sukhodol," so many different kinds of jam are offered at a fancy tea that it is impossible for the guests to taste them all at one helping. They must repeatedly approach the table in order to sample the vast assortment.

In *Anna Karenina,* Princess Shcherbatskaya admonishes Agafia Mikhailovna to pour the finished jam into jars and cover them with paper moistened with a little rum to prevent the jam from growing moldy. This practice is still followed in most Soviet homes, although today the moistening agent is more often vodka. Only commercially prepared jams are hermetically sealed, but vegetables and other highly perishable preserves have to be. This is accomplished by a rather cumbersome capping process requiring both patience and strength, since Mason-type jars are not available. The prepared foods are then hidden away in the most unlikely places—under tables and beds and chairs, in all available nooks and crannies—to be triumphantly pulled out and proffered to guests almost as soon as they walk through the door.

BASIC BOUILLON
🏹 *BUL'YON* 🏹

Soup is a mainstay of the Russian cuisine, and the comforting smell of broth simmering on the back burner is encountered in virtually every Russian home. The recipe below is for a basic meat stock, to be served alone as a first course or used as the basis for other, more intricate concoctions. Beef stock, like fish stock, is a staple item in Russian cookery, one that should always be ready for unexpected guests.

*2 pounds meat**	*2 large onions, quartered*
4 cups cold water	*2 bay leaves*
12 black peppercorns	*6 carrots, scraped*
6 sprigs parsley	*1 tablespoon salt*

Place all the ingredients except the salt in a large stockpot and bring to a boil, skimming off any scum that rises to the surface. Reduce the heat to low and stir in the salt.

Simmer, covered, for 2 to 3 hours, until the meat is tender and the liquid has been reduced by half. Strain the broth. Cut the meat and the carrots into serving-sized pieces and divide among the soup bowls. Pour the broth over to serve.

Yield: About 2 cups.

NOTE: If the stock is going to be frozen, do not return the meat and carrots to it after straining.

*If a beef broth is desired, use beef shins or chuck with some bone left in; for a chicken broth, use a stewing hen, adding all of the giblets except the liver.

BASIC FISH STOCK
⚔ *KREPKII BUL'YON IZ RYBY* ⚔

This fish stock is sometimes served with tiny pies as the soup course, but more often than not it forms the base for Russia's famous fish soups. It's a good idea always to keep some on hand in the freezer.

1 tablespoon butter
1 small onion, coarsely chopped
1 carrot, scraped and coarsely chopped

2 ounces mushroom trimmings

2 pounds fish, including trimmings (at least one fish head is recommended for best flavor)

3 cups cold water
1 cup dry white wine

2 sprigs parsley
2 sprigs dill
1 bay leaf
6 white peppercorns
¾ teaspoon salt
1 tablespoon freshly squeezed lemon juice

Sauté the onion, carrot and mushroom trimmings in the butter.

In a large stockpot place the remaining ingredients; add the sautéed vegetables. Bring to a boil, skimming off any foam that rises to the surface.

Cook partially covered over medium heat for 30 to 40 minutes. Strain through muslin.

Yield: 1 quart.

CRANBERRY JUICE
🌿 *KLYUKVENNYI MORS* 🌿

A refreshing cold drink that is also good mulled.

1 pound cranberries
4 cups water
1 cup sugar

¼ cup freshly squeezed lemon juice
Zest of half a lemon, in a long spiral

Rinse the cranberries. Place them in a large saucepan with the water and bring to a boil. Boil for about 5 minutes, or until the skins have burst.

Meanwhile, line a colander with cheesecloth. When the cranberries have burst, strain the juice through the colander, letting it drip into a bowl for a few minutes. Then gently press the cranberries to extract the remaining juice. (If a very clear juice is desired, strain once again through clean cheesecloth.)

Return the juice to a clean saucepan and bring to a boil with the sugar. Simmer for just 1 or 2 minutes, stirring to dissolve the sugar. Let cool.

When the juice has cooled, stir in the lemon juice and the lemon spiral. Chill and serve.

Yield: About 1 quart.

SPICED HONEY DRINK
⚔ SBITEN' ⚔

Sbiten' is an ancient Russian drink. I first tasted it in Azov, a sleepy town in the Don River delta. Azov was once a strategically important city, guarding the entrance to Russia's waterways and the site of a great battle against the Turks in the eighteenth century. Stone ruins still stand overlooking the water, and a charming restaurant, The Fortress Ramparts, has been built on the promontory. The restaurant is decorated in the Old Russian style, with ornately carved window shutters and long wooden benches. In keeping with its decor and the history of the town, The Fortress Ramparts serves old Russian specialties, including this spiced hot drink.

4 cups water	2 cinnamon sticks
½ cup sugar	½ teaspoon dried mint flakes
½ cup honey	1 teaspoon grated lemon rind
6 whole cloves	
8 whole cardamom pods, peeled	Nutmeg

Bring all the ingredients except the nutmeg to a boil in a large saucepan. Simmer, covered, for 15 minutes. Then cool to room temperature.

Once the *sbiten'* has cooled, strain it. Reheat to serve. Grate some fresh nutmeg into each cup.

Yield: 4 servings.

BARREL-CURED SAUERKRAUT
✹ *KVASHENAYA KAPUSTA* ✹

Russian families once required whole cartloads of cabbage to accommodate their yearly sauerkraut-making. Although the process of shredding
so many heads of cabbage was laborious, it ensured a constant supply
throughout the winter, to be eaten plain, mixed with other vegetables or
added to the inevitable *shchi*. The sauerkraut was put up in large oaken
barrels, whose scent permeated the fermenting cabbage. Black currant or
cherry leaves were often layered with the cabbage, further contributing
to its final flavor. Unfortunately, neither oaken barrels nor black currant
leaves are as readily available as they once were, so now we must settle
for a glazed crock and a slightly more prosaic sauerkraut. Still, it's good!
Try adding spices, such as caraway, bay leaves, cardamom or peppercorns,
to vary the flavor.

> *2 heads of white cabbage,*
> *about 4 pounds each*

> *4 tablespoons coarse or pickling*
> *salt*

The day before you plan to begin making sauerkraut, remove the cabbage
to room temperature and let it sit for 24 hours so that the leaves won't
be brittle. When ready to make the sauerkraut, remove the outer leaves
of the cabbage, then rinse each head and cut into quarters. Remove the
cores and shred the cabbage finely.

Place the shredded cabbage in a large bowl and add the salt, mixing to
distribute it evenly. Let stand for about 15 minutes.

Pack the salted cabbage firmly into a 4-gallon crock, pressing down on
it with a wooden spoon. Brine will start to form almost immediately.

Place a clean cloth over the top of the cabbage. On top of the cloth
place a plate that just fits inside the rim of the crock. Weight the plate
down with a jar filled with water or another heavy weight. The brine
should rise about 2 inches above the saucer, thus keeping air from reaching the fermenting cabbage.

Leave the crock at room temperature (about 70°F.) Bubbles will form,
showing that fermentation is taking place. Each day, remove the cloth
and any scum that has appeared on the surface. Rinse the cloth out and
replace it, and replace the heavy weight on the plate.

If there seems to be a lack of brine at any time (that is, less than 2 inches above the cabbage), add 1 cup of water in which 2 teaspoons of coarse salt have been dissolved.

The fermentation process will take anywhere from 2 to 6 weeks, depending on the room temperature. When the sauerkraut is done, bubbles will stop rising to the surface even though it is still fermenting. Taste the cabbage, and if it is soured enough for your taste, then it is ready and can be refrigerated.

Yield: 2 gallons.

NOTE: The right amount of salt is important. Too little salt results in a soft sauerkraut; too much salt prevents fermentation. Uneven distribution of salt may result in the growth of yeast with a pinkish color.

The top layer of the sauerkraut may turn brown from exposure to air as the cloth is changed, but this layer may be discarded when the sauerkraut is ready to be refrigerated or eaten.

SOUR CABBAGE
KISLAYA KAPUSTA

Sour cabbage differs from sauerkraut in that it sits only long enough to sour, not ferment, and so is easier to prepare. Sour cabbage salad is practically an institution in the Soviet Union, garnishing meals at both lunch and dinner. Here I must break the taboo against mentioning unappetizing food in cookbooks, for sour cabbage, as prepared in all too many Soviet cafeterias, can be truly dismal. At its best, the salad is tart and refreshing. One learns early on either to develop a taste for it (a wise idea, since other vegetables are few and far between) or to successfully avoid it. The recipe given here is guaranteed foolproof, however, and makes a salad to put any Soviet café to shame.

2 pounds white cabbage
1 large carrot, scraped
1 large tart apple, peeled and
    cored
1 tablespoon salt

2 small bay leaves
8 black peppercorns

8 allspice berries
¼ teaspoon caraway seed
¼ teaspoon dill seed

Thinly sliced onions
Sugar
Vegetable oil

Shred the cabbage, carrot and apple very finely. (This is most easily done in a food processor.) Put the shredded vegetables and apple in a large bowl and sprinkle with the salt. Let stand for 1 hour, then squeeze the juice out through a strainer, reserving it. There should be 1¾ cups of expressed juice.

Place one fourth of the shredded vegetables in a 1-quart jar. Top with half a bay leaf, 2 peppercorns, 2 allspice berries, and one fourth of the caraway and dill seeds. Cover with more shredded vegetables and apple and continue the process until there are 4 layers.

Pour the reserved juice over the layered cabbage; it should cover it.

Cover the mouth of the jar with cheesecloth and let stand at room temperature for 4 days. Then cover the jar and refrigerate until ready to serve.

To serve, cut a few thin slices of onion. Toss each portion of sour cabbage with some onion, a dash of sugar and a few drops of vegetable oil.

Yield: 8 servings.

BARREL-STYLE DILL PICKLES
𝕏 *SOLYONYE OGURTSY* 𝕏

The pickled cucumber is a recurrent character in the cast of Russian foods. These sour pickles are so widespread that Chichikov in Gogol's *Dead Souls* is only mildly surprised to find his hostess' hand reeking of pickle brine when she proffers it to him in greeting. Actually, the brine is put to as good a use as the pickles: for some, it's a sure cure for hangovers; for others, it has a cosmetic effect. I once asked my grandmother, then seventy-two years old, how she kept her skin so wrinkle-free. The secret, she explained, was a daily dose of the fermented brine from the pickle barrel, rubbed into her skin. This treatment explained the unusual smell I'd always associated with my grandmother, but the astringent quality of the brine did seem to work wonders.

Although the cosmetic benefits of these pickles may not be for everyone, I can certainly recommend their gustatory delights. They are tart and crisp, as good as any you'll find at a delicatessen. Just be sure to scrub your hands well after dipping into the barrel, lest you begin to resemble Chichikov's hostess.

8 pounds unwaxed pickling
   cucumbers, preferably small
2 fistfuls fresh dill with seeds
   (about 40 sprigs)
1 pound pickling salt (1½
   cups)
6 quarts water
2 whole bulbs of garlic, peeled,
   the cloves halved (about 18
   cloves)

3 teaspoons black peppercorns
2 teaspoons crushed dried hot
   pepper (or 10 small hot red
   peppers)
3 teaspoons coriander seed
2 teaspoons mustard seed
8 bay leaves
Thick chunk of rye bread
   (without preservatives)

Wash a 2-gallon crock or barrel. Wash the cucumbers, making sure that none of them have brown spots or bruises. Place half of the dill on the bottom of the crock. Stand the cucumbers on end in the crock as tightly as they will fit, in a single layer.

Dissolve the pickling salt in the water and pour half of it over the cucumbers. Add half of the garlic, peppercorns, hot pepper, coriander seed, mustard seed and bay leaves.

Pack the remaining cucumbers into the crock, standing them on end. Add the rest of the salt water, spices and dill. Place the chunk of rye bread on top. The salt water should completely cover the pickles. Run the blade of a knife down into the crock a few times to make sure there are no pockets of air. If the salt water does not cover the cucumbers, add a little more in the same proportions.

Place a saucer over the pickles, laying it right in the brine, and place a heavy weight on top of the saucer. Then cover the crock loosely with a cloth. Once again, make sure the cucumbers are completely immersed in the brine.

Keep the crock at room temperature, about 70°F. Every day remove any scum that has formed on top of the brine, each time washing out the cloth, then replacing the saucer, weight and cloth.

Half-sour (*malosol'nye*) pickles will be ready in 3 to 4 days. For fully soured pickles, wait 8 to 9 days. When the pickles are as sour as you like, pack them into jars, along with the brine and spices, and refrigerate.

SALTED MUSHROOMS
SOLYONYE GRIBY

This excellent method of preserving mushrooms makes even the mildest champignons come alive. For a more sensational taste, try salting wild forest or field mushrooms.

> 1 pound mushrooms
> 2 tablespoons salt
> Bay leaves
> Black peppercorns
>
> Fresh dill
> Whole cloves
>
> ½ cup hot water

Take firm, unblemished mushrooms. Rinse them lightly. Place a layer of mushrooms, steps up, in a 2-quart crock. Sprinkle them with salt and desired amounts of seasonings. Continue layering the mushrooms (always stems up) with the salt and the seasonings, until the crock is full.

Pour the hot water over all, shaking the jar gently to dissolve the salt. Weight the top layer of mushrooms down with a plate on which something heavy has been placed. Close the jar tightly. Place in a cool, dark place.

After a few days check to see that the mushrooms are immersed in the liquid. If not, add a little more water and salt.

The mushrooms will be ready after 1 month.

Yield: 1 pound salted mushrooms.

DRIED MUSHROOMS
SUSHONYE GRIBY

The best dried mushrooms are those that have been freshly gathered from the woods and fields. To dry them, simply wipe them off with a damp cloth to remove all traces of dirt; do not wash. Remove the stems and, if desired, peel the caps. If the weather is sunny, spread the mushrooms on brown paper and leave them to dry in the sunshine for 2 or 3 days, taking them in at night as soon as it begins to grow damp. The mushrooms should be covered with fine cheescloth to protect them from insects and should be turned occasionally. Once they are dry, thread them on twine and hang them in the sun or in a well-ventilated room until they have dried out completely, at which time they may be transferred to airtight jars and stored.

If the weather is not sunny, the mushrooms may be spread on a screen and dried in a 140°F oven for several hours, until dry.

To reconstitute, soak the dried mushrooms in warm water to cover for at least 30 minutes, then drain and use as directed. The soaking liquid may be added to soups and stews.

SOUSED APPLES
🦊 *MOCHONYE YABLOKI* 🦊

Very Russian, with a taste like wine.

4 pounds small tart apples	*2 quarts water*
Oak leaves (or black currant	*⅓ cup honey*
or cherry leaves)	*1 tablespoon pickling salt*

Wash the apples and layer them with the leaves in a 2-quart crock.

Bring the water, honey and salt to a boil. Then cool to lukewarm. Pour the liquid over the apples. Place a weight on the top layer of apples to keep them immersed.

Place the crock in a large kettle (the apples are likely to ferment very actively at first; the liquid that bubbles out of the crock can then be poured back in to cover the apples). Cover the crock but do not seal tightly.

Check the apples after a few days to make sure they are immersed in the liquid; if not, add more. Store in a cool, dark place for 1 month.

Yield: 2 quarts.

PICKLED EGGPLANTS
🏵 *BAKLAZHAN MARINOVANNYI* 🏵

I first tasted pickled eggplants in Rostov-on-Don. They were a gift from a cheerful old gentleman whose head I remember being as round, smooth and shiny as the eggplants he offered me, though perhaps I am confusing my impressions. This is an unusual pickled dish that looks lovely when served, since the carrot retains its bright orange color.

2 small eggplants (1 pound each)	*16 black peppercorns*
	10 allspice berries
	¼ teaspoon mustard seed
3 large carrots, scraped	*½ teaspoon crushed hot red pepper*
6 large cloves garlic	
	½ teaspoon pickling salt
4 cups white wine vinegar (herb-flavored is nice)	*½ cup olive oil*
4 bay leaves	*1 long stalk of celery*
3 cloves garlic, slightly crushed	

Rinse the eggplants and cut in half lengthwise. Place them in a baking dish, skin side up. Rub the skins with vegetable oil. Pour 1 inch of water into the bottom of the pan, then bake the eggplants at 350°F for 20 minutes. Set aside to cool.

Meanwhile, grate the carrots and garlic together.

Bring the vinegar to a boil with the spices. Boil, covered, for 10 minutes. Cool. Then stir in the olive oil.

When the eggplants have cooled, scrape out some of the pulp, leaving a thick shell of at least 1 inch on both the bottom and the sides. Stuff each half with the mixture of grated carrot and garlic.

Cut the celery into 6 very thin strips. Carefully reassemble the eggplants, taking care not to lose any filling. Tie each eggplant with 3 strips of celery, securing them with toothpicks, if necessary.

Turn a scalded 2-quart container on its side and slip the eggplants into it, side by side. Turn the container upright and pour the cooled vinegar mixture over the eggplants. Seal.

Leave to ripen in a cool, dark place for 3 weeks before eating. Chill well before serving, cut into crosswise slices.

Yield: 2 pickled eggplants.

SPICED PICKLED CHERRIES
✖ VISHNYA MARINOVANNAYA ✖

When Peter the Great returned from Holland intent upon Westernizing his nation, he introduced many innovations, one of which was the practice of serving pickled fruits with meat. Although not all of Peter's measures met with equal delight among the populace, the Russians took readily to the idea of eating pickled fruits. These cherries provide a lively accompaniment to roast meat or chicken.

2 pounds sweet cherries
3 cups cider vinegar
1½ cups sugar
1 cup water
¼ teaspoon mace

½ stick cinnamon
4 allspice berries
4 whole cardamom pods, peeled
2 tablespoons kirsch (clear
  cherry brandy)

Wash the cherries and remove the stems, but do not pit them. Place them in a crock and cover with the vinegar. Let stand overnight, then drain, pouring the vinegar into a saucepan.

Bring the vinegar to a boil with the sugar, water, mace, cinnamon, allspice and cardamom. Simmer for 15 minutes. Cool, then stir in the kirsch. Pour the pickling liquid over the cherries and let stand for 3 days.

After 3 days, drain the cherries and bring the liquid to a boil once again. Allow it to cool and then pack the cherries into sterilized preserving jars. Pour the pickling liquid over them and seal the jars. Let stand for 1 month before using.

Yield: 2 quarts.

BLACK CURRANT CONSERVE
CHORNAYA SMORODINA S SAKHAROM

The high vitamin C content of black currants contributes to their popularity in the citrus-starved Soviet Union, where they are often stirred with sugar and aged for several weeks. I was offered this conserve in homes from Leningrad to Alma-Ata. It is usually prepared in batches large enough to last throughout the winter, and since its sugar content is so high, it needs no refrigeration. Serve this with roast meat for dinner, or in a small jam dish with tea.

Black currants   *Sugar*

The proportions to use are 1 part black currants to 2 parts sugar (or less, to taste).

Pick the currants over, discarding any damaged ones. Wash them, and then grind coarsely together with the sugar in a food processor or meat grinder. Pack into jars and let stand at least 1 month before eating.

VARIATION: In one variation I tasted, the black currants are left whole. They are mixed with sugar and then left to sit for at least 3 months before serving, so that the sugar can penetrate them completely.

KIEV-STYLE RASPBERRY JAM
🦗 *MALINOVOYE VAREN'YE V KIEVSKOM MANERE* 🦗

As propounded by Princess Shcherbatskaya in *Anna Karenina*.

1 pound fresh raspberries   *3 cups sugar*
1 tablespoon cognac

Place half of the raspberries in a shallow pan. Sprinkle with a little cognac and half of the sugar. Top with the remaining berries and the rest of the cognac and sugar. Refrigerate overnight. The berries should give off quite a bit of juice.

The next day, bring the berries, along with their juice, to a boil over high heat, then remove from the heat and let stand for 15 minutes. Bring to a boil again, remove from the heat and let the berries stand for 15 minutes more. Then bring to a boil for a third time and cook the berries over low heat, skimming off any scum that rises to the surface. Cook gently, shaking the pan lightly from time to time, for about 20 minutes, or until the berries are translucent and the syrup thickens.

Let cool slightly before pouring into jars so that the berries won't rise to the top. Cover the jars with waxed paper soaked in rum and tie with a cord to fasten; or seal the jars.

Yield: 1 pint.

APRICOT JAM
𝓎 *ABRIKOSOVOYE VAREN'YE* 𝓎

A golden jam with bits of whole fruit suspended in it.

1 pound fresh apricots	*1 cup blanching water*
2 cups sugar	*1 tablespoon vodka*

Blanch the fruits in boiling water to loosen their skins, then peel them. Cut them in half and remove the pits. Place 1 dozen of the pits in a muslin bag and tie it with string. Drop the apricots into cold water into which a little lemon juice has been squeezed.

In a saucepan bring the sugar and 1 cup of the blanching water to a boil. Boil for a few minutes to make a light syrup. Cool the syrup slightly, then add the halved apricots and the bag of pits. Bring to a boil over high heat, then remove the pan from the heat and let stand for 15 minutes.

Bring the mixture to a rolling boil again, then once more remove the pan from the heat and let stand for 15 minutes.

Bring to a boil for the third time, then pour the mixture into a shallow ceramic or earthenware bowl. Cover the syrupy fruit and let stand overnight.

The next day, strain the mixture, catching the syrup in a saucepan. Bring the syrup to a boil, then pour it hot over the fruit, which has been returned to the ceramic bowl. Cover; let stand overnight.

The third day, repeat the procedure, straining the fruit and bringing the syrup to a boil. Poor the hot syrup over the fruit once again.

On the fourth day, remove the bag with the pits. Then bring the entire mixture—both syrup and fruit—to a boil over high heat. Reduce the heat and cook slowly until the fruit is transparent and the syrup has thickened, about 30 minutes.

Remove from the heat; stir in the vodka. Let the jam cool slightly until a thin skin forms on the surface, then stir the jam for a few minutes (this prevents the fruit from floating to the top of the jars). Pour into jars and seal.

Yield: 1 pint jam.

ROSE PETAL JAM
VAREN'YE IZ ROZOVOGO TSVETA

Making this jam is almost as enjoyable as eating it: the simmering petals infuse the air with their fragrance.

8 ounces rose petals	*2 cups water*
2 lemons	*1½ cups sugar*

Early in the morning pick fresh, sweet-smelling pink or red roses. Trim off the white base of the petals and discard. Rinse the petals, then drain.

Slice the lemons very thinly. Place them in a pan with the water. Cover and bring to a boil. Simmer for 15 minutes, then remove the lemon slices and discard them.

Bring the lemon water to a boil again and stir in the sugar until dissolved. Add the rose petals and cook until they are transparent and the liquid is syrupy, about 10 minutes. Pour into jars and seal.

Yield: 1½ pints.

RUSSIAN-STYLE MUSTARD
GORCHITSA

Russian mustard is particularly pungent. The name comes from the verb *gorchit'*, "to have a bitter taste." The addition of sugar relieves the bitterness, but the piquancy of the mustard remains intact. Use it sparingly!

4 tablespoons powdered dry mustard (Coleman's is good)	*3 teaspoons freshly squeezed lemon juice*
2 teaspoons water	*1 teaspoon vegetable oil*
	3 tablespoons sugar
6 tablespoons boiling water	*Pinch of salt*

In a small bowl combine the mustard powder and the 2 teaspoons of water to make a paste.

Slowly pour the 6 tablespoons of boiling water over the paste and let stand for 15 minutes. Then pour the water off.

Stir in the remaining ingredients until the mustard is smooth. Store in the refrigerator.

Yield: ¼ cup.

PREPARED HORSERADISH
🐾 KHREN 🐾

In Russian, a *staryi khren,* literally "old horseradish," refers to a person who has been through a lot but has not lost his sharp bite. When properly refrigerated, this tangy homemade horseradish will retain *its* bite for up to several weeks.

1 6-ounce piece of horseradish root (about half of a large root)

½ cup white vinegar
½ teaspoon salt

Peel the horseradish root. Grate it coarsely by hand, then place it in a blender or food processor along with the vinegar and salt. Grate it very finely, until a fairly smooth puree has been formed. Let chill at least 2 hours before using.

Yield: About 1 cup prepared horseradish.

VARIATIONS:

1. Beet Horseradish: Boil one small beet until tender. Peel and grate it finely. Stir into 1 cup Prepared Horseradish. This horseradish has a lovely rose color.
2. Apple Horseradish: Peel, core and finely grate one large apple. Stir it into 1 cup Prepared Horseradish. This horseradish has a somewhat sweeter and milder taste.

CRANBERRY-HORSERADISH RELISH
KLYUKVA S KHRENOM

This relish is a good condiment to serve on the *zakuska* table with cold boiled beef; if you are not planning a Russian-style meal, it tastes equally good with pot roast.

1 pound cranberries
1 cup light brown sugar
½ cup prepared horseradish
(preferably homemade, or
use bottled horseradish,
drained)
Juice of 1 lemon

Chop the cranberries medium fine (this is most easily done when they are frozen). Stir in the remaining ingredients and mix well. Place the relish in the refrigerator and let chill at least 2 days before serving.

Yield: About 4 cups.

HOMEMADE DAIRY PRODUCTS
MOLOCHNYE PRODUKTY

One of the triumphs of the Russian kitchen is its imaginative use of dairy products. Even though many of these can now be bought ready-made, they still taste better when prepared at home.

· I ·
RUSSIAN COTTAGE CHEESE
TVOROG

Tvorog is the name for the dry curds from soured milk so indispensable to Russian baking. It forms the basis for many uniquely Russian dishes, from the glorious Easter *paskha* to the homely *syrniki* (cheese pancakes), but *tvorog* may also be enjoyed on its own, topped with sour cream and sugar as a sweet, or mixed with paprika and caraway seed for a savory snack. *Tvorog* is not difficult to make at home, but if necessary, baker's cheese, or less successfully farmer cheese, may be substituted.

❀◇

METHOD 1 (FOR THE BEST HOMEMADE *tvorog*):

1 quart unpasteurized milk   *1 quart heavy cream*
(available from a farm or
from health-food stores)

Heat the milk and cream together gently, and when just warm pour into a glass bowl. Place the bowl in a warm spot (in winter, this could be on a radiator). Let the mixture stand, uncovered, for 24 hours,* until a watery liquid appears at the bottom of the bowl. Strain the milk through cheesecloth.

Hang the curds in the cheesecloth over a bowl in the refrigerator; let drip for a few more hours, until the curds are dry. Transfer to a bowl and cover with plastic wrap.

Yield: About 1½ pounds.

METHOD 2 (A QUICKER AND EASIER VERSION).†

1 quart buttermilk

Place the buttermilk in its unopened carton in a deep pot and fill the pot with water. Bring to a boil, then boil gently for 30 minutes. Remove from the heat but leave the carton of buttermilk in the water. The next morning, open the carton and turn the contents out into a colander. The whey will quickly drain off and *tvorog* will be left. Store in the refrigerator.

Yield: Approximately ½ pound.

---

* Do not let the milk sit out for more than 24 hours or it will take on a bitter taste.
† This quick version of *tvorog* is excellent for eating plain. It is not, however, as suitable for baking as the *tvorog* made by Method 1. Therefore, for the *tvorog*-based recipes in this book, Method 1 is preferred.

· II ·
HOMEMADE SOUR CREAM
⚙ *SMETANA* ⚙

Just as Russian *tvorog* is unique, so is Russian sour cream. The commercially prepared product we usually buy bears only a superficial resemblance to it. The difference is in both texture and flavor. True *smetana* will not clump when added to hot soups, such as *borshch;* nor will it ever overwhelm a dish. Although commercial sour cream may be substituted in most of the recipes in this book, when sour cream is called for as a garnish, try making your own. You'll be pleasantly surprised.

4 cups heavy cream   *2 tablespoons buttermilk*

Stir the buttermilk into the cream. Let stand for 24 hours in a warm place. Then stir to blend, and refrigerate.

Yield: About 1 pound.

· III ·
HOMEMADE KEFIR
⚙ *KEFIR* ⚙

Kefir is another well-loved dairy product that the Russians have enjoyed for centuries. For a refreshing drink, serve it ice-cold, plain or flavored with fruit syrup.

2 cups light cream (or half and   *2 tablespoons buttermilk*
half)

Heat the cream until it is lukewarm, then stir in the buttermilk. Let stand for 24 hours in a warm place, then refrigerate. Serve very cold, sweetened or plain.

• IV •
BAKED MILK
✿ *VARENETS* ✿

Varenets is as rich and sweet as condensed milk. The Russians consider it a special treat for coffee, and the skin that forms during baking is prized by connoisseurs. *Varenets* may be served either warm from the oven or chilled. Its name comes from the Russian *varit'*, "to cook," the same root that is found in *samovar*.

4 cups whole milk

Preheat the oven to 300°F. Pour the milk into a large shallow earthenware baking dish. Bake for about 2 hours, or until the milk has turned a deep pinkish color, occasionally stirring the skin that forms back into the milk. Leave the final skin in place.

Yield: 1 pint.

KVASS
⚔ *KVAS* ⚔

In Russia, commercially brewed beer still has not presented a serious challenge to the well-loved homemade kvass, which ranks second only to vodka as a popular libation. (In a unique nineteenth-century religious sect, it outranked even vodka. The believers were known as *kvasniki*, since they eschewed all drinks except kvass.)

A typical street scene in any Soviet city, large or small, is a kvass truck parked on a shady corner, surrounded by a crowd of people eager to quench their thirst. Usually the lines are made up of male workers who seem to be idling away the working day, but sometimes women join the crowd, too, net bags in hand. A kvass truck's long cylindrical tank is usually painted bright yellow, with stenciled red letters proclaiming its contents—*KBAC*—to the passersby. Even on gray, wintry days the tank shines like a beacon, offering good spirits to those who would imbibe— and there's never a shortage of customers. The truck is often equipped

✧⟩

with its own glasses (cursorily rinsed in cold water after each use), but true aficionados bring their own glasses—or jugs—to fill.

The root of the Russian word *kvas* means "to ferment," and the brew may be made from any number of fruits or vegetables. The most common type of kvass, and the kind sold on street corners, is made from fermented black bread. Special herbs are often added to enliven the brew, and it is said that the best kvass of all is made in Russian Orthodox monasteries, where the secret ingredient is ostensibly a dash of "religious feeling."

The recipes below are for three very different kinds of kvass. The first, made from cranberries, has a taste reminiscent of good dry champagne and may be served as a refreshing summertime drink. The second, a black bread kvass, can also be drunk straight, but I prefer to use it as the base for cold Russian soups like *okroshka* and *botvin'ya,* as the taste for this strong homemade brew is an acquired one. The final recipe is for a beet kvass, which is not meant to be drunk at all but rather to add color and flavor to soups and stews, such as *borshch* and *vereshchaka.*

· I ·

CRANBERRY KVASS

✿ *KVAS KLYUKVENNYI* ✿

1 pound cranberries	*½ teaspoon cream of tartar*
7 cups boiling water	*1 package active dry yeast*
1 cup sugar	*6 raisins*

Crush the berries with a potato masher or the back of a wooden spoon. Pour the boiling water over them, then cover the container and let them stand undisturbed for 12 hours.

Strain the berries through muslin, but do not press down on the berries very much to extract more juice. To the clear liquid add the sugar, the cream of tartar and the yeast, which has been dissolved in a little of the liquid. Stir well to mix. Cover the container, and let stand in a warm place for 8 hours.

The next day, strain the liquid once more through muslin and pour into a large bottle. Add 6 raisins to the bottle. Seal. Leave at room temperature for 8 hours, then refrigerate until ready to drink.

Yield: ½ gallon.

• II •
BLACK BREAD KVASS
✿ KVAS SUKHARNYI DOMASHNII ✿

1½ pounds stale black bread,   *½ cup sugar*
   cubed   *1 teaspoon cream of tartar*
1½ tablespoons dried mint   *1 package active dry yeast*
1 small lemon, cut into chunks   *8 grains of white rice*
10 cups boiling water

Place the bread cubes on a baking sheet and toast in a 325°F oven for about 20 minutes, or until dry. Transfer to a large crock. Sprinkle the mint over the toasted cubes. Add the lemon. Pour the boiling water over all, and cover the crock tightly. Let stand for 5 to 6 hours.

Strain the liquid through cheesecloth, pressing down on the bread with the back of a spoon in order to extract as much liquid as possible, but without pushing sediment through. To the strained liquid add the sugar, the cream of tartar and the yeast, which has been dissolved in a little of the liquid. Stir well to mix. Cover the container, and let stand undisturbed for 8 hours.

The next day, strain once more through cheesecloth and pour into a 1-quart bottle. Add the 8 grains of rice. Seal. Let stand for 8 hours more at room temperature. Then strain once more through cheesecloth into a clean bottle and refrigerate until ready to use.

Yield: 1 quart.

· III ·
BEET KVASS
⚙ *SVEKOL'NYI KVAS* ⚙

4 pounds beets, tops removed   *Lukewarm water*

Scrub the beets, then peel and cut them into cubes. Place the cubes in a 1-gallon crock. Bring water to a boil and let cool to lukewarm. Then pour enough water over the beet cubes to cover them. Cover the crock, and let stand undisturbed for several days.

After a few days, lift the cover and check the liquid. Skim off any scum or mold that has formed. (The fermenting process is very active, so do not be alarmed to find that mold has grown on the liquid.) Repeat this process every 4 to 5 days.

The kvass will be ready in two weeks. It should give off a sour smell and be a deep red color. Skim the top of the liquid until it is free of scum, then strain the liquid through cheesecloth into a clean jar. Store in the refrigerator or, if desired, freeze.

Yield: 2 quarts.

NOTE: A quicker, though less potent, kvass from beets may be made by *grating* the beets and covering them with warm water. Cover the crock and keep it in a warm place. The kvass will be ready in 3 to 4 days.

PLUM CORDIAL
🎿 *SLIVOVAYA NASTOIKA* 🎿

In Russia, closely guarded recipes for fruit liqueurs and brandies have been passed down from generation to generation, and even today Russians delight in regaling their guests with homemade *nalivki* and *nastoiki*. As sage a writer as Chekhov causes one of his characters to claim: "I can tell you truthfully . . . that homemade brandy is better than any champagne. After the first glass, your sense of smell enlarges, envelops your whole being. It's a great illusion. It seems to you that you're no longer sitting at home in your easy chair, but are somewhere in Australia, astride the softest imaginable ostrich." In other words, homemade brandy is potent stuff! This plum cordial is simple to prepare. The only hard part is waiting six weeks to enjoy it.

> *2½ pounds red or purple plums*   *6 cups vodka*
> *3 cups sugar*

Cut the plums in half but do not pit them. Place them in a 2-quart container. Pour the sugar over the plums, then add the vodka. Cover the container tightly and turn it to distribute the sugar evenly throughout. Let the plums stand in a cool, dark place for 6 weeks, turning the container occasionally if the sugar has settled on the bottom.

Strain the liquid from the plums and bottle it.

Yield: About 1½ quarts.

VARIATION: To make homemade peach brandy, take 2½ pounds ripe, blemish-free peaches and about 2 cups of sugar, depending on the sweetness of the peaches. Blanch the peaches in boiling water to loosen the skins, then peel. Pack the whole peaches into a 3-quart container, alternating with half of the sugar. Cover the container loosely and let stand for several hours, until the sugar has dissolved and juice has been drawn from the peaches. Then add the remaining sugar, stirring to mix well. Cover the container loosely again and let stand until all the sugar is dissolved. The syrup should cover the peaches; otherwise they will turn brown. Cover the container, but not too tightly to allow for the release of carbon dioxide. Wrap the container in heavy brown paper and store in a cool, dark place. Test after two months to see if the brandy is ready; it will take from two to three months. The peaches themselves rival the brandy in flavor, and make an excellent topping for ice cream or pound cake.

DRIED FISH
✖ VYALENAYA RYBA ✖

The windows of apartment buildings in the provincial cities of the Soviet Union are often adorned with bunches of fish that have been hung out to dry, adding a homely touch to an otherwise drab urban landscape. The Russians dry all kinds of fish, as long as it is very fresh, but especially prized is the Don River's *rybets* (vimba), with its delicate flesh. This dried fish makes a perfect summertime picnic when served with boiled potatoes and plenty of beer or kvass.

For every 2 pounds of very fresh fish (such as cod or haddock, but any favorite will do):

3 tablespoons salt	*1 tablespoon sugar*

Rub the salt and the sugar all over the cleaned fish, both inside and out. Place in a pan and let stand for 4 days at room temperature.

Rinse the fish lightly. Then hang it to dry for 2 or 3 days, until it is firm to the touch. (Test for firmness by pressing the flesh with your fingers; this is a sign that the fish is ready.) The fish will have the best flavor if hung in the sun, but if it is rainy or cold, the fish may be wrapped loosely in cheesecloth and set on the radiator. (Turn it occasionally to allow air to circulate.) If the air is not particularly clean, it is best to wrap the fish loosely in cheesecloth even when it is hung outside.

To serve, cut the fish into long, diagonal slices about 1 inch thick. It is a stunning dish when the slices are reassembled and placed on a platter along with the fish head, surrounded by fresh greens. Store any leftover fish in the refrigerator.

Yield: One 2-pound fish will serve 4 people.

TOASTED SUNFLOWER SEEDS
🌾 *SEMECHKI* 🌾

No picture of the Russian peasant is quite complete unless it also depicts a handful of sunflower seeds. The love of these crisp seeds is near-universal, and even though it is considered gauche to crunch them in public, the floors of public buildings—especially waiting rooms—bear testimony to their popularity. The careful observer can always spot the site of an erstwhile line from the sunflower hulls strewn over the ground. One of my favorite memories of the Soviet Union is of a tiny girl boarding a train, her hair done up in bright ribbons, proudly clutching her refreshment for the long train ride ahead, a sunflower head almost as big as herself. Most Russians eat the seeds raw, cracking the hulls with their teeth, but they are even better toasted.

*1 cup sunflower seeds in the
hull*

*2 tablespoons butter
Salt to taste (optional)*

Melt the butter. Toss the seeds in it to coat well.

Preheat the oven to 325°F. Turn the seeds out onto a baking sheet, separating them. Bake them for 15 to 20 minutes, or until just golden.

Eat the seeds as is out of your hand, or shell them and salt them, if desired.

Yield: 2 snack-size servings.

☙ · VI · ☙

SPECIALTIES FROM
THE REPUBLICS

*M*any non-native dishes have crept into the Russian cuisine
and taken hold. In metropolitan Moscow it is no longer unusual to find
Georgian-style chicken, Uzbek pilaf, or Estonian cream cake on a restaurant menu. The Russians, with their love of the exotic, have eagerly
embraced these new foods and adapted them as festive dishes in their
own kitchens.

In all there are fifteen republics that make up the Soviet Union.
Three are Slavic: Russia (including Siberia), Ukraine and Byelorussia
(White Russia). The Baltic republics are three formerly independent
nations hugging the coast of the Baltic Sea: Latvia, Lithuania and Estonia.
To the south lies the second smallest republic, Moldavia, which is akin
to Rumania in both language and culture. The Caucasus, an extensive
mountain range, lends its name to the three Caucasian republics: Georgia,
Armenia and Azerbaidzhan. And extending deep into the steppes and
mountains of continental Asia are the five Central Asian republics:
Tadzhikistan, Uzbekistan, Turkmenia, Kirghizia and Kazakhstan. Within
each republic live numerous ethnic groups, each attempting to preserve
its own culinary heritage in the face of ever-more centralized (and less
efficient) food distribution.

The original Russian cuisine is distinguished by the use of dough to enclose fillings in various guises and shapes; by the love of the sour and the abundant use of sour cream; by the variety of salted vegetables and sweetened fruits accompanying meat and fish. Of all the national cuisines, the Ukrainian, with its inventive soups and robust breads, is closest to the Russian. The Ukraine is, in fact, the breadbasket of the Soviet Union, boasting a rich black soil, the chernozem, which yields high-quality grains and vegetables. It is also renowned for its thick dark honey, contributing to the excellence of Ukrainian sweets. And the true home of borshch (beet soup), so often considered typically Russian, is actually the Ukraine.

Oddly enough, the Russians came to know (and love) Ukrainian cookery through literature. Gogol's tales, written in Russian, are rich with mouth-watering descriptions of Ukrainian eating, vivid enough to stimulate even the most indifferent palate. Nikolai Gogol is rightly considered a master of literature, and perhaps more attention should be paid him in the culinary world as well, for he was reputed to be as excellent a cook as he was a writer. Thanks in large part to Gogol's writings, when the Russians think of the Ukraine they think of abundance: fresh vegetables, savory stews, thick soups, imaginative pies, fragrant breads, pastries dripping with honey. But even this abundance accounts for only a part of the Ukraine's culinary renown. It is also famed for its sausages—and what varieties there are! Kazimir Malevich, the founder of the suprematist school of modern painting, grew up in the Ukraine. In his autobiography, Malevich indulges in descriptions of Ukrainian life at the turn of the century. One of the most vivid, even lurid, scenes depicts a marketplace full of the temptations of a small Ukrainian town.

> Oh, the whole glorious town of Konotop glistened with fat! At the market and at the station, behind long rows of tables, sat women called "lard-sellers" who reeked of garlic. Heaped on the tables were mounds of lard of all different kinds—smoked and unsmoked with a good rind. There were rings of sausage: Cracow-style, stuffed with large chunks of meat and pork fat, blood sausage, and grain sausage with a smell so strong it inflamed a man's glands. There was ham rimmed with fat, kasha cooked thick with lamb suet and cut into rounds to resemble buns, and country sausage with gristle. The lard-sellers glistened in their greasy clothes, reflecting the rays of the sun.
>
> I'd buy a ring of sausage for five kopecks and break it into pieces, eating it the way people at the market eat. I didn't even glance at the lamb, which cost only a kopeck and a half per pound, nor at the meat.

Pork and fish were the best foods at the market, especially the dried sea-roach at two kopecks a piece, large chunks with fatty red backbone and roe. I liked to eat the pork and the fish with white bread. Or I'd buy a small suckling pig from the lard-seller for forty kopecks—already roasted, with a crisp brown rind stippled with fat. The rind, baked just right, crackled under my teeth. It was easy enough to consume the whole pig in secret from those at home, awaiting me for dinner.

In Konotop, among this Ukrainian fat and garlic, I grew . . .

Of course, such an abundance of fat is no longer pleasing to Western taste. I can recall my own initial aversion to a large chunk of freshly salted lard atop a slice of sour black bread proudly offered me by a Ukrainian family. Not wanting to refuse their hospitality, I accepted the sandwich. To my great relief the lard was quite palatable, and had I been free of my deeply instilled preconceptions about cholesterol and animal fats, I might even have found it tasty.

The Ukrainians are not the only people versed in the art of charcuterie. Byelorussia has long been known for its skillful butchers. Butchers were in especially great demand among the large Jewish population, which required kosher cuts of meat. (My own great-grandfather was a butcher in a Byelorussian village, and it was in his shop that the young Marc Chagall played as a child. My family likes to think that the sides of beef and live chickens must have impressed themselves upon the boy's mind, to find later expression as the whimsical chickens and cows in his scenes of village life.) Russians from as far as Rostov-on-Don will travel to Minsk in the heart of Byelorussia in search of the meat reputed to be there; in their own cities the shelves are more often bare.

As one might expect, the people of the Baltic nations traditionally consume a good deal of fish. Especially prized is the tiny Baltic herring, with a flesh so delectable it is actually sweet. During the summer, city-trapped Leningraders flock to the Baltic coast to enjoy its riches, along with the excellent dairy products produced farther inland. Butter and cream are used liberally in Baltic cookery. One favorite dessert common to all three Baltic states is a simple combination of dark rye bread crumbs mixed with fantastic amounts of fresh sweet cream.

If the Ukraine is the Soviet Union's breadbasket, then surely the tiny landlocked republic of Moldavia is its corn bushel, for most of the corn produced in the Soviet Union is grown on Moldavia's fertile plains. No wonder, then, that corn is a staple in Moldavia, eaten with the same relish Russians evince for buckwheat. In season it is eaten fresh from the cob, but a year-round dish is cornmeal pudding, or *mamaliga,* the Moldavian *polenta.* Moldavia also produces some very good wine, the best coming from a variety of grapes known as "lady's fingers."

Moldavia, the Ukraine, Byelorussia, the Baltic republics and Russia are all on the European continent. Traveling 800 miles south and east from Kishinev one crosses the conventional boundary between Europe and Asia, finding oneself in the heart of Transcaucasia, where the Soviet republics of Georgia, Armenia and Azerbaidzhan lie. Here East meets West in a lively mingling of cultures, and the mixing of traditions is evident also in the food.

Russians have long considered the people of the Caucasus exotic. The dark-eyed women, the temperamental men who dance daringly and gracefully with unsheathed swords, impressed themselves upon the Russian imagination long ago. And life in the beautiful Caucasus *does* seem exotic and mysterious to the outside observer: ancient vendettas are still acted upon, and people routinely live beyond a hundred years of age (though one wonders why these two facts wouldn't tend to cancel each other out). Watching a wedding celebration in Armenia, I sensed an otherworldliness—in all probability, people had celebrated in just this way centuries before. That day I had traveled to an old monastery in the hills beyond Yerevan, Armenia's capital. The weather was hot and hazy; in the distance the tip of Mount Ararat poked through the clouds, reminding me of biblical times. The melancholy sound of a reed pipe and other woodwinds carried through the air with haunting insistence. Soon a lively procession rounded the corner of one of the monastery's narrow streets. It was headed by a finely arrayed man leading a white lamb by the collar. The lamb wore a red ribbon and its ear had been slashed, marking it for sacrifice. The parade continued through the streets, accompanied by wailing instruments, and ended up in a shady grove on the banks of a small stream outside the monastery walls. The women in the group began to spread brightly patterned tablecloths on the ground and unpack baskets of wine, cheese, breads and fruit. The mood was gay and anticipatory, enhanced rather than restrained by ritual. Suddenly the leader of the procession drew out a long knife from his belt and with a single flourish cut off the lamb's head, holding it triumphantly on high for all to see. The musicians immediately broke into festive song, and everyone started dancing and passing around goatskins of red wine. Before long I could detect the exquisite smell of skewered lamb grilling on the coals: *shashlyk,* the Armenian contribution to international cuisine. Even now, when I think of Armenia, I smell the lamb roasting and see the people dancing in the grass, people full of enthusiasm for life and for good food.

To the Russians, Armenia is not the only exotic southern republic. Georgia is even more so, and it is Georgian cookery that Russians prefer over all other ethnic cuisines. For them it plays the same role French cookery does for many Americans and Europeans—they consider it the height of chic and culinary taste. And a visit to Georgia's capital, Tbilisi, confirms this impression.

The city is dissected by the Kura River, and on the cliffs overlooking the water one can sip strong Turkish coffee and taste the local sweets at an open-air café. Tbilisi's main street is dotted with snack bars, offering the famed Georgian cheese bread *khachapuri,* and restaurants where one can dine on such excellent Georgian appetizers as *lobio* (kidney beans in a plum sauce) and platters of the wonderful Georgian cheese *suluguni,* served with fresh coriander and scallions. One of the highlights of the city is its marketplace, which takes up two entire floors of an old ware- house. Vendors come from all over Georgia to sell their produce, vying with one another to make the most attractive displays of food, hoping to catch the customer's eye and thereby his business. The competition seems greatest among the vendors of *khmeli-suneli,* a characteristically Georgian spice mixture. These vendors are usually older women dressed in bright scarves and shawls. They spoon the spice mixture into high mounds and place themselves decoratively behind. The coriander, dill, pepper and other spices that make up the mixture give off a heady aroma, and the experience of simply standing in the marketplace and breathing in the smells is vivid. Most Georgian families hoard the secret of their own private blend of *khmeli-suneli,* and the mixtures at the market range in hue from a deep mossy green to a bright mustard yellow. I returned from the market with five different blends of *khmeli-suneli,* all gifts from the generous Georgian people who pitied this poor American, unaware of the delights of their native spice.

The Georgians are indeed a generous people, and they rival the Russians in hospitality. In Georgia, love and respect for a guest are expressed in- directly through elaborate ritual, and this ritual is enacted around the dining table as toast after toast is raised. Georgian-style toasting is not merely the *pro forma,* albeit sincere, toasting of the Russian meal; it is rather an art in itself, a competition that can—and usually does—go on for hours, each toast-maker trying to outdo the rest with the beauty and expressiveness of his toast. Luckily, Georgian wine is excellent and, unlike vodka, can be enjoyed glass after glass.

Georgia produces the best wines in the Soviet Union. Especially prized are its aromatic red wines, such as Kindzmarauli (reputedly Stalin's favorite) and Teliani, the preferred wine of the literati. Teliani in particular has found favor among the great poets of the Soviet period. The poet Nikolai Zabolotsky is known to have consumed large quantities of it, invariably offering it to his guests, while Osip Mandelstam even wrote a poem about it.

Traveling deeper into continental Asia one enters the Central Asian republics, where the mountains and steppes are peopled by literally hundreds of different nationalities. The cookery of these peoples has much more in common with traditional Eastern cuisine than it does with the Western. Russia first felt the influence of Eastern cookery in the thirteenth century, when the Mongol hordes came storming across the Asian steppes, carrying with them exotic teas, spices and cooking implements. Later, with Russia's acquisition of Astrakhan in the sixteenth century and Siberia in the seventeenth century, the Eastern influences became even more strongly felt, especially the Tatar influence. To paraphrase Napoleon's famous statement "Scratch a Russian and you'll find a Tatar," one might say "Try Russian food and you'll taste the Eastern influence." Such basic foods as noodles, dried fruits, lemons and jams, so prevalent in Russian cookery, are all of Eastern origin.

One of the oldest Central Asian cities is Bukhara, in the republic of Uzbekistan. Bukhara also boasts a lively marketplace, and the Uzbeks in native garb make it even more colorful than Tbilisi. The market is a gathering place where not only money is traded but gossip as well. Turbaned heads tilt together, ear to mouth. The market features row upon row of dried fruits: raisins dark brown and yellow, plump and wizened; apricots, figs, dates and nuts. Some stalls sell balls of hard cheese the size of marbles and as easily popped in the mouth. Since the sights at the market can make one quite hungry, it is best to follow one's nose to a vat of steaming *plov* (pilaf), an Uzbek specialty, prepared outdoors over wood fires. Or one can visit an Eastern tearoom, or *chai-khana,* where customers sit at low tables on pillows and rugs. It is an enchanting experience to sit and chat over a leisurely pot of green tea, sipped from bowls, especially if the tea is served at a central Bukhara teahouse over-looking a glassy reflecting pool that mirrors an ornate carved mosque.

Bukhara lies in the flat steppe of Uzbekistan, and it is not until much farther east that mountains begin; yet still one is within the borders of the Soviet Union. In the Altai Mountains bordering China lie the re-publics of Kazakhstan and Kirghizia, once inhabited by nomadic tribes known for their daring. The tribes of Kirghizia were also known for their ability to consume large drafts of *koumiss* (fermented mare's milk). All male visitors to the tribes were expected to down at least one, if not two, of the vessels containing *koumiss,* vessels holding up to three pints apiece (a test of the visitor's bravado!). Today this potent beverage is hard to find in the city, but the people of the mountains still swear by it. The casual tourist to Frunze, the capital of Kirghizia, or Alma-Ata, the capital of Kazakhstan, is more likely to taste *samsa* (fried peat pies resembling *pirozhki*) or *lagman* (a meat and noodle stew) than *koumiss.* Or perhaps he will simply enjoy one of the many varieties of apples for which Alma-Ata is famous—the name of the city means "Father of Apples."

No book on Russian cuisine could be considered complete without at least mentioning some of the various foods that have influenced its de-velopment and that are today enjoyed in the heart of Mother Russia. Here, then, is a random sampling of recipes from the different republics.

SIBERIAN DUMPLINGS
SIBIRSKIE PEL'MENI

Almost every national cuisine boasts its own version of boiled dumplings wrapped around pockets of seasoned meat. *Pel'meni* are the Siberian specialty, now popular throughout the Soviet Union. Moscow alone has several *pel'mennye,* cafés specializing in these dumplings. *Pel'meni* are practical for the harsh Siberian winter. Prepared in large quantities, they can be buried in the snow, where they keep for months on end, ready to boil up at a moment's notice.

Siberians swear by a mustard and vinegar sauce for *pel'meni:* place a spoonful of hot mustard on the edge of each plate and mix it with concentrated vinegar to taste. Muscovites prefer a milder garnish, slathering butter and sour cream on the dumplings in lavish amounts. *Pel'meni* are most often served steaming hot, mounded high on a platter, but they may also be eaten in chicken broth.

When making *pel'meni,* it's wise to make a lot. As one Russian saying goes, "You can never have too many *pel'meni.*" And once you've tasted these wonderful dumplings, you're bound to agree.

DOUGH

3 cups flour	*2 whole eggs*
1 teaspoon salt	*¼ cup warm water*

FILLING

1½ pounds ground beef and	*12 tablespoons (1½ sticks)*
pork, mixed	*butter, melted*
1 medium onion	*Russian-style mustard*
1 teaspoon salt	*Strong vinegar*
Freshly ground pepper to taste	*Sour cream*

To make the dough, mix together the flour and the salt in a medium-sized bowl. Make a well in the center and pour in the eggs and water. Toss the mixture together, then knead by hand until the dough holds together. Form the dough into a ball and place it on waxed paper or a floured surface. Cover the dough with an overturned bowl and let stand at room temperature for 1 hour.

To prepare the filling, in a food processor or meat grinder grind the beef, pork, onion, salt and pepper very finely, until there is a smooth mass with no lumps. Set aside to "season" while the dough is resting.

Divide the dough into four pieces. Working with one piece at a time, roll the dough out onto a floured board as thinly as possible (¹⁄₁₆ inch thick or less) and with a cookie cutter or a glass cut out 2-inch rounds. Place a heaping teaspoon of the meat filling on each round. Bring one edge of the round over to meet the other and seal the edges tightly, forming a half-moon. Then take the two pointed edges and bring them together in the center of the half-moon, along its straight edge. Lift these edges slightly so that a round ball is formed. Make sure that the edges are securely pressed together in the center. As each ball is formed, place it on a clean dish towel.

If you are not going to boil the *pel'meni* right away, cover them with a dish towel so that they don't dry out. When ready to serve, bring a large kettle of salted water to a boil. Add a teaspoon of vegetable oil to the water to keep the dumplings from sticking. When the water has reached a rolling boil, drop in the *pel'meni* and boil them gently for 5 minutes, or until they rise to the top of the water. Make sure not to crowd them in the kettle; they may be cooked in several batches.

Drain the *pel'meni* and immediately pour the melted butter over them. Bring them to the table piled high on a platter, and let each person choose his own garnish: mustard and vinegar, or sour cream and more butter.

Yield: 8 to 10 dozen.

VARIATIONS:

1. To serve the *pel'meni* in chicken broth, boil them as directed above in salted water. When they are done, transfer them to a bowl with hot chicken broth and serve each bowl with a generous dollop of sour cream.

2. A delicious way to eat any leftover *pel'meni* is to fry them in butter until golden brown. Serve with the above garnishes.

3. In Central Asia *pel'meni* are made with a filling of fresh greens. Mix together scallions, fresh coriander, sorrel and spinach in desired proportions. Chop the greens finely and season with salt and pepper. Place a generous teaspoonful of the chopped vegetables on each round of dough. Shape the *pel'meni* as directed above and boil in salted water. Serve with plenty of melted butter.

UKRAINIAN STEAMED CABBAGE SOUFFLÉ
❦ *NAKIPLYAK IZ KAPUSTY* ❦

A festive, delicious way with cabbage.

1 head of white cabbage (about 2 pounds), with large outer leaves intact	1¼ teaspoons salt
	Freshly ground white pepper to taste
¾ cup milk	Dash of cayenne pepper
4 tablespoons butter	1 teaspoon marjoram
1 large onion, finely chopped	3 egg yolks
½ cup fine dry bread crumbs	5 egg whites
1 teaspoon sugar	

Core the cabbage and peel off the large outer leaves. Blanch them in boiling water for 5 minutes to soften. Drain and set aside.

Cut the rest of the cabbage into chunks and place the chunks in a large pan. Pour the milk over the cabbage and simmer, covered, for about 30 minutes, or until tender. Drain the cabbage and chop finely.

Meanwhile, sauté the chopped onion in the butter. In a large bowl mix together the chopped cabbage, sautéed onions (along with all the butter from the frying pan), the bread crumbs, seasonings and egg yolks.

Beat the egg whites until stiff but not dry. Fold them into the cabbage mixture.

Spread a large clean linen dish towel on a table. On the towel arrange the blanched cabbage leaves in an overlapping pattern, making a circle large enough to contain the soufflé filling. Pile the filling in the center, making sure that there are no openings in the cabbage-leaf circle through which the filling could seep out. Carefully fold the leaves up to cover the filling. Then bring the ends of the dish towel together in the center and tie them securely with kitchen string.

Place the towel-wrapped cabbage in a colander to retain its round shape. Place the colander in a large, deep kettle over a few inches of water. If the lid of the kettle will not close over the colander, use aluminum foil to cover the pot, sealing it tightly.

Bring the water to a boil and simmer the cabbage for 50 minutes. Then remove the cabbage from the colander and untie the string. Open the dish towel and place a plate over the cabbage leaves. Invert the plate to unmold the soufflé and peel off the towel from the top.

To serve, cut the soufflé into wedges.

Yield: 8 servings.

BRAISED CHICKEN WITH PRUNES
🌾 *KURITSA, TUSHONAYA S CHERNOSLIVOM* 🌾

The original recipe for this Ukrainian dish calls for prunes that have been dried over a smoky wood fire, imparting a dusky flavor to the chicken. The commercially processed prunes substituted here yield a somewhat subtler taste.

1 2½- to 3-pound broiler, cut up	*2 slices of lemon, seeded*
Salt, pepper to taste	*1 cup rich chicken stock*
2 tablespoons butter	*½ cup dry white wine*
2 tablespoons olive oil	
	½ pound prunes
	1½ cups water
2 large carrots, scraped and chopped	*1 tablespoon freshly squeezed lemon juice*
2 large onions, sliced	
4 small cloves garlic, crushed	*2 tablespoons butter*
4 sprigs parsley	*2 tablespoons flour*
2 bay leaves	*2 teaspoons sugar*

Season the chicken with salt and pepper to taste. In a large, heavy frying pan heat the 2 tablespoons of butter together with the olive oil. Add the chicken pieces and fry until golden, about 15 minutes. Then transfer them to a plate and keep warm.

Add the carrots, onions and garlic to the frying pan and cook over medium heat until soft but not brown, about 8 minutes. Then return the chicken pieces to the pan, skin side up. Place the parsley, bay leaves and lemon slices on top of the chicken. Pour in the stock and dry white wine all at once. Cover the pan. Bring to a boil, then simmer for about 30 minutes, until the chicken is tender.

While the chicken is simmering, combine in a saucepan the prunes, the 1½ cups of water and the lemon juice. Bring to a boil, uncovered, and simmer until the prunes are plump and tender, about 15 minutes. Drain and set aside.

When the chicken is done, transfer it with a slotted spoon to a plate and keep warm. Strain the broth from the frying pan into a bowl, pressing down hard on the vegetables with the back of a spoon to extract all their juice. Set aside.

In the frying pan melt the remaining 2 tablespoons of butter. Add the flour and stir to make a roux. Cook for about 3 minutes, or until the flour browns slightly. Gradually add the reserved broth, stirring constantly, and bring to a boil. Simmer until slightly thickened, then stir in the sugar. Test for seasoning. When the sauce is done, add the chicken and prunes to it, and heat through.

Serve the chicken on a large platter, garnished with the prunes and about half of the sauce. Pass the remaining sauce in a sauceboat.

Yield: 4 servings.

UKRAINIAN PORK STEW
☙ VERESHCHAKA ☙

This Ukrainian peasant stew comes from a very old recipe, making use of the best local products—pork, beets and rye bread. In some households it is prepared just before Lent and served over *blini* during the Butter Festival (*maslenitsa*) celebrations.

3 thick slices of bacon	2 cups Beet Kvass
2 onions, coarsely chopped	2 cups fresh rye bread crumbs,
1 pound boneless pork loin,	crusts removed
cut into strips	
Salt, pepper to taste	Fresh parsley or dill

In a heavy kettle fry the bacon until just slightly crisp. Remove the bacon from the fat and set aside.

Fry the chopped onion in the bacon drippings until golden. Then add the strips of pork, turning to brown them on all sides. Add salt and pepper to taste.

Crumble the bacon into the kettle, then pour in the kvass. Cover the pot and bring to a boil. Simmer, covered, for 30 minutes, then stir in the rye bread crumbs and simmer for 30 minutes more.

Transfer the stew to a serving bowl and garnish with fresh dill or parsley. Serve with boiled potatoes.

Yield: 4 servings.

NOTE: If no Beet Kvass is on hand, 2 cups of beef stock may be poured over 2 grated beets in a saucepan. Bring to a boil, then remove the pan from the heat and let stand for 1 hour. Strain and add to the stew in place of the kvass. This makes quite an acceptable substitute, though the flavor of the stew will not be as rich.

UKRAINIAN DUMPLINGS
✖ *VARENIKI* ✖

These excellent Ukrainian dumplings were purportedly the writer Gogol's favorite food, and he was a connoisseur. In true Russian philosophical style, he is said to have mused on occasion over the inconceivability of life without his beloved *vareniki*. Others who have lived in the Ukraine are likely to share Gogol's sentiments: the painter Malevich, long after his Ukrainian childhood had passed, still fondly recalled boiled *vareniki* with cherries, slathered with sour cream and dark Ukrainian honey.

Vareniki are a very adaptable food, changing with the seasons. They are perhaps most glorious in midsummer, when served stuffed with fresh berries, cherries or plums. In autumn, field mushrooms are likely to replace the summertime fruits, while the heavier demands of a cold winter call for buckwheat groats and sauerkraut. But throughout the year Ukrainians serve the most popular *vareniki* of all—filled with cottage cheese (*tvorog*), they make a savory main course or a slightly sweetened dessert.

3 cups flour	*2 egg yolks*
½ teaspoon salt	*1 cup plus 2 tablespoons water*

Place the flour and salt in a bowl and make a well in the center. Gradually add the egg yolks and water and work with your hands until a fairly stiff dough is formed, adding more water if necessary. Knead the dough on a lightly floured surface, then place under an overturned bowl and let rest for 1 hour.

Roll the dough out very thinly, to $\frac{1}{16}$-inch thickness or less. Cut into 4-inch rounds. Place desired filling on each round, then shape into half-moons, crimping the edges with a fork to seal. Place on a dish towel and cover with another towel until ready to boil.

Bring a large pot of salted water to a boil, then drop in the *vareniki* and boil gently until they rise to the surface, about 5 minutes. Remove with a slotted spoon and serve immediately.

TVOROG FILLING

1 pound Russian Cottage Cheese (tvorog) *or farmer cheese*	*2 tablespoons sour cream*
2 egg yolks	*6 tablespoons sugar (optional)*
Pinch of salt	*1 teaspoon grated lemon rind (optional)*

Mix together well all the ingredients, adding the sugar and lemon rind if sweet dessert *vareniki* are desired. Place 1 teaspoon on each round of dough. Seal. Boil as directed above. Serve these *vareniki* with plenty of melted butter and sour cream, and, if desired, browned bread crumbs.

CHERRY FILLING

2 pounds sour cherries	*1 cup sugar*
¼ cup sugar	*¼ cup cornstarch*
	¼ cup flour

Pit the cherries and mix them with the ¼ cup of sugar.* Let stand in a warm spot (in the sun) for several hours, stirring occasionally.

The cherries will produce about ⅔ cup of juice. Add enough water to make 2 cups. Place in a saucepan and stir in the remaining sugar. Dissolve the cornstarch in a little of the liquid. Bring the syrup to a boil, then stir in the dissolved cornstarch, mixing well. Simmer for 5 minutes. Keep warm over low heat.

Dredge the cherries in the ¼ of cup flour. Place 2 cherries on each round of dough. Seal. Boil as directed above. Serve with the cherry sauce or with buckwheat honey. These are very sweet!

Yield: About 8 to 10 dozen dumplings.

---

* Canned sour cherries may be used if no fresh ones are available. Use 2 1-pound cans of cherries. Drain the liquid and reserve it to add to the juice produced by the cherries. Proceed as directed above.

UKRAINIAN SWEET BRAID
🦐 *BULKA* 🦐

Honey often figures as a temptation in Nikolai Gogol's Ukrainian tales. In one tale, "Viy," some young seminarians visit a marketplace, where they are lured by a stunning array of home-baked goods. The peasant women cajole them to buy bread, one offering her special poppy-seed buns, another claiming that *her* loaf has been sweetened with real honey. The recipe below is for a typical Ukrainian sweet loaf, one even the strictest seminarian cannot resist.

1 package active dry yeast	½ cup sour cream
Pinch of sugar	1 teaspoon salt
¼ cup warm water	Grated rind of 1 lemon
	6 to 7 cups all-purpose flour
½ cup milk	
8 tablespoons butter, cut into	1 egg yolk
bits	1 tablespoon water
3 whole eggs, beaten	Blanched sliced almonds
½ cup honey	

Dissolve the yeast and sugar in the warm water until bubbly.

Scald the milk; stir in the butter and let cool to lukewarm. Then add the milk mixture to the yeast, along with the eggs, honey, sour cream, salt and lemon rind. Stir in the flour, ½ cup at a time, adding enough to make a soft dough.

Turn the dough out onto a floured board and knead until smooth and elastic, about 10 minutes. Place in a greased bowl, turning dough to grease the top. Cover and let rise in a warm place until doubled in bulk, about 2 hours.

Punch down the dough and let rise again until doubled in bulk, about 1 hour.

Turn the dough out onto a floured board and divide it in half. Divide each half into three balls of equal size. Roll each ball out between your palms into a rope about 12 inches long. Braid three ropes together, and place the loaf on a greased baking sheet. Repeat with the remaining dough.

Cover the loaves and let rise until doubled in bulk, about 40 minutes.
Preheat the oven to 375°F. Brush the loaves with a glaze made by
beating the egg yolk with the water. Sprinkle the almonds over the loaves.
Bake for 35 minutes, or until nicely browned on top.
Yield: 2 loaves.

UKRAINIAN HONEY CAKE
✠ MEDIVNYK ✠

The famous Ukrainian *myod*, "honey," lends its name to this excellent
cake, rich with dates and nuts, a native specialty. *Medivnyk* is traditional
for Christmas but is baked throughout the year because it's so popular.
Hawkers set up their rickety stands in the streets of Kiev, selling slices
of *medivnyk* by the gram. In the summer the stands are often surrounded
by swarms of honeybees, bewitched by the heavy smell of honey in the
air; but the hawkers are expert at selling their luscious cake without ever
getting stung.

8 tablespoons butter	*Grated rind of 1 orange*
1 cup dark brown sugar	*1 cup sour cream*
1 cup dark honey	*1 teaspoon cinnamon*
4 eggs, separated	*½ teaspoon nutmeg*
2½ cups flour	*½ cup currants*
2 teaspoons baking soda	*1 cup chopped walnuts*
1 teaspoon baking powder	*½ cup chopped pitted dates*
Pinch of salt	

Cream the butter and sugar together until light and fluffy, then beat in
the honey. Beat in the egg yolks one at a time, mixing well after each
addition. Stir in the flour, baking soda, baking powder and salt. Mix
well. Add the orange rind and sour cream, beating until the batter is
smooth. Then stir in the cinnamon, nutmeg, currants, walnuts and dates.
Whip the 4 egg whites until stiff but not dry and fold them into the
batter.
Preheat the oven to 300°F. Prepare a 10-inch tube pan by greasing it

and then lining the bottom and sides with brown paper. Grease the paper. Pour the batter into the pan, spreading it evenly.

Bake the cake for 1 hour and 15 minutes, or until a cake tester comes out clean. Remove the outer part of the pan and let the cake cool (upright) in the tube section. When completely cool, remove the cake from the pan.

Wrap the cake in aluminum foil and let age at room temperature for 2 days before serving. (It may be eaten sooner, but the flavor won't be as rich.)

Yield: 1 large cake.

NOTE: Buckwheat honey, if available, is the best choice for this cake. Clover honey will not give it as distinctive a taste.

PRUNES STUFFED WITH CHEESE
⚜ CHERNOSLIV, FARSHIROVANNYI TVOROGOM ⚜

A lovely Byelorussian dessert, as served at the Minsk restaurant in Moscow.

½ *pound prunes*	4 *tablespoons sugar*
½ *pound* Russian Cottage Cheese (tvorog) *or farmer cheese*	¼ *cup chopped walnuts*
	2 *tablespoons plum brandy*

Pour boiling water over the prunes and soak them, covered, until they have swelled. Drain. If the prunes have not been pitted, carefully remove the pits with a sharp knife, leaving the prunes as intact as possible. Dry them on paper towels.

Mix the *tvorog* with the sugar. With a pastry tube, fill the prunes with the sweetened *tvorog*.

Place the prunes in a lightly greased baking dish. Preheat the oven to 350°F. Sprinkle the walnuts over the prunes, then bake for 20 minutes. Remove from the oven and sprinkle with the plum brandy, flaming it if desired. Serve hot.

Yield: 6 servings.

◆>◆◆◆◆◆◆◆◆◆◆◆◆◆◆◆◆◆◆◆◆◆◆◆◆◆◆◆◆◆◆

ESTONIAN POTATO SALAD
⚔ ROSSOL'YE ⚔

Here's one more potato salad to round out your repertoire, this one tarter and heartier than its Russian cousin.

1 salt herring

2 boiling potatoes (1 pound)
1 Bermuda onion, chopped
1 large tart apple, cored and chopped, but not peeled
2 large dill pickles, chopped
1 8-ounce jar of pickled beets chopped
½ pound ham, chopped

2 teaspoons dry mustard

2 tablespoons cider vinegar
¼ cup reserved juice from pickled beets
1 teaspoon sugar
½ cup sour cream
½ teaspoon salt
Freshly ground white pepper to taste

2 hard-boiled eggs, sieved
Parsley

The night before making the salad, soak the salt herring in milk or buttermilk to cover. The next day, rinse it, remove the backbone, and chop coarsely.

Boil the potatoes in salted water until tender. While still warm, peel them and chop coarsely. Put them in a large bowl.

Add the onion, apple, pickles, beets, ham and herring. Mix well.

To make the dressing, mix the dry mustard with the vinegar until smooth. Stir in the reserved beet juice. Add the sugar, sour cream, salt and pepper. Mix well.

Pour the dressing over the salad and toss until all the ingredients are coated. Cover the bowl with aluminum foil and let stand at room temperature for 1 hour, then chill in the refrigerator for at least 6 hours, or overnight, before serving.

Just before serving, mound the salad on a large platter and garnish with the sieved hard-boiled eggs. Strew some parsley around the base of the salad.

Yield: 8 to 10 servings; more if served as a *zakuska*.

LATVIAN APPLE PUDDING
🌿 YABLOCHNAYA ZAPEKANKA 🌿

Rye flour is not just for bread, as proved by this delicious cake-like pudding. Variations of this dessert are found throughout the Baltic states.

4 medium apples, cored and diced	½ teaspoon baking powder
4 tablespoons unsalted butter	Pinch of salt
1 cup sugar	1 egg
	1 teaspoon vanilla extract
1¼ cups white flour	
¾ cup rye flour	½ cup chopped nuts
1 teaspoon baking soda	

Lightly grease and flour a round 9-inch baking dish. Preheat the oven to 350°F.

In a light skillet, melt the butter. Remove the pan from the heat and stir in the sugar until well blended. Then stir in the prepared apples. Set aside.

In a medium-sized bowl mix together the white flour, rye flour, baking soda, baking powder and salt.

Beat the egg until frothy and stir in the vanilla extract. Beat the egg into the apple mixture, which should have cooled somewhat.

Stir in the dry ingredients, mixing well. Finally, stir in the nuts. Turn the batter into the prepared baking dish. Bake the pudding at 350°F for 35 to 40 minutes, until a tester comes out clean.

Serve with fresh sweet cream, if desired.

Yield: 8 to 10 servings.

CORNMEAL PUDDING
✠ MAMALYGA ✠

Traditionally, Moldavian cornmeal pudding is cooked slowly over a low fire and stirred with a wooden spoon reserved especially for this dish. *Mamalyga* lovers also insist that the cooled pudding should never be cut with a knife, but with string, so as not to destroy its texture.

1 cup yellow cornmeal	*2½ cups boiling water*
1½ teaspoons salt	*3 tablespoons butter*
1½ cups cold water	

In a large saucepan combine the cornmeal and salt. Pour the cold water over the cornmeal and stir until well mixed. Add the boiling water, stirring constantly, and bring the mixture to a boil. Stir in the butter. Cook over low heat until slightly thickened, then cover and simmer for 12 to 14 minutes. Serve immediately, topped with butter, grated cheese, or gravy.

Yield: 4 servings.

VARIATIONS:

1. Add 1 cup feta cheese to the hot cornmeal and spread the mixture in a greased oven-proof casserole. Top with ½ cup sour cream and bake uncovered at 375°F for 15 minutes.

2. To make *mamalyga* a meal in itself, prepare it as in the variation above, and top each portion (there will be 4) with a freshly poached egg.

3. Pour the hot cornmeal into a greased 9 x 9-inch baking dish and let harden. Chill. The next day cut into squares and fry in butter over low heat until golden on both sides. Serve with syrup or jam. (This is a good use for leftover pudding as well.)

4. To make *mamalyga* dumplings, shape cold *mamalyga* into balls and with a finger make an indentation in each ball. Stuff with chopped cooked ham, crumbled bacon, chopped hard-boiled egg or chopped cooked mushrooms. Seal with more *mamalyga* and dredge with flour. Deep fry in hot oil (360°F) until golden, about 5 minutes.

5. Cheese dumplings are made by taking 1 cup of cold *mamalyga* and adding to it ½ cup of grated cheese. Form into balls. Take some plain *mamalyga* and mold a thin layer of it around each cheese ball. Dredge with flour and deep fry as directed above.

STUFFED PEPPERS, MOLDAVIAN STYLE
PERETS, FARSHIROVANNYI V MOLDAVSKOM STILE

The Moldavians love peppers, which grow in abundance in their small republic. In the recipe below, two kinds of peppers—green bell and hot red—are joined in a lively combination. After chopping some hot red pepper for the filling, there's no need to waste the rest. Instead, do as the Moldavians do: place the pepper in a glass, cover it with vodka and let stand for 24 hours. Then remove the pepper and transfer the vodka to a jar, which should be stored in the refrigerator. The next time you feel a cold coming on, drink about 6 ounces of this fiery vodka before bedtime—by morning all your ills will be gone!

4 large bell peppers
½ of a small head of white cabbage
1 large onion
3 medium carrots
5 tablespoons olive oil

4 tablespoons parsley, chopped
Salt, freshly ground black pepper and fresh dill to taste
¼ teaspoon minced hot red pepper (or more, to taste)
¼ pound brynza cheese, grated

Slice the tops off the bell peppers about 1 inch down from the top and remove the seeds and membrane. Parboil the peppers in salted water for 3 to 4 minutes, then set aside on paper towels to drain. They should still be firm.

Shred the cabbage, onion and carrots finely. (The shredding disk on a food processor is ideal for this.) Place the vegetables in a large frying pan, in which the olive oil has already been heated. Toss them well to coat with the oil. Add the parsley, salt, black pepper, dill and red pepper. Cook, stirring occasionally, for 5 to 7 minutes, or until the vegetables are soft but not mushy.

Preheat the oven to 350°F. Place the drained peppers upright in a deep casserole. Spoon the vegetable mixture into the cavities, packing it firmly. Pour about ¼ inch of water into the bottom of the casserole. Top each stuffed pepper with a handful of grated cheese.

Cover the casserole and bake for 30 minutes. Then remove the lid and put the peppers under the grill for a few minutes, until they are browned and bubbly.

Yield: 4 servings.

NOTE: If brynza is unavailable, substitute 4 ounces of any favorite sharp cheese.

TATAR MEAT PIES
⚔ PEREMECH ⚔

These succulent meat pies are Tatar in origin, very much like the Kazakh *belyashi* enjoyed throughout Russia. This recipe was given to me by a dear Tatar friend, Zainab, whose house is hung with heavy Oriental carpets and whose kitchen never fails to produce delectable surprises. These *peremech,* typical for a Tatar meal, should be eaten straight from the frying pan, juicy and hot.

DOUGH

2 eggs	*Pinch salt*
½ cup sour cream	*Pinch sugar*
6 tablespoons light cream (or half and half)	*2½ cups flour*

FILLING

1 pound boneless beef chuck, with only a little fat	*1 clove garlic*
	1 teaspoon salt
1 onion	
	Vegetable oil for frying

To make the dough, beat the eggs until light, then beat in the sour cream, light cream, salt, sugar and flour. Knead until smooth and elastic. Wrap the dough in waxed paper and refrigerate overnight before using.

To prepare the filling, grind finely in a food processor or meat grinder the beef chuck, onion, garlic and salt.

Next prepare the meat pies. Working with one quarter of the dough at a time (leave the rest in the refrigerator), roll out each piece into a 12-inch rope. Cut each rope into 6 pieces, then roll the pieces into balls between the palms of your hands. Flatten the balls slightly, and on a floured surface, roll each ball out into a round 3½ to 4 inches in diameter.

Spread 1 tablespoon of meat mixture on each round, leaving 1 inch around the edges.

To shape the meat pies, gather the dough in little pleats all the way around the patty, using an upward, folding motion. The result should be a round, flat pastry with a hole the size of a quarter in the middle. As each patty is made, place it on a linen cloth and cover with another cloth so that the pastries do not dry out.

Pour vegetable oil into a large skillet to a depth of ½ inch. Heat it, and once it is hot add the *peremech,* a few at a time, hole side down. Cook the meat pies, turning once, for about 15 minutes, or until golden brown.

Yield: 2 dozen meat pies.

CRIMEAN MEAT PIES
🦐 *CHEBUREKI* 🦐

Chebureki are native to the Crimea. This recipe comes from the town of Simferopol, where the pies are a source of passion and pride. *Chebureki* should always be eaten out of the hand—never with knife and fork—so that the first bite sends a spurt of hot juice right into the mouth.

DOUGH

2½ cups flour
1 teaspoon salt

1 generous tablespoon
   vegetable oil
1 cup water

FILLING

6 ounces beef
¼ pound well-larded lamb
1 clove garlic
1 small onion
12 sprigs of parsley, leaves only
1¼ teaspoons salt

Freshly ground black pepper
  to taste
6 tablespoons water

Vegetable oil for frying

To make the dough, mix together the flour and salt, then stir in the oil. Add the water to make a soft dough. Turn the dough out onto a floured board and knead until smooth and elastic. Wrap in plastic wrap and refrigerate for at least 2 days before using.

To prepare the filling, in a meat grinder or food processor grind together the beef, lamb, garlic, onion and parsley till the mixture is fine and smooth. Stir in the salt, pepper and water. Set aside.

Next, cut the dough into 16 equal pieces. On a floured board, roll each piece out thinly to a circle 6 to 8 inches in diameter. (The thinner the dough, the crisper the pies will be.)

Spread a generous tablespoon of the filling on half of each circle, then fold the other half over the filling to enclose it, forming a half-moon. Seal the edges well with the tines of a fork.

Heat ½ inch of oil in a large frying pan. Fry the *chebureki,* two at a time, until golden, turning once. Serve immediately.

Yield: 4 to 6 servings.

CIRCASSIAN CHICKEN
🐎 *KURITSA PO-CHERKESSKI* 🐎

The Circassian people, renowned for their beauty and bravery, inhabit the mountainous regions of the Caucasus. Legend has it that this chicken was named for a beautiful Circassian peasant girl who lovingly ground the nuts by hand in preparing this dish for her lover, a prince of some kind who would come to her at midnight. Unfortunately, the legend ends there. We'll never know whether the girl's devoted cookery made a princess out of her, but Circassian Chicken still makes a legendary entrée, perfect for a fancy luncheon—or even a special midnight meal.

2 whole chicken breasts
  (2½ pounds)
1 quart cold water
1 bay leaf
1 onion, quartered
1 carrot, scraped and cut in half
½ teaspoon tarragon
6 black peppercorns
1 teaspoon salt
2 sprigs parsley

1 cup walnut halves
1 cup hazelnuts
2 tablespoons olive oil

1 small onion, finely chopped
1 clove garlic, crushed
2 slices home-style white bread,
  crusts removed
¼ cup heavy cream
¼ teaspoon paprika
¼ teaspoon salt
Freshly ground white pepper
  to taste
Dash of cayenne pepper
1 cup of the chicken stock

Soft-leaved lettuce, parsley,
  walnut halves

Place the chicken breasts in a stockpot, pour the cold water over them, and add the bay leaf, onion, carrot, tarragon, peppercorns, salt and parsley. Simmer for 45 minutes, or until the chicken is tender. Remove the chicken and strain the broth. Return the broth to the pot and cook it over high heat until reduced by half. Reserve 1 cup.

Remove the skin from the chicken breasts, bone them and cut the flesh into strips.

Pour boiling water over the walnut halves and slip off the thin skins. (This is a tedious process, but a necessary one, because the skins will make the sauce taste bitter. The hazelnuts do not need to be peeled.) Then place the walnuts on a baking sheet in a warm oven to dry out.

When the walnuts have dried out, grind them together with the hazelnuts in a food processor or nut grinder.

In a large frying pan sauté the onion and garlic in the olive oil until golden. Soak the bread in the cream, then add it to the sautéed onions without squeezing the liquid from it. Stir in the ground nuts, paprika, salt, white pepper, cayenne and the reserved stock. Mix well. Cool to room temperature.

Spread a serving platter with leaves of lettuce. Place a layer of the chicken strips in the center of the platter, the strips radiating out like the spokes of a wheel. Cover the chicken with a layer of the nut sauce, then top with another layer of chicken, this one also radiating out from the center and overlapping the bottom layer.

Top the chicken with more nut sauce and continue in this manner until all of the meat has been used, reserving enough sauce to decorate the top of the mound. Spread the remaining sauce over the top, piling it somewhat higher in the middle, and garnish with chopped parsley and walnut halves.

Serve at room temperature or very slightly chilled. The chicken may be prepared a day ahead of time and chilled, covered, in the refrigerator overnight, but it must be brought to almost room temperature before serving; otherwise its flavor will not come through.

Yield: 6 servings.

ARMENIAN FLAT BREAD
⚜ *LAVASH* ⚜

Lavash has been baked for centuries in Armenia. The raw, flat rounds of dough are traditionally slapped onto the sides of a hot cylindrical oven, the *tonir*, where they bake in less than 5 minutes, but nowadays the bread is more often baked in large modern ovens. *Lavash* is an excellent crisp bread to serve with cheese or soup.

1 cup unbleached white flour	*4 teaspoons vegetable oil*
1 cup whole-wheat flour	*⅔ cup milk*
2 teaspoons salt	*Sesame seeds or poppy seeds*

In a bowl mix together the white flour, whole-wheat flour, and salt. Drizzle the oil over the flour, and with the palms of your hands, rub the oil into the flour until it is well incorporated. Make a well in the center and pour in the milk. Mix with your hands to form a dough.

Turn the dough out onto a floured board and knead for 5 to 10 minutes, until smooth and pliable. Cover the dough with an overturned bowl and let stand at room temperature for at least 30 minutes. (It may be refrigerated at this point, if necessary.)

Cut the dough into 8 pieces. Taking 1 piece at a time, knead the dough and press it into a round on a floured board. With a rolling pin, roll out the round until the dough is 8 inches in diameter. Sprinkle it generously with sesame or poppy seeds, then roll it out once more with the rolling pin (it will have contracted a little), pressing the seeds firmly into the dough.

Preheat the oven to 400°F. As the rounds are finished, place them on large baking sheets. Bake for 10 to 12 minutes, or until lightly browned on top. Do not overbake. Cool on racks before serving.

Yield: 8 pieces of bread.

NOTE: Unbaked rounds of *lavash* may be frozen between sheets of waxed paper. As needed, unwrap and bake as directed.

VARIATION: *Lavash* may also be used as a soft sandwich bread to wrap around meat or cheese. Moisten the rounds of baked bread on both sides under cold running water, until they are moist but not soggy. Wrap them in a damp towel and let stand until soft, about 45 minutes.

CAUCASIAN SKEWERED LAMB
❧ *SHASHLYK* ❧

Shashlyk is the wonderful skewered grilled lamb made throughout the Caucasus and Central Asia. Its name comes from the word *shashka,* "sword," since *shashlyk* was once the fare of mountain tribesmen who roasted meat on their swords over open fires. The aroma of roasting lamb is one hard to resist: in Solzhenitsyn's *Cancer Ward,* when Oleg is finally released from the hospital, he is given an allowance of 5 rubles a day. But once tempted by the irresistible odor of grilling *shashlyk* from a curbside brazier, Oleg cannot help relinquishing three of his precious rubles for a skewer of meat. The meat is grilled to perfection—still rosy, not charred.

To grill *shashlyk* to perfection at home, simply put it over hot coals and serve it rare.

2 pounds boneless shoulder or leg of lamb, cut into 2-inch cubes	*1 teaspoon salt*
	Freshly ground black pepper to taste
	1 bay leaf, crushed
2 cups pomegranate juice	*1 teaspoon crushed thyme*
¼ cup olive oil	*2 cloves garlic, crushed*

Mix together the pomegranate juice, olive oil, salt, pepper, bay leaf, thyme and garlic. Marinate the lamb overnight in this mixture. The next day, place the meat on skewers, alternating, if desired, with cubes of eggplant, which have been salted and drained.

Grill over hot coals for about 10 minutes. Serve with pilaf and Sour Plum Sauce (see below).

Yield: 4 to 6 servings.

VARIATION: To make *shashlyk karsky,* buy a whole rack of lamb and cut it into large serving-sized pieces, about 3 x 5 inches. Alternate the lamb on skewers with fresh lamb kidneys. Grill as directed above.

SOUR PLUM SAUCE
✹ SOUS TKEMALI ✹

¾ pound fresh sour plums
6 tablespoons pomegranate
  juice
3 small cloves garlic

1 tablespoon chopped fresh
  coriander
1 tablespoon chopped fresh basil
Salt, hot pepper sauce to taste

Bring the plums to a boil in water and simmer until soft, about 6 to 8 minutes. Drain the plums, then peel and pit them.

In a bowl mash the plums and then stir in the remaining ingredients. Transfer the mixture to a saucepan. Bring to a boil, then simmer uncovered for 20 to 25 minutes.

Serve at room temperature. This sauce is best when made 1 day ahead of serving time and allowed to meld overnight.

CAUCASIAN SKEWERED BEEF
⚔ BASTURMA ⚔

Like the more familiar *shashlyk, basturma* is a grilled specialty from the Caucasus, made with beef instead of lamb. The meat is left to season overnight in a highly spiced marinade, then cooked quickly over hot coals.

2 pounds boneless beef sirloin,
  cut into 2-inch cubes

1 large onion, grated
1 teaspoon salt
3 black peppercorns, crushed
2 cloves garlic, crushed
2 tablespoons chopped fresh
  coriander

1 tablespoon chopped fresh basil
1¼ cups olive oil
¾ cup freshly squeezed lemon
  juice

Fresh tomatoes, scallions

Place the meat cubes in a large bowl. (They should be at room temperature.)

Mix together thoroughly the onion, salt, peppercorns, garlic and herbs. Combine the olive oil and lemon juice, and stir in the onion mixture. Pour over the meat.

Marinate overnight or preferably for 24 hours. Grill over hot coals for about 10 minutes, turning once. The meat should still be pink inside.

Serve garnished with sliced tomatoes and scallions. A simple rice pilaf makes a nice accompaniment to this meal.

Yield: 4 to 6 servings.

AZERBAIDZHAN LAMB PATTIES
🗡 *LYULYA-KEBAB* 🗡

Yet another grilled treat from the Caucasus.

2 pounds boneless lamb shoulder, with some fat left on	*Freshly ground black pepper*
	Cayenne pepper
	Basil
2 large onions	
2 tablespoons freshly squeezed lemon juice	*Scallions*
	Tomatoes
1 teaspoon salt (or more, to taste)	*Lemon wedges*

In a food processor or meat grinder finely grind the lamb and onions. Then stir in the lemon juice and salt and add the black pepper, cayenne pepper and basil to taste.

Shape the mixture into sausage-shaped patties about 4 inches long and 2 inches wide. Chill for 2 hours.

Prepare the coals in a grill. When they are hot, skewer the lamb patties, pressing the meat firmly with your hands to make sure it adheres to the skewers. Grill over hot coals for about 10 minutes, turning to brown all sides. The lamb should still be pink inside.

Serve the patties garnished with fresh scallions, tomatoes and lemon wedges on a bed of fresh greens.

Yield: 4 to 6 servings.

VARIATION: Wrap the patties in softened Armenian Flat Bread (*lavash*) and serve them as sandwiches.

GEORGIAN CHEESE PIE
💥 *KHACHAPURI* 💥

In Tbilisi, many restaurants cater to the Georgians' love for this rich cheese pie. On Tbilisi's main thoroughfare there is a café that can be reached only by descending a steep flight of stairs into a subterranean room. In spite of its windowless location, the café shimmers with an abundance of gilded mirrors and polished marble walls and floors. The *khachapuri* there are served hot from the oven, and they're a good 8 inches in diameter—more than enough for even the heartiest eater. The pies may be ordered plain or with an egg baked on top.

Khachapuri is a versatile pie. Serve it with salad for supper or wrap it hot in layers of newspaper and foil to take along on a picnic. And if you should have the patience, shape the *khachapuri* into bite-sized pieces and serve them as a striking hors d'oeuvre.

DOUGH

¾ cup milk
1½ packages active dry yeast
½ teaspoon honey
6 tablespoons butter, at room temperature

¼ teaspoon ground coriander
1½ teaspoons salt
2 cups flour

FILLING

1½ pounds brick cheese
1 egg

2 tablespoons butter

Heat the milk to lukewarm. Dissolve the yeast and honey in 4 tablespoons of the milk. Set aside to soften for 10 minutes. Then stir in the remaining milk. Add the 6 tablespoons of butter, coriander, salt and flour, mixing well.

Turn the dough out onto a floured board and knead until smooth and elastic, about 10 minutes. Place in a greased bowl, turning dough to grease the top. Cover and allow to rise in a warm place until doubled in bulk, 1½ to 2 hours.

To prepare the filling, grate the cheese in a food processor or blender. Beat in the egg and the 2 tablespoons of butter until a smooth, fluffy puree has been formed. (You may have to do this in several batches.) Set aside.

When the dough has doubled in bulk, punch it down and then let rise again until doubled in bulk, about 45 minutes. Punch down the dough and divide into 6 equal pieces. Let stand for 10 minutes.

On a floured board, roll each piece of dough out to a circle 8 inches in diameter. Grease 6 4-inch cake or pie pans. Center one 8-inch round of dough in each pan.

Divide the cheese mixture into 6 equal parts. Spread the filling on each circle of dough, heaping it higher in the center. Then begin folding the edges of the dough in toward the center, moving in a clockwise direction, allowing each fold of dough to overlap the previous one, until the cheese mixture is completely enclosed in the pleated dough. Grasp the excess dough in the center of the pie and twist it into a topknot to seal.

Preheat the oven to 375°F. Let the pies stand for 10 minutes, then bake for 35 to 40 minutes, until browned. Slip the *khachapuri* out of the pans and serve immediately.

Yield: 6 servings.

VARIATION: To make *khachapuri* with egg, follow the instructions above for shaping the pies, but instead of making a tall topknot, flatten the knot so that the surface of the pie is relatively level. Bake the pies as directed. When they are done, crack one raw egg onto the top of each pie. Return to the oven and continue baking for another 5 minutes or so, until the eggs are set. Serve at once.

CHICKEN TABAKA
☗ *TSYPLYATA TABAKA* ☗

For garlic lovers, a Georgian classic.

4 1-pound squabs or Rock Cornish game hens	12 large cloves garlic, crushed
	4 tablespoons butter
Salt, freshly ground black pepper to taste	2 tablespoons olive oil

SAUCE

½ cup rich beef stock	6 large cloves garlic

First, make the sauce. Pound the 6 large garlic cloves in a mortar to make a paste and gradually add enough hot stock (approximately ½ cup) to make a thin sauce. Let stand at room temperature while the chicken is being prepared.

To prepare the hens, pat each hen dry and turn breast side down on a large cutting board. With a sharp knife, cut along both sides of the backbone down its entire length to free it. Then turn the hen over and break the backbone away from the keel bone, which holds the two sides of the breast together. Remove the backbone and the keel bone, along with any adhering cartilage.

Next, push back the chicken skin to reveal the thigh joint. With a sharp knife make a cut halfway through the joint so that it can be straightened out. Then, using the knife, make a small slit on each side of the breast just below the rib cage. Push the tips of the drumsticks through these slits, one on each side, so that the knobby ends of the drumsticks protrude on the skin side.

Place the prepared hens between sheets of waxed paper and pound lightly with a meat pounder to flatten slightly. Remove the waxed paper, and salt the hens liberally. Dust with pepper and rub with the crushed garlic.

In one or two large frying pans heat the butter and oil over medium-high heat. Place the hens, skin side up, in the pans and immediately reduce the heat to medium low. Cook for 1 minute, then turn so that the skin side is down.

Place a heavy kettle or frying pan over the chicken pieces (if using a 12-inch frying pan for the chicken, top it with a 10-inch one) and weight it down with a heavy can or a bowl filled with water. Cook the hens over medium-low heat for 20 minutes, then turn them, weighting them down once more. Cook for 5 minutes more.

Transfer the hens to a platter and serve at once with the garlic sauce. Sour Plum Sauce (*tkemali*) also makes a good accompaniment to the chicken.

Yield: 4 servings.

NOTE: Chicken Tabaka is meant to be eaten with the fingers. It's a nice idea to provide finger bowls of warm lemon-scented water so that the diners can unabashedly dig in.

CHICKEN CHAKHOKHBILI
✠ *CHAKHOKHBILI IZ KUR* ✠

A young girl's future was once determined by her skill in preparing chicken by this old Georgian method. When she came of marriageable age, each Georgian girl was given a whole chicken and told to prepare *chakhokhbili* from it. Only if she could cut the chicken up into seventeen precise pieces was she considered ready for matrimony.

Fortunately, times have changed. Here, for modern ease of preparation, the chicken is divided into only eight pieces, but the beauty and taste of the dish have not been lost. It is well suited for dinner parties, as it must be prepared a day ahead and reheated before serving.

1 3-pound chicken, cut into eight pieces	3 large onions
	4 large cloves garlic
2 teaspoons salt	6 tablespoons parsley
¼ teaspoon ground thyme	4 tomatoes
Freshly ground black pepper to taste	1 lemon
	4 bay leaves
3 tablespoons butter	¼ cup dry white wine

Mix the salt with the thyme and pepper. Season the chicken pieces all over. Set aside while preparing the vegetables.

Slice the onions, mince the garlic and parsley, peel, seed and slice the tomatoes into eighths. Cut the lemon into thin slices (there should be about 10 slices).

Then brown the chicken in a large frying pan in the butter. Lightly grease a baking dish large enough to hold all of the chicken in a single layer. Place half of the onion slices on the bottom of the baking dish, and top with the browned chicken.

Strew the remaining onion slices, as well as the garlic, tomatoes, parsley and lemon, over the chicken. Tuck in the bay leaves. Pour the wine over all.

Preheat the oven to 350°F. Cover the chicken and bake for 1 hour.

Leave the chicken to cool to room temperature, then refrigerate overnight before serving. Reheat to serve.

Yield: 4 generous servings.

GEORGIAN-STYLE KIDNEY BEANS
🦂 *LOBIO* 🦂

Lobio means "bean" in Georgia, where the legumes are put to imaginative use. Here are two traditional ways of preparing kidney beans, one with a sweet plum sauce, the other with plenty of herbs.

· I ·
SAVORY KIDNEY BEANS
⚙ *LOBIO* ⚙

1 cup small dried kidney beans
¼ teaspoon salt
1 clove garlic, halved
¼ teaspoon crushed hot red
   pepper
½ teaspoon crushed basil
½ teaspoon crushed mint
2 tablespoons red wine vinegar

1 medium onion, finely
   chopped
2 small tomatoes, peeled, seeded
   and chopped
2 tablespoons fresh coriander,
   chopped

1 clove garlic, minced
1 teaspoon salt
Freshly ground black pepper
   to taste
¼ teaspoon crushed hot red
   pepper
¼ teaspoon crushed basil
¼ teaspoon crushed mint
3 tablespoons chopped parsley
2 tablespoons red wine vinegar
2 tablespoons olive oil

¼ pound crumbled feta cheese

Soak the beans in water to cover overnight. The next day, bring to a boil with the ¼ teaspoon of salt, 1 clove garlic, ¼ teaspoon of red pepper, ½ teaspoon each of basil and mint, and 2 tablespoons of vinegar. Simmer until just tender, about 1 hour. Drain.

While the beans are still warm, stir in the remaining ingredients except the cheese. Let stand at room temperature until cool, then stir in the feta cheese. Refrigerate for several hours or overnight before serving.

Yield: 6 to 8 servings.

• II •
KIDNEY BEANS WITH PLUM SAUCE
❀ LOBIO TKEMALI ❀

1 cup small dried kidney beans
1 clove garlic, halved
¼ teaspoon crushed hot red
  pepper
¼ teaspoon salt
1 bay leaf
2 tablespoons red wine vinegar

1 clove garlic, minced

¼ teaspoon crushed hot red
  pepper
½ teaspoon salt
Freshly ground black pepper
  to taste
2 teaspoons chopped fresh
  coriander
2 tablespoons red wine vinegar
⅓ cup plum jam

Soak the beans overnight in ample water to cover. The next day, bring to a boil with 1 clove of garlic, ¼ teaspoon of red pepper, ¼ teaspoon of salt, the bay leaf, and the 2 tablespoons of vinegar. Simmer until just tender, about 1 hour. Drain.

While the beans are still warm, stir in the remaining ingredients. Let stand at room temperature until cool. Then refrigerate several hours or overnight before serving.

Yield: 6 servings.

GEORGIAN-STYLE CAULIFLOWER
⚔ TSVETNAYA KAPUSTA S YAITSOM ⚔

An innovative approach to cauliflower.

1 small cauliflower (1 pound),
  separated into flowerets
4 tablespoons butter
2 small onions, finely chopped
4 tablespoons butter
4 tablespoons minced parsley

2 tablespoons minced fresh
  coriander
2 large eggs, beaten
Salt, freshly ground white
  pepper to taste

Steam the cauliflower over boiling water for 10 minutes. Drain.

Meanwhile, in a large frying pan sauté the onions in the 4 tablespoons of butter until golden. Add the remaining 4 tablespoons of butter and stir in the cauliflower, turning the flowerets to coat with the butter. Cook, covered, for 10 minutes more, until tender.

Stir in the parsley, coriander and eggs. Toss to coat, cooking only until the eggs are done. Season to taste.

Yield: 4 servings.

UZBEK-STYLE PILAF
🜉 *UZBEKSKII PLOV* 🜉

Plov is what we know as pilaf, an Eastern dish really, but very popular in Russia as well. I first tasted Uzbek-style *plov* in Bukhara, where vast quantities of the rice are kept steaming all day in iron cauldrons hung over outdoor fires. For 1 ruble, a bowl is heaped high with rice and vegetables, either pumpkin and squash, or carrots and onion with just a hint of saffron, as in the recipe below. *Plov* is perfect for entertaining, since it is simple to prepare and feeds a crowd. Serve it liberally strewn with sliced raw onion, with wedges of hot flat bread on the side.

2 pounds boneless shoulder or leg of lamb, with some fat*

2 tablespoons olive oil

2 large onions (¾ pound), cut into julienne strips

3 carrots (½ pound), cut into julienne strips

2½ cups raw rice

4½ cups boiling water

1 teaspoon crushed red hot pepper or ½ teaspoon adzhika (see below) to taste

3 teaspoons salt

⅛ teaspoon saffron

Freshly ground black pepper to taste

Raw onion, sliced paper-thin

---

* If the lamb is extremely lean, ask the butcher to give you some fat. It lends great flavor to this dish.

Cut the lamb into chunks. Heat the olive oil in a large Dutch oven. Stir in the lamb and brown on all sides. Remove to a platter and keep warm.

Stir the onions and carrots into the fat remaining in the pan, adding a little more olive oil if necessary. Cook over medium heat for 10 to 15 minutes, until the vegetables are tender but not brown. Then return the lamb to the pot and stir in the raw rice. Cook, stirring, for 5 minutes, or until the rice begins to turn golden in color. Then pour in the boiling water, stirring to mix well.

Add the red pepper, salt, saffron and black pepper. Cover the pan; cook over low heat for 20 minutes, until the rice is done.

Serve liberally garnished with paper-thin slices of raw onion.

Yield: 6 to 8 servings.

NOTE: To make *adzhika,* grind together equal amounts of red bell peppers, cleaned and seeded, and hot red peppers, including seeds. Add crushed garlic to taste. Store in a covered container in the refrigerator.

KAZAKH LAMB AND NOODLE STEW
🐟 *LAGMAN* 🐟

A flavorful combination of vegetables and lamb, *lagman* is a cross between a soup and a stew.

2 pounds boneless lamb, cut
    into 1-inch chunks
¼ cup olive oil

2 onions, chopped
4 large cloves garlic, chopped
1 large carrot, scraped and
    chopped
1 small green pepper, chopped
1 medium red pepper, chopped

½ eggplant (½ pound),
    unpeeled and chopped
¼ cup tomato puree
4½ tablespoons cider vinegar
4 cups beef stock
½ teaspoon dried hot red
    pepper
Salt, freshly ground black
    pepper to taste

NOODLES

1½ cups flour	*1 tablespoon melted butter*
½ teaspoon salt	
½ cup minus 1 tablespoon	*Scallions*
water	

Brown the lamb in the olive oil; transfer the meat to a dish and keep warm.

To the oil remaining in the pot add the onions, garlic and carrot. Cook over medium heat for 10 minutes.

Then add the peppers and eggplant. Cook 5 minutes longer. Stir in the tomato puree, vinegar, beef stock and seasonings. Return the lamb to the pot. Cover and simmer for 1½ hours.

To make the noodles, mix together the flour and the salt. Make a well in the center and pour in the water. Knead for a few minutes to make a rather firm dough. Cover the dough with an upturned bowl and let stand for 1 hour. Roll the dough out paper-thin. Cut into long strips for noodles. Boil the noodles in salted water until tender, then toss with the melted butter.

Place a portion of noodles in each soup plate, then pour some of the lamb mixture over. Garnish each serving with chopped scallions.

Yield: 6 servings.

✠ · VII · ✠

SITTING AROUND
THE SAMOVAR

*A house is beautiful not because
of its walls, but because of its
cakes.*

—OLD RUSSIAN SAYING

*P*icture a brass urn with wooden handles, its high patina reflecting
the warmth of a cozy room. The face of this urn, emblazoned with medals
and etched with the likeness of the tsar, tapers down to an ornate spigot.
This is the samovar, the symbol of Russian hospitality at its best.

In Russian *samovar* means "self-cooker." Contrary to popular belief,
tea itself is not made in the samovar; the samovar serves only to heat
water and keep it hot. Nor is the samovar a strictly Russian discovery.
The idea was first introduced by the invading Mongol hordes in the
thirteenth century, hence the samovar's exotic appearance and resemblance
to the Mongolian hot pot. But tea-loving Russians found it too efficient
to be ignored, and by the late eighteenth century the samovar had been
adapted to everyday use and become an essential part of Russian life. It
was always kept burning, ready to refresh guests with a cup of hot tea.

The samovar works on a simple principle. Within the central body is
a wide tube. The tube is filled with hot coals or charcoal, and water is
poured into the body of the urn surrounding it. The coals efficiently heat
the water, the only drawback being the smoke they produce. In the
summertime the samovar was always heated outdoors to avoid smoking
up the house. But in the winter it was too cold to carry it outside, so
most families used a pipe extension that fit onto the large Russian stove
and carried the soot and fumes out through the stove's chimney. Many

poor peasant families, however, had only a makeshift hole in the roof of their cottage through which the smoke lazily drifted out, much of it remaining in the cottage and settling in a thick layer below the ceiling. Cottages with only a roof hole were known as *chornye izby* (black cottages), while those outfitted with a chimney extension were called *belye* (white).

Once the water boils, the samovar is brought to the table. The tea is brewed separately and made into a strong concentrate, or *zavarka*. *Zavarka* is brewed in a tiny teapot, which is kept warm on top of the samovar. To make tea, a small amount of the concentrate is poured into each cup, and the cup is filled with hot water from the samovar's spigot. In this way the strength of the tea can be adjusted according to taste.

The hostess traditionally presided over the samovar, pouring the tea into porcelain cups for the ladies and glasses for the men. The glasses were inserted into *podstakanniki,* metal or filigreed silver holders, so that the tea could be held comfortably. Noble families often had their own unique *podstakanniki* designs. Children were permitted—in fact, encouraged—to drink tea from their saucers, so as not to burn their lips. Today tea is usually served in glasses at restaurants and cafés, and in cups at home. But children still drink from their saucers.

My Russian friends were rather horrified to learn that I drink my tea "straight." (Actually I prefer a slice of lemon in it, but since lemon is often hard to come by in the Soviet Union today, I stopped asking for it, having learned my lesson my first week in Moscow when I stopped at a café for some tea. The menu offered two types: plain tea or tea with lemon. I was surprised to see lemon on the menu and assumed that the food situation must be better than I'd heard. When the waitress came for my order, I requested the tea with lemon. She looked at me with disbelief, then with disdain. "Lemon?" she repeated scornfully. "Next you'll be asking for a slice of orange in your tea!" When she plopped the tea down in front of me, it was plain, but she was kind enough to suggest adding sugar to it.) The Russians love sugar in their tea. They say it brings out the flavor of the leaves. In fact, there are three Russian idioms used only in conjunction with tea:

pit' chai vnakladku: "to drink tea with sugar in it";
pit' chai vpriglyadku: "to drink tea without any sugar at all";
pit' chai vprikusku: "to drink tea with a cube of sugar clenched between
        the teeth."

This third method was a favorite among peasants and no doubt largely responsible for their high incidence of tooth decay. Even today many Russians swear by a cube of sugar between the teeth for the greatest satisfaction from a cup of tea.

Another very Russian way of drinking tea is with jam. And the jam in the Soviet Union is marvelous—very thick, with whole pieces of fruit suspended in it. The jam is served alongside the tea on tiny, flat crystal jam dishes called *rozetki*. It can either be eaten right from the dish or spooned into the tea itself, giving the brew a fruity aroma and flavor.

Often a slice of apple replaces lemon in tea—a favorite choice, because not only are the Russians fond of apples, the autumnal fragrance of the fruit also reminds them of their national poet, Alexander Pushkin, whose favorite season was the fall.

If one should catch a cold in Omsk or Tomsk, one is advised to drink plenty of tea with raspberry jam. Or else add a teaspoon of red wine to the tea—it relaxes one as it helps the cold symptoms disappear.

An old Hanukkah custom among Russian Jews is to serve flaming tea. A cube of sugar is saturated with brandy and placed in a teaspoon with a little more brandy. The teaspoon is then balanced across the rim of a full cup of tea. A lighted candle is passed around to ignite the cubes, which are then dropped, flaming, into the tea.

The Russians drink mainly black tea, the best of which is grown on the mountain slopes of Georgia and Azerbaidzhan. In Central Asia, however, green tea predominates. It is said to be refreshing even on the hottest of desert days. Most of the tea in the Soviet Union is sold loose, or in packets, but occasionally one encounters *plitochnyi chai* (brick tea). This tea is made of inferior leaves, which have been pressed into bricks, often with a design imprinted on the surface. Brick tea is the standard brew of Siberian exiles, who sometimes use so much of it that it produces a narcotic effect, helping them to endure their hardship.

Tea drinking is still a favorite pastime in the Soviet Union. Most cities and towns have tearooms (and most of the tearooms are less than imaginatively named either Samovar or Russian Tea). Often they are decorated in the Old Russian style, with brightly painted ceilings and embroidered tablecloths. Typically the tearooms contain one or two huge samovars standing several feet tall. On top of the samovars perch tea cozies made in the round shape of Russian peasant women with disarming faces. Behind the samovars stand the real thing—rotund, matronly women dispensing the tea. After sitting down with one's tea, one can choose from a variety of sweets displayed on the tables.

Making a good cup of tea is an art in itself, a task not to be taken lightly. It is essential to start with leaves of high quality. Loose tea will not lose its flavor if stored in a tightly sealed container away from moisture and strong-smelling foods. These are the steps to follow in making a perfect cup of tea in the Russian manner:

Bring a kettle of water to a boil—but just barely. The kettle should not whistle, and there should not be much steam.

While the water is heating, rinse the teapot with very hot water and then keep it warm in a warm oven or under a cozy. It should not be allowed to cool off. It is important, too, that the teapot be porcelain or ceramic; metal imparts an off taste to the tea.

Sprinkle the loose tea into the warm teapot, using not less than 1 teaspoon of tea for each cup of water, plus 1 teaspoon for the pot.

Pour in the just-boiled water to half-full. Close the lid of the teapot and cover the entire pot with a clean linen towel or napkin. Let the tea steep for 4 to 5 minutes. Then fill the pot with water and immediately pour the tea into cups.

(If making a *zavarka*—the concentrate—instead of a pot of regular-strength tea, use 1 teaspoon of tea for every ½ cup of water. Cover and let steep for 5 minutes. Do not add any more water to the pot.)

Following are some recipes that traditionally grace the Russian tea table. For inveterate coffee drinkers, these desserts will taste just as good with a cup of coffee, although the experience won't be quite as Russian.

RUSSIAN TEA COOKIES
PECHEN'YE CHAINOYE

The Russians have a notorious sweet tooth, and even a cup of tea must be accompanied by jam at the very least. Happily, this craving for sweets has produced a wonderful variety of tea cookies and cakes, such as the cookies below, simple to prepare and rich with butter.

¼ cup unsalted butter

½ cup sugar

1 egg

½ teaspoon vanilla extract

1 cup flour

Pinch of salt

½ teaspoon baking powder

¼ teaspoon mace

⅛ teaspoon ground coriander

Candied orange rind

Preheat the oven to 375°F. Cream the butter and sugar together until light and fluffy. Beat in the egg and vanilla extract.

Sift together the dry ingredients and add to the butter mixture, mixing well.

Drop by scant teaspoonfuls onto lightly greased and floured cookie sheets. Top each cookie with a piece of candied orange rind, pressing down slightly to flatten the cookie.

Bake for 8 to 10 minutes, until lightly browned.

Yield: 3 dozen small cookies.

MERINGUE TEA COOKIES
PECHEN'YE CHAINOYE S MERINGOI

A plain tea cookie made fancy with meringue, jam and nuts.

6 tablespoons unsalted butter

½ cup sugar

1 egg yolk

½ teaspoon vanilla extract

1 tablespoon light cream

1 cup cake flour

1 teaspoon baking powder

¼ cup tart apricot jam

MERINGUE

1 egg white

¼ cup sugar

¾ teaspoon cinnamon

⅓ cup finely chopped pecans

Cream the butter with the ½ cup of sugar until light and fluffy. Beat in the egg yolk, vanilla extract and cream. Sift together the flour and baking powder, then stir them into the butter mixture, blending well. Form the dough into a ball. Wrap in waxed paper and chill in the refrigerator for at least 1 hour.

When the dough is firm, roll it out on a floured board to ¼-inch thickness. (Since the dough will be somewhat sticky, make sure the board and rolling pin are well floured.) Cut into rounds with a 2-inch cookie cutter. Place the rounds on a lightly greased cookie sheet about 1 inch apart.

Preheat the oven to 350°F. Spread each round with a thin layer of apricot jam, and then top with meringue.

To make the meringue, beat the egg white until stiff, gradually beating in the sugar, 1 tablespoon at a time. Whip in the cinnamon, then fold in the pecans.

Spread the meringue over the jam, leaving an outer rim of dough visible around the edge of the cookies. Bake for 12 to 15 minutes, until browned. Let cool on the cookie sheet for about 3 minutes, then transfer to wire racks to cool. These cookies are best when very fresh.

Yield: 2 dozen cookies.

SUVOROV COOKIES
🦅 *PECHEN'YE SUVOROVSKOYE* 🦅

Aleksandr Suvorov was a great Russian military commander, who found fame during the Russo-Turkish Wars of the late eighteenth century. Exactly how these dainty biscuits came to be named after him has been lost to history, but we do know that the recipe is an old one, dating back to his time. These biscuits are very elegant for tea.

½ cup unsalted butter	Pinch of salt
2 cups flour	
¼ cup sugar	¼ cup thick jam (raspberry
½ cup plus 2 tablespoons	or apricot)
heavy cream	Confectioners' sugar

Cut the butter into the flour. Add the sugar, cream, and salt. Form the mixture into a ball and wrap in waxed paper. Chill for at least 1 hour in the refrigerator.

On a floured board, roll out the dough ⅛ inch thick. Using a flower-shaped cookie cutter (or other decorative shape), cut out the dough into cookies about 1½ inches in diameter. Place on ungreased cookie sheets.

Preheat the oven to 375°F. Bake the cookies for 10 to 12 minutes, until golden around the edges. Remove from the cookie sheets and cool on wire racks.

To assemble, sandwich two cookies together with a layer of thick jam, putting the two flat sides together. Dust with confectioners' sugar before serving.

Yield: 5 dozen small cookies.

ALMOND RINGS
𝕏 KOL'TSO MINDAL'NOYE 𝕏

These crisp cookies were a mainstay of my diet in the Soviet Union. I used to frequent a bakery where a cup of tea or juice could be had along with an assortment of baked goods. The first time I entered the shop I came face to face with a surly saleswoman, who slapped the cookies down on the counter so hard that they crumbled. I wisely decided to take this only as a sign of their freshness and continued to frequent the shop, each time asking for the same two almond rings. Before long the saleswoman and I were great friends, and she always set aside the cookies with the most almonds for me.

1 cup butter	2 egg yolks, lightly beaten
½ cup sugar	1 cup finely chopped almonds
2 small eggs	¼ cup sugar
2 cups flour	

Cream the butter and the ½ cup of sugar until light and fluffy. Beat in the eggs, then stir in the flour. Mix well. Form into a ball and refrigerate for 1 to 2 hours, until firm.

Preheat the oven to 375°F. On a floured pastry board, roll out the dough to ½-inch thickness. Cut out rounds with a 4-inch cutter, preferably a fluted one. Then take a 1-inch round cutter and cut a hole out of the center of each cookie.

Transfer the cookies to a greased cookie sheet and brush with the lightly beaten egg yolks, then sprinkle with a mixture of the chopped almonds and sugar.

Bake for 12 to 15 minutes, until golden.

Yield: 1½ dozen large cookies.

HAZELNUT RUSKS
𝕏 SUKHARIKI 𝕏

Crisp and slightly sweet, these rusks are lovely on the afternoon tea table or with morning coffee.

2 eggs	1¼ cups hazelnuts, coarsely
¾ cup sugar	chopped
1 cup flour	

Beat the eggs and the sugar until light and fluffy. Dredge the nuts with the flour; blend them into the egg mixture.

Preheat the oven to 300°F. Grease an 8-inch loaf pan. Pour the batter into the pan and bake at 300°F for 50 minutes.

Turn the loaf out of the pan and wrap it in a moist dish towel. Let the loaf stand for 4 hours. Then cut it into slices about ⅓ inch thick.

Preheat the oven to 250°F. Place the slices on a cookie sheet and bake until lightly browned and crisp, about 3 hours.

Yield: 2 dozen.

COTTAGE CHEESE TARTLETS
☙ *VATRUSHKI* ☙

These wonderful tartlets always disappear fast. Though they may be made larger (Gogol's Chichikov feasted on *vatrushki* "at least as big as a dinner plate, if not larger"), I find the diminutive size perfect for eating by hand. A classic accompaniment to *borshch,* these tartlets can also inspire a tea or *zakuska* table.

DOUGH

2 *cups flour*
2 *tablespoons sugar*
½ *teaspoon salt*

8 *tablespoons butter*
2 *egg yolks*
¾ *cup (scant) sour cream*

FILLING

1½ *pounds* Russian Cottage
    Cheese (tvorog) *or farmer*
    cheese
3 *egg yolks*
¼ *teaspoon salt*
6 *tablespoons sugar*

6 *tablespoons sour cream*
6 *tablespoons raisins*

1 *egg yolk*
1 *tablespoon cold water*

To make the dough, mix together the flour, sugar and salt. Cut in the butter. Work in the yolks and sour cream. (The mixture will be slightly sticky.) Wrap the dough in waxed paper and chill for at least 30 minutes before using.

To prepare the filling, beat the 3 egg yolks into the cheese. Stir in the salt, sugar, sour cream and raisins, blending well. Chill.

Roll the dough out on a floured board to ⅛-inch thickness. With a cookie cutter, cut out 4-inch rounds. On each round, place 2 heaping tablespoons of filling, spreading it to within 1 inch of the edges.

Bring the edges of the dough up around the filling in gentle folds, leaving the filling exposed and making a narrow border of dough. Place on a greased baking sheet.

Preheat the oven to 375°F. Brush the tartlets with the egg yolk, which has been mixed with the cold water. Bake for 25 minutes until the filling is puffed and the dough golden.

Yield: 20 tartlets.

NOTE: If the *vatrushki* are to be served as an accompaniment to *borshch*, cut down on the sugar and omit the raisins entirely.

WALNUT CRESCENTS
🌿 *ROGALIKI* 🌿

Rogaliki, "little horns," are a specialty of southern Russia and the Ukraine. This recipe was given to me by a motherly woman named Margarita, who throughout my stay in the Soviet Union kept trying to fatten me up with goodies from her kitchen, such as these excellent pastries stuffed with sugar and nuts.

PASTRY

2 cups flour
1 package active dry yeast
14 tablespoons unsalted butter
  (1¾ sticks)

2 egg yolks
1 cup (scant) sour cream

FILLING

1½ cups (heaping) walnut
  pieces
¾ cup sugar

2 egg whites
Pinch of salt

In a medium-sized bowl mix together the flour and the yeast. Cut in the butter until the mixture resembles coarse meal. Stir in the egg yolks and sour cream and with your fingers mix until the dough holds together. (The less you work this dough, the more tender it will be.) The dough will be sticky. Shape it into a ball, wrap in waxed paper and refrigerate for at least 2 hours.

Meanwhile, to prepare the filling, fry the walnuts in a frying pan over low heat for about 5 minutes to release their flavor, being careful not to burn them. Then grind them coarsely along with the sugar.

Beat the egg whites with the salt until stiff but not dry. Fold into the nut mixture.

Preheat the oven to 350°F. Divide the dough into 3 parts. With a floured rolling pin, on a well-floured board, roll out each part into a circle ⅛ inch thick. Cut 10 pie-shaped wedges out of each circle. Spread the wedges with the filling, then roll them up like croissants, starting at the wide end.

Place the *rogaliki* point side down on a lightly greased baking sheet, turning the edges in slightly to form crescents. Bake for 15 to 20 minutes, until puffed and golden.

Yield: 30 pastries.

VARIATION: Spread the dough with thick jam instead of the nut filling. Proceed as directed above.

RAISIN BUNS
🦎 *BULKA S IZYUMOM* 🦎

A superb choice for morning coffee or tea.

1 package active dry yeast	*2 eggs, well beaten*
¼ cup warm water	*2¾ cups flour*
½ cup light cream	
¼ cup sugar	*8 ounces cream cheese, at room*
1 teaspoon salt	*temperature*
4 tablespoons unsalted butter,	*⅓ cup light cream*
at room temperature	*1½ cups seedless raisins*
Grated rind of 1 lemon	
	2 tablespoons melted butter

Dissolve the yeast in the warm water. Heat the ½ cup of cream to just below boiling, then pour it over a mixture of the sugar, salt and butter in a mixing bowl, stirring until the butter melts. Cool to lukewarm.

Stir in the yeast, lemon rind, eggs and enough flour to make a soft dough. Cover the bowl and chill the dough in the refrigerator for 3 to 4 hours, or until it is workable. (The dough may be held overnight in the refrigerator.)

Meanwhile, beat the cream cheese until smooth. Stir in the ⅓ cup of cream, mixing well. Beat out any lumps, then stir in the raisins.

Roll the dough out on a floured board to ⅛-inch thickness. Cut it into squares. Place a heaping tablespoon of the cream cheese filling in the center of each square. Bring the edges together in the center and pinch to seal. (If desired, the buns may be placed in the refrigerator and chilled overnight to be baked fresh in the morning; or they may be baked now.)

Grease a large baking sheet. Place the buns on it and brush them with the melted butter. Let rise, covered, until doubled in bulk.

Preheat the oven to 400°F. Bake the buns for 12 minutes, or until lightly browned.

These buns are best when still slightly warm.

Yield: 2 dozen.

SWEET BOILED BUNS
☙ BUBLIKI ❧

In the 1920s Soviet Russia instituted its New Economic Policy (NEP), permitting a certain degree of private enterprise. A new breed of Soviet citizen, the wily enterpreneur, emerged, wheedling the public to buy wares of often dubious quality. Many less sophisticated sellers also took to the streets in an attempt to peddle their goods, and for a while the cities were once again full of all manner of colorful hawkers.

One of the most popular products of this era was the *bublik,* sold hot from portable ovens and immortalized in a contemporary song, "Bublichki," in which a young girl bewails her father's drunkenness and the fact that she must eke out her livelihood selling buns on the street.

The well-loved *bubliki* are actually bagels, boiled until puffy and then baked to a golden finish in the oven. The recipe presented here is a less common version of these popular buns. A sweet, enriched dough is boiled in flavored milk before baking, resulting in a light and dainty bun.

¼ cup unsalted butter

½ cup sugar

3 egg yolks

1½ teaspoons baking powder

Pinch of salt

¼ teaspoon mace

1½ cups flour

4 cups milk

2 teaspoons vanilla extract

1 egg yolk, beaten

Pearl sugar

Cream the butter and sugar. Beat in the 3 egg yolks. Stir in the baking powder, salt, mace and enough flour to make a firm dough. Divide the dough into 12 pieces. Shape each piece into a ring 2 inches in diameter.

In a deep pot bring the milk and vanilla extract to a boil. Then drop in the rings of dough, a few at a time, and cook them in the boiling milk until they rise to the surface, which will take only a minute.

With a slotted spoon, transfer the rings to a cookie sheet and brush them with the beaten egg yolk, then sprinkle with the pearl sugar.

Preheat the oven to 300°F. Bake the *bubliki* until they are puffed and brown, about 30 minutes. Transfer to racks to cool.

Yield: 1 dozen buns.

YEAST-RAISED LEMON CAKE
LIMONNYI TORT

A tart lemon filling is sandwiched between the layers of this wonderfully fragrant loaf. Sliced thin and served with a cold fruit soufflé, it makes an elegant ending to a light meal.

1 package active dry yeast

¼ cup warm milk

1 tablespoon sugar

2 tablespoons flour

1 egg

1 cup butter, cut into bits, at
   room temperature

2¼ cups flour

1 whole lemon

1 cup sugar

GLAZE

½ cup plus 1 tablespoon
confectioners' sugar

1 tablespoon hot water

¼ teaspoon vanilla extract

Curls of lemon rind
Tiny raspberries or strawberries

Dissolve the yeast in the milk; gradually add the 1 tablespoon of sugar and the 2 tablespoons of flour. Cover and let stand in a warm place for 1 hour, until bubbly.

Stir in the egg, butter and remaining flour. The dough will be *very* soft. Place it in a greased bowl and let rise until doubled in bulk, about 1½ hours.

While the dough is rising, prepare the filling. Cut the whole lemon into eighths and remove any pits. Then, in a food processor or meat grinder, grind the lemon, including the rind. Stir in the 1 cup of sugar and set aside.

Generously grease a large cookie sheet. When the dough has risen, punch it down. Then take two thirds of the dough and press or roll it out into a circle 7 inches in diameter, flouring it lightly from time to time to make it more manageable, if necessary. Place the circle of dough on the cookie sheet. Pinch the edges of the circle up all the way around, making a rim high enough to contain the lemon filling. Pour in the filling.

Press or roll the remaining dough into a circle 6 inches in diameter, which will fit over the lemon filling, covering it completely and meeting the outer rim of the larger circle. Pinch the edges of the top and bottom layers of dough together to seal.

Preheat the oven to 375°F. Let the cake rise for about 20 minutes, then bake it for 25 minutes, or until nicely browned.

Remove the cake from the oven. While it is still warm, swirl the glaze over it, which has been made by combining the confectioners' sugar, hot water and vanilla extract. After about 20 minutes carefully transfer the cake to a rack to continue cooling. Serve at room temperature, decorated with tiny berries along the seam of the cake and lemon curls on top.

Yield: About 12 servings.

NOTE: In spite of the yeast, this is a rather flat cake, about 1 inch high.

APPLE CAKE WITH CHOCOLATE GLAZE
🏂 *YABLOCHNYI PIROG* 🏂

My friend Sonya, an excellent cook, gave me this recipe for an apple cake that has been made for generations in her family. I first tasted it when we returned to her small Moscow apartment after a day of cross-country skiing in the countryside. The weather was bitterly cold, and as soon as we'd taken off our wet clothes, Sonya brewed a fresh pot of tea and offered this delightful cake along with it.

¾ pound apples, pared, cored,
 and thinly sliced
3 eggs
1 cup sugar
1 cup flour

¼ teaspoon salt
1 teaspoon baking soda
1½ teaspoons freshly squeezed
 lemon juice
½ teaspoon cinnamon

GLAZE

4 tablespoons butter
2 tablespoons milk
½ cup confectioners' sugar,
 sifted

2 tablespoons unsweetened
 cocoa powder

Chopped walnuts (optional)

Preheat the oven to 350°F. Grease and lightly flour a 9-inch springform pan.

Beat the eggs with the sugar. Stir in the flour and the salt. Dissolve the baking soda in the lemon juice and add to the batter. Stir in the cinnamon, mixing well. Finally, stir in the apples.

Pour the batter into the prepared pan and bake for 1 hour, until browned, or until a cake tester comes out clean.

Prepare the glaze 5 minutes before the cake is removed from the oven. Melt the butter over low heat in a small saucepan. Stir in the milk, confectioners' sugar and cocoa powder. Bring the mixture just to a boil, then spread it over the top of the cake while the cake is still hot.

Decorate the top of the cake with chopped walnuts, if desired.

Cool to room temperature before serving.

Yield: 10 servings.

CRANBERRY-APPLE ROLL
☙ *RULET S KLYUKVOI* ☙

Here a tender pastry crust encloses tart apples and berries in a very Russian dessert, and a lovely one.

PASTRY

¾ cup butter, at room
   temperature
6 ounces cream cheese, at
   room temperature

1 egg yolk
1½ cups flour
¼ teaspoon salt

FILLING

1 cup cranberries (¼ pound)
½ cup (scant) sugar
2 tablespoons honey
1 tablespoon water
Grated peel of ½ lemon
2 tablespoons flour

¼ teaspoon cinnamon
2 large tart apples, pared, cored
   and finely chopped

1 egg yolk, beaten

Cream the butter and cream cheese together. Beat in the egg yolk. With your hands work the flour and salt into the butter mixture until a soft dough has been formed. Shape into a ball, wrap in waxed paper and chill for at least 30 minutes before rolling out.

To make the filling, place the cranberries, sugar, honey, water, lemon peel, flour and cinnamon in a heavy saucepan. Bring to a boil and cook, stirring, until the cranberries burst, about 10 minutes. Remove from the heat and stir in the apples.

Roll the dough out and trim it to a 9 x 18-inch rectangle. Leaving a 3-inch-wide strip down the center of the dough, cut 3-inch-long strips radiating out from the center down both sides of the dough. (Use a fluted pastry cutter if you have one.) Thus there will be a 3-inch-wide center strip with approximately 12 fluted ribbons on either side of it.

Spread the filling along the center strip. Then, alternating sides, fold in the fluted strips at an angle, each one overlapping the next, so that the filling is completely covered.

Transfer the roll to a greased baking sheet using two spatulas. Brush with the beaten egg yolk.

Preheat the oven to 375°F. Bake the roll for approximately 1 hour, if necessary covering it with foil toward the end of the baking so that it doesn't brown too much. Transfer the roll to a rack while still slightly warm. Serve at room temperature.

Yield: About 10 servings.

NOTE: This pastry will also make 1 dozen *pirozhki*.

APRICOT TART
ABRIKOSOVYI PIROG

Butter, sour cream, jam and nuts join forces once again in this excellent tart.

2 cups flour	Grated rind of ½ lemon
8 tablespoons butter	2 egg yolks, lightly beaten
⅛ teaspoon salt	4 teaspoons sour cream
½ cup sugar	
¾ teaspoon baking powder	1 cup thick apricot jam
1 tablespoon freshly squeezed	⅓ cup sliced blanched almonds
lemon juice	1 egg yolk, beaten

Cut the butter into the flour, then add the salt, sugar and baking powder. Stir in the lemon juice, rind, 2 egg yolks and sour cream, mixing well to form a soft, sticky dough. Set aside one third of the dough for the lattice top.

Lightly grease a baking sheet and place a greased 9½-inch flan ring on it. (Or use a false-bottomed tart pan.) Pat the larger piece of dough evenly into the flan ring, covering the bottom and sides.

Spread the jam over the top of the dough, then sprinkle the almonds over the jam.

Press out the remaining piece of dough and either cut or mold it into pieces to make a lattice crust. Brush the top of the tart with the beaten egg yolk.

Preheat the oven to 350°F. Bake the tart for 25 minutes, or until golden. Cool to room temperature before serving.

Yield: 6 to 8 servings.

POPPY-SEED TORTE
🏿 *MAKOVYI TORT* 🏿

A beautiful and delicate torte, which separates into three ribboned layers upon baking.

1 cup poppy seeds	3 ounces semisweet chocolate,
1¼ cups boiling water	grated
8 egg yolks	6 egg whites, beaten
1 cup heavy cream	
1 cup sifted confectioners'	Fine bread crumbs
sugar	
1 cup potato starch	Powdered sugar
6 bitter almonds, ground	Chocolate curls

Pour the 1¼ cup of boiling water over the poppy seeds in a bowl to scald them. Let soak for 1 hour, then drain through cheesecloth. Set aside to drain well.

Beat the egg yolks until light and lemon-colored, then beat in the cream. Gradually add the sugar and potato starch, continuing to beat well. Stir in the ground almonds and grated chocolate, then add the drained poppy seeds, mixing well.

Beat the egg whites until stiff but not dry. Fold them into the cake batter. The mixture will be quite loose.

Preheat the oven to 325°F. Grease and dust with bread crumbs a 10-inch springform pan. Pour the cake mixture into the pan and bake for 45 minutes.

Cool the torte completely before removing the outer ring of the pan. Dust the top of the torte with powdered sugar and decorate with chocolate curls.

Yield: 10 servings.

RUSSIAN CARAMEL TORTE
🏵 *TORT "TYANUCHKI"* 🏵

A favorite of the Russian expatriates living in Scandinavia, this fabulous torte is so popular that Finland's largest confectionery firm, Fazer, produces it commercially. The name comes from its topping, *tyanuchki,* an old-fashioned white fudge that is left to cook for long hours until thick and caramel-colored. So sleek is this topping, it looks like liquid marble. Serve the torte in small portions. It is very, very rich.

6 tablespoons unsalted butter
¾ cup (heaping) sugar
3 eggs, separated
1½ cups blanched almonds

6 bitter almonds
3 boiled potatoes (1½ pounds;
 to yield 1 pound mashed)
Pinch of salt

TOPPING

½ cup heavy cream
6 tablespoons sugar
3 tablespoons corn syrup
2 tablespoons unsalted butter

½ teaspoon vanilla extract

Apricot jam
Sliced almonds (optional)

Cream the butter and sugar. Beat in the egg yolks. Grind the blanched almonds together with the bitter almonds. Mash the potatoes and leave them to cool slightly. Add the almonds, potatoes and salt to the butter mixture, beating well until there are no lumps left in the batter (this will take some work). Beat the egg whites until stiff but not dry and fold them into the batter.

Preheat the oven to 350°F. Grease and flour two 8-inch round cake pans; cover the bottoms of the pans with rounds of waxed paper and grease the waxed paper. Pour the batter into the pans and bake for 1 hour, until a cake tester comes out clean.

Prepare the topping while the cake is baking. In a heavy saucepan combine the cream, sugar and corn syrup. Cook over medium heat, stirring, until the sugar has dissolved. Then cook slowly for 50 minutes, until the mixture is thick and caramel-colored (a candy thermometer will register 220°F). Remove from the heat and stir in the 2 tablespoons butter and vanilla extract. Cool slightly.

Turn the cake layers out onto a rack and let cool. Then spread a thin layer of jam between the layers and assemble them. Pour the caramel topping over all, letting it drip down the sides and then smoothing it with a spatula until the cake is entirely coated. Decorate with sliced almonds, if desired.

Refrigerate for 24 hours before serving.

Yield: 10 to 12 servings.

VARIATION: Prepare only the topping and serve it warm over fresh cranberries or pears.

"MOTHER-IN-LAW" TORTE
🗡 "SVEKRUKHA" 🗡

The recipe for this festive torte, reserved for special occasions in Russia, was given to me by my cousin Roma, who works as a pathologist but whose avocation is baking. He regularly turns out flaky *pirogi* with wild-mushroom stuffing and tender *pirozhki* filled with chopped cabbage and eggs. This torte is Roma's specialty. It was his mother who passed the recipe on to him, so Roma's wife, Raya, dubbed the cake "Mother-in-Law" Torte. It's a favorite with children, as evidenced by the clamorous cries of Roma's two children when the torte appears on the table.

CAKE LAYERS

14 tablespoons unsalted butter
  (1¾ sticks)
5 tablespoons sugar
½ teaspoon salt

1 cup walnuts, ground
2 tablespoons sour cream
2 cups flour

FILLING

4 tablespoons unsalted butter
¼ cup sugar
½ teaspoon vanilla extract
1 small egg, slightly beaten
¼ cup sour cream

¼ cup walnuts, heated slightly
  in a frying pan to release
  their flavor, then finely
  chopped
1 tablespoon cognac

CHOCOLATE GLAZE

2 tablespoons milk
¼ cup sugar

1 (scant) teaspoon unsweetened cocoa powder
1 tablespoon unsalted butter

To make the cake layers, melt the butter, then pour it into a mixing bowl. Stir in the sugar, salt, walnuts and sour cream, mixing well. Then stir in the flour until it is well blended. The dough will be loose.

Preheat the oven to 350°F. Spread two baking sheets with aluminum foil and grease the foil.

Divide the dough into 4 parts. On the foil, pat out 4 rounds, each ¼ inch thick and 8 inches in diameter. Bake the rounds for about 15 minutes, until browned around the edges.

Cool the rounds before removing them from the foil, since they are very fragile.

To make the filling, cream the butter and sugar until light. Gradually stir in the vanilla extract, egg and sour cream. Add the nuts and the cognac, beating well. This filling will be very loose, so chill it for at least 10 minutes in the refrigerator before spreading it on the cake layers.

Spread the buttercream filling between the cooled cake layers. To prepare the glaze, pour the milk into a small saucepan. Mix together the sugar and cocoa powder and add to the milk. Bring to a boil and simmer for 10 minutes, stirring constantly. Remove from the heat and stir in the butter. Immediately spread the glaze over the top layer of the torte.

Place the torte in the refrigerator and chill for several hours before serving.

Yield: 12 servings.

GLACÉED APRICOTS
❦ *ZASAKHARENNYE ABRIKOSY* ❦

Perfect for eating out of your hand or for decorating lavish tortes.

1 cup sugar
½ cup hot water
Pinch of cream of tartar

Dash of salt
4 ounces dried apricot halves

Combine the sugar, water, cream of tartar and salt in a heavy saucepan. Bring to a boil, stirring until the sugar dissolves, and cook until the mixture registers 290°F on a candy thermometer (hard-crack stage).

Immediately remove the syrup from the heat and dip the apricots into it, one at a time. This is most easily done by grasping the edge of each apricot half with a pair of tweezers.

As each apricot is dipped, place it on a lightly buttered drying rack or marble slab to harden. If the syrup should become too thick, heat it gently until it loosens again.

Yield: About 2 dozen candies.

NOTE: These apricots must be prepared in dry weather; otherwise the sugar coating will not harden.

ALMOND CARAMELS
✕ MAKAGIGI ✕

These chewy caramels come from Ukrainian kitchens, but their name suggests a Turkish origin.

¼ cup sugar
8 tablespoons butter
⅓ cup honey (preferably
buckwheat)

1½ cups blanched almonds,
coarsely chopped

In a large frying pan melt the sugar and cook it over low heat, stirring constantly, until it has caramelized (turned light golden brown). Be very careful not to let the sugar burn.

Stir in the butter and the honey and cook the mixture at the barest simmer for 5 to 8 minutes, stirring constantly, until a bit of the mixture dropped into a glass of ice water holds a pliable ball (firm-ball stage on a candy thermometer).

Stir in the almonds and drop by teaspoonfuls onto a buttered marble slab or well-buttered waxed paper. Cool.

Yield: 3 dozen candies.

APPLE CONFECTIONS
🎏 *PASTILA* 🎏

Pastila are a cross between candy and meringue cookies. They are light, airy puffs with a delicate apple flavor, the adornment of elegant tea tables since the mid-nineteenth century.

> 3 large, tart green apples
>   (1¼ pounds)
> 1 teaspoon fresh lemon juice
> 1 cup sugar
> ¼ teaspoon (scant) almond
>   extract
>
> ¼ teaspoon cinnamon
> 2 egg whites
> Yellow food coloring (optional)
> Flour

Steam the apples whole and unpeeled over boiling water until tender, about 25 to 30 minutes. (It's all right if the apples fall apart.)

Put the apples through a vegetable mill. Stir in the lemon juice, sugar, almond extract and cinnamon.

Beat the egg whites until stiff but not dry. Stir them into the apple mixure, along with 16 drops of yellow food coloring if a pale yellow tint is desired. Beat the mixture at high speed with an electric mixer for at least 5 minutes, until fluffy, or for 10 to 15 minutes by hand.

Preheat the oven to 150°F. Spread a sheet of aluminum foil on a baking sheet. Grease it lightly and then dust with flour. Drop the apple foam by tablespoonfuls onto the foil.

Bake for about 6 hours in a slow oven, until the confections are dry. Then transfer them to a wire rack to cool.

Yield: About 5 dozen confections.

NOTE: The *pastila* look especially lovely when served in fluted paper candy cups displayed on an epergne.

INDEX

Abrikosovaya, 24
Abrikosovaya nachinka, 73
Abrikosovoye varen'ye, 214
Abrikosovyi pirog, 285
Almond
   Caramels, 291
   Rings, 275
Anise Vodka, 24
Anisovaya, 24
Appetizers. *See* Zakuski
Apple(s)
   Baked
      with Jam, 187
      Souffléed, 188
   Cake with Chocolate Glaze, 283
   Charlotte, Baked, 111
   Confections, 292
   Cranberry-, Roll, 284
   Dumplings, 165
   Filling (for *pirozhki*), 74
   Fritters, 189
   Pudding, Latvian, 246
   Roast Goose with, 141
   Soused, 209
   Turkey Breast with, 90
Apricot(s)
   Filling (for *pirozhki*), 73
   Glacéed, 290

Jam, 214
Tart, 285
Vodka, 24
Armenian Flat Bread, 254
Aspic, Cold Fish in, 34
Azerbaidzhan Lamb Patties, 257

Baba au Rhum, 110
Baked Apple Charlotte, 111
Baked Apples
   with Jam, 187
   Souffléed, 188
Baked Fish with Horseradish, 174
Baked Milk, 220
Baklazhan farshirovannyi, 103
Baklazhan marinovannyi, 210
Baklazhannaya ikra, 40
Barley, Mushroom and, Soup, 161
Barrel-cured Sauerkraut, 203
Basic Bouillon, 199
Basic Fish Stock, 200
Basic Raised Pirozhki Dough, 68
Basic Tomato Sauce, 50
Basturma, 256
Beans, Kidney
   with Plum Sauce, 264
   Savory, 263

Beef
  in Cold Meat and Vegetable Soup, 164
  in Crimean Meat Pies, 250
  Filling (for *pirozhki*), 71
  Hussar-style, 97
  in Mixed Meat Soup, 160
  in Moscow-style Beet Soup, 159
  in Russian-style Hamburgers, 173
  Skewered, Caucasian, 256
  Stew
    with Horseradish Sauce, 172
    with Rum, 99
  Stroganoff, 95
  in Tatar Meat Pies, 249
  in Ukrainian-style Beet Soup, 157
Beet(s)
  Kvass, 223
  Mayonnaise, Cauliflower with, 53
  Salad, 184
  Soup
    Cold, 162
    Moscow-style, 159
    Ukrainian-style, 157
  Sweet and Sour, 50
  Vinaigrette of, 51
Bef-stroganov, 95
Berries
  and Cream, 117
  with Sour Cream, 117
  see also Names of berries
Beverages (alcoholic)
  Egg Toddy, 192
  Plum Cordial, 224
  Wine Bowl, 150
  see also Vodkas
Beverages (nonalcoholic)
  Cranberry Juice, 201
  Hot Chocolate, Russian, 149
  Spiced Honey Drink, 202
Bezdrozhzhevoye testo, 69
Bitki, 173
Black Bread
  Kvass, 222
  Russian, 168
Black-Currant
  -Bud Vodka, 24
  Conserve, 212
Blinchiki, 78
Blini, 135

Blueberry
  Ice Cream, 148
  Kisel', 189
Borshch moskovskii, 159
Borshch ukrainskii, 157
Bouillon, Basic, 199
Braised Chicken with Prunes, 237
Braised Rabbit in Sour Cream, 91
Bread(s)
  Black
    Kvass, 222
    Russian, 168
  Flat, Armenian, 254
  Kulich
    Cake-like, 133
    Traditional, 131
  Name Day Loaf, 146
  Rye, 170
  Sourdough White, 171
  Ukrainian Sweet Braid, 242
  Yeast-raised Lemon Cake, 281
  see also Buns
Bubliki, 280
Buckwheat Groats, 166
  with Mushrooms and Cream, 104
Buffalo Grass Vodka, 25
Bulka, 242
Bulka s izyumom, 279
Buns
  Lark-shaped, 137
  Raisin, 279
  Sweet Boiled, 280
Buterbrod s syomgoi, 31
Buterbrody s rediskoi, 54
Butter, Egg and, Sauce, Cod with, 94

Cabbage
  Filling (for *pirozhki*), 71
  Leaves, Stuffed, 176
    Jewish Sweet-and-Sour Style, 176
  with Noodles and Poppy Seeds, 179
  Soup, 155
  Sour, 204
    see also Sauerkraut
  Steamed, Soufflé, Ukrainian, 236
  Stuffed Whole, 178
Cake(s)
  Apple, with Chocolate Glaze, 283
  Baba au Rhum, 110
  Cheesecake. *See* Paskha
  Doughnuts, 147

Honey, Ukrainian, 243
Lemon, Yeast-raised, 281
-like Kulich, 133
Queen, 108
see also Tortes
Calf's Liver, Roast Whole, 102
Canapés of Smoked Salmon, 31
Caramel(s)
Almond, 291
Torte, Russian, 287
Carrot
Filling (for pirozhki), 73
Salad, 185
Casserole of Mashed Potatoes, 180
Caucasian Skewered Beef, 256
Caucasian Skewered Lamb, 255
Cauliflower
with Beet Mayonnaise, 53
Georgian-style, 264
with Mayonnaise, 52
Caviar
Eggplant, 40
Fresh Salmon Roe, 26
Halibut Steaks with, 92
Mushroom, 43
Yellow (Crookneck) Squash or Zucchini, 42
Celeriac Salad, 186
Chainaya, 25
Chakhokhbili iz kur, 261
Champagne, Sturgeon Soup with, 63
Charlotte(s)
Apple, Baked, 111
Malakoff, 113
Chebureki, 250
Cheese
Garlic-, Spread, 55
Pancakes, Russian, 191
Pie, Georgian, 258
Prunes Stuffed with, 244
see also Cottage cheese
Cheesecake. See Paskha
Chernosliv, farshirovannyi tvorogom, 245
Cherry(ies)
Filling (for vareniki), 241
Sauce, Sturgeon with, 93
Spiced Pickled, 211
Veal Stew with, 100
Vodka, 24
Chesnochnaya, 24
Chestnut Puree, 135

Chicken
Braised, with Prunes, 237
Chakhokhbili, 261
Circassian, 252
in Cold Meat and Vegetable Soup, 164
Cutlets, 87
Kiev, 84
and Mushrooms en Cocotte, 38
Pie, Russian, 81
in Russian Salad, 45
Spring, with Gooseberry Sauce, 88
Stuffed with Parsley and Lemon, 87
Tabaka, 260
Circassian Chicken, 252
Chocolate Glaze, Apple Cake with, 283
Chornaya smorodina s sakharom, 212
Chornyi khleb, 168
Clear Fish Soup, 64
Cocktail Sausages in Tomato Sauce, 42
Cod with Egg and Butter Sauce, 94
Cold Beet Soup, 162
Cold Fish in Aspic, 34
Cold Fruit Soup with Dumplings, 165
Cold Meat and Vegetable Soup, 164
Cold Raspberry Soup, 67
Cold Stuffed Eggplant, 103
Confections
Almond Caramels, 291
Apple, 292
Glacéed Apricots, 290
Conserve, Black Currant, 212
Coulibiac of Salmon, 77
Cookies
Almond Rings, 275
Deep-fried "Twigs," 142
Gingerbread, Russian, 143
Hazelnut Rusks, 276
Mint, 145
"Pigtails," 70
Suvorov, 274
Tea
Meringue, 273
Russian, 272
Walnut Crescents, 278
Cordial, Plum, 224
Coriander Vodka, 24
Cornmeal Pudding, 247
Cottage Cheese
Russian, 217
Ukrainian-style, 182
Tartlets, 277

Cranberry(ies)
-Apple Roll, 284
Frosted, 120
Horseradish Relish, 217
Juice, 201
Kisel', 191
Kvass, 220
Cream
Berries and, 117
Mushrooms and, Buckwheat Groats with, 104
sour. *See* Sour cream
Tsarina's, The, 116
Crimean Meat Pies, 250
Cucumbers in Sour Cream, 183
Currant, Black
-Bud, Vodka, 24
Conserve, 212

Deep-fried "Twigs," 142
Desserts
Apples
Baked, with Jam, 187
Baked, Souffléed, 188
Charlotte, Baked, 111
Fritters, 189
Berries
and Cream, 117
with Sour Cream, 117
Blueberry
Ice Cream, 148
Kisel', 190
Charlotte Malakoff, 113
Compote of Dried Fruits, 138
Cottage Pudding, Russian, 192
Cranberry(ies)
-Apple Roll, 284
Frosted, 120
Kisel', 191
Fruit Pudding, Russian, 190
Guriev Kasha, 114
Prunes Stuffed with Cheese, 244
Rhubarb Mousse, 119
Strawberry(ies)
Kisel', 190
Romanov, 118
Tsarina's Cream, The, 116
Wheat Berries with Honey and Nuts, 139
see also Cakes; Cookies, Pies (sweet)

Dill
Garlic-and-, Vodka, 24
Marinade, Turbot in, 33
Pickle(s)
Barrel-style, 206
Kidney and, Soup, 66
Sauce, Herring in, 28
Dilled Onions, 54
Dough(s)
Pirozhki, Basic Raised, 68
Short, for Sweet Pirozhki, 70
see also Pastry
Doughnuts, 147
Dragomirovskaya kasha, 104
Dried Fish, 225
Dried Fruits, Compote of, 138
Dried Mushrooms, 208
Sauce, 181
Drinks. *See* Beverages
Drochona, 192
Drozhzhevoye testo, 68
Dumplings
Apple, 165
Cold Fruit Soup with, 165
"lazy," 192
mamalyga, 247
Siberian, 233
Ukrainian, 240

Egg(s)
and Butter Sauce, Cod with, 94
Mushroom-stuffed, 47
Salad, Russian, 47
Toddy, 193
Eggplant(s)
Caviar, 40
Cold Stuffed, 103
Pickled, 210
Estonian Potato Salad, 245
Eugenia Torte, 107

File indeiki s yablokami, 90
Filling(s)
savory, for *pirozhki,* 71–73
sweet, for *pirozhki,* 73–75
for *vareniki,* 241
Fish
Baked, with Horseradish, 174
Cold, in Aspic, 34

Dried, 225
Pies, Small, 75
Soup, Clear, 54
Stock, Basic, 200
see also Names of fish
Flat Bread, Armenian, 254
Flounder, in Baked Fish with Horseradish, 174
Forshmak, 37
Frankfurters, in Mixed Meat Soup, 160
Fresh Ham Cooked with Hay, 134
Fresh Salmon Roe Caviar, 26
Fritters, Apple, 180
Frosted Cranberries, 120
Fruit(s)
Dried, Compote of, 138
Soup, Cold, with Dumplings, 165
see also Names of fruits

Garlic
-Cheese Spread, 55
-and-Dill Vodka, 24
Georgian Cheese Pie, 258
Georgian-style Cauliflower, 264
Georgian-style Kidney Beans, 263
Glacéed Apricots, 290
Glaze, Chocolate, Apple Cake with, 283
Gogol'-mogol', 193
Golubtsy, 176
Goose, Roast, with Apples, 141
Gooseberry Sauce, Spring Chicken with, 88
Gorchitsa, 215
Grechnevaya kasha, 166
Gribnaya ikra, 43
Gribnaya nachinka, 72
Gribnoi sous, 181
Griby, marinovannye v tomatnom souse, 44
Griby v smetane, 104
Gur'evskaya kasha, 114
Guriev Kasha, 114
Gus' zharenyi s yablokami, 141

Halibut
in Baked Fish with Horseradish, 174
Steaks with Caviar, 92
in Estonian Potato Salad, 245
Fresh, Cooked with Hay, 134
in Mixed Meat Soup, 160
Hamburgers, Russian-style, 173
Hazelnut Rusks, 276
Herb Vodka, 24

Herring
in Dill Sauce, 28
in Estonian Potato Salad, 245
in Mustard Sauce, 29
Pickled, 27
Potato and, Bake, 175
Roast Meat and, Soufflé, 37
in Sour Cream, 28
Homemade Kefir, 219
Homemade Sour Cream, 219
Honey
Cake, Ukrainian, 243
Drink, Spiced, 202
and Nuts, Wheat Berries with, 139
Walnut-, Filling (for pirozhki), 75
Horseradish
Baked Fish with, 174
Cranberry-, Relish, 217
Mustard and, Mayonnaise, Cauliflower with, 52
Prepared, 216
Sauce, Beef Stew with, 172
Hot Chocolate, Russian, 149
Hussar-style Beef, 97

Ice Cream, Blueberry, 148
Ikra iz kabachkov, 43

Jam(s)
Apricot, 214
Baked Apples with, 186
Raspberry, Kiev-style, 213
Rose Petal, 215
Sour Cream and, Pie, 105
Juice, Cranberry, 201

Kakao s yaichnym zheltkom, 149
Kapusta farshirovannaya, 178
Kapusta s lapshoi i makom, 179
Kartofel'naya zapekanka, 180
Kartofel' solomkoi, 96
Kartofel' s selyodkoi, 175
Kazakh Lamb and Noodle Stew, 266
Kasha, Guriev, 114
Kefir, Homemade, 219
Khachapuri, 258
Khleb iz pshenichnoi muki, 171
Khlodnik, 163
Kholodets, 41
Khren, 216
Khvorost, 142

Kidney(s)
and Dill Pickle Soup, 66
in Madeira, 39
Kidney Beans
with Plum Sauce, 264
Savory, 263
Kievskie kotlety, 84
Kiev-style Raspberry Jam, 213
Kisel'(s)
Blueberry, 190
Cranberry, 191
Strawberry, 190
Kislaya kapusta, 204
Kislaya kapusta gribami i smetanoi, 182
Kletski, 165
Klyukva s khrenom, 217
Klyukva s sakharom, 120
Klyukvennyi mors, 201
Kol'tso mindal'noye, 275
Koriandrovaya, 24
Korolevskii tort, 108
Koryushki v tomatnom souse, 32
Kosichki, 70
Krashaya ikra, 26
Krem tsaritsy, 116
Krendel, 146
Krepkii bul'yon iz ryby, 200
Krolik, tushonyi v smetane, 91
Kryushon, 150
Kulebyaka, 77
Kulich
Cake-like, 133
Traditional, 131
Kuritsa, farshirovannaya prtrushkoi, 87
Kuritsa po-cherkesski, 252
Kuritsa, tushonaya s chernoslivom, 237
Kurnik, 81
Kut'ya, 139
Kvashenaya kapusta, 203
Kvas klyukvennyi, 221
Kvass
Beet, 223
Black Bread, 223
Cranberry, 221
Kvas sukharnyi domashnii, 222

Lagman, 266
Lamb
in Crimean Meat Pies, 250
and Noodle Stew, Kazakh, 266
Patties, Azerbaidzhan, 257

Skewered, Caucasian, 255
in Uzbek-style Pilaf, 265
Lark-shaped Buns, 137
Latvian Apple Pudding, 246
Lavash, 254
"Lazy" dumplings, 192
Lemon
Cake, Yeast-raised, 281
or Orange Vodka, 25
Parsley and, Chicken Stuffed with, 87
Soup, Russian, 65
Lenivye vareniki, 192
Limonnyi tort, 281
Limonovka, 25
Liver
Calf's, Roast Whole, 102
Pâté, Russian, 36
Lobio, 263
Lobio tkemali, 264
Luk marinovannyi, 54
Lyulya-kebab, 257

Machanka, 182
Madeira, Kidneys in, 39
Makagigi, 291
Makovaya nachinka, 74
Makovyi tort, 286
Malinnik, 67
Malinovoye varen'ye v kievskom manere,
213
Mamalyga, 247
Marinade, Dill, Turbot in, 33
Marinated Mushrooms, 44
Marinated Smoked Salmon, 30
Mayonnaise(s)
Beet, Cauliflower with, 53
Cauliflower with, 52
Mustard and Horseradish, Cauliflower
with, 52
and Sour Cream Sauce, 35
Meat(s)
Mixed, Soup, 160
Pies
Crimean, 250
Tatar, 249
Roast, and Herring Soufflé, 37
and Vegetable Soup, Cold, 164
Medivnyk, 243
Meringue Tea Cookies, 273
Milk, Baked, 220
Mint Cookies, 145

Mixed Meat Soup, 160
Mochonye yabloki, 209
Morozhenoye s chernikoi, 148
Moscow-style Beet Soup, 159
"Mother-in-law" Torte, 288
Mousse, Rhubarb, 119
Mushroom(s)
  and Barley Soup, 161
  Caviar, 43
  Chicken and, en Cocotte, 38
  and Cream, Buckwheat Groats with, 105
  Dried, 208
    Sauce, 181
  Filling (for *pirozhki*), 72
  Marinated, 43
  Salted, 208
  and Sour Cream, Sauerkraut with, 182
  in Sour Cream, 104
  -stuffed Eggs, 49
Muss iz ravenya, 119
Mustard
  and Horseradish Mayonnaise,
    Cauliflower with, 52
  Sauce, Herring in, 29
  Russian-style, 215
Myaso po-gusarski, 97
Myatnye pryaniki, 145

Nachinka iz kapusty, 71
Nachinka iz rublenogo myasa, 71
Nachinka iz zelonogo luka, 72
Nakiplyak iz kapusty, 236
Name Day Loaf, 146
Noodle(s)
  Lamb and, Stew, Kazakh, 266
  and Poppy Seeds, Cabbage with, 179
Nuts, Honey and, Wheat Berries with, 139

Olad'i, 189
Ogurtsy v smetane, 183
Okroshka, 164
Onions, Dilled, 54
Open-faced Radish Sandwiches, 54
Orange, Lemon or, Vodka, 25
Osetrina pod vishnyovym sousom, 93

Paltus po-astrakhanski, 92
Paltus v marinade s ukropom, 33
Pancakes
  Cheese, Russian, 191
  Russian, 135

Parsley and Lemon, Chicken Stuffed with,
  87
Pashtet iz pechonki, 36
Paskha
  Maria Nikolaevna's, 128
  Pink, 130
Paskha tsarskaya, 129
Pastila, 292
Pastry
  Puff, 77
  Sour Cream, for Pirozhki, 69
  see also Doughs
Pâté, Liver, Russian, 36
Pechen'ye chainoye, 272
Pechen'ye chainoye s meringoi, 273
Pechen'ye suvorovskoye, 274
Pechonaya ryba s khrenom, 174
Pechonye yabloki s varen'em, 187
Pepper Vodka, 25
Peppers, Stuffed, Moldavian Style, 248
Peremech, 249
*Perets, farshirovannyi v moldavskom
    stile*, 248
Pertsovka, 25
Pickle(s)
  Dill
    Barrel-style, 206
    Kidney and, Soup, 66
  Soused Apples, 209
  Spiced Pickled Cherries, 211
  Pickled Eggplants, 210
  see also Relishes
Pickled Eggplants, 210
Pickled Herring, 27
Pie(s) (savory)
  Cheese, Georgian, 258
  Chicken, Russian, 81
  Coulibiac of Salmon, 77
  Fish, Small, 75
  Meat
    Crimean, 250
    Tatar, 249
  Russian, 67
Pie(s) (sweet)
  Apricot Tart, 285
  Sour cream and Jam, 105
"Pigtails," 70
Pilaf, Uzbek-style, 265
Pink Pashka, 130
Pink Potato Salad, 47

Pirozhki
  Dough, Basic Raised, 68
  fillings for
    savory, 71–72
    sweet, 73–75
  Sour Cream Pastry for, 69
Plum
  Cordial, 224
  Sauce, Kidney Beans with, 264
  Sour, Sauce, 256
Pochki v madere, 39
Pokhlyobka, 161
Ponchiki, 147
Poppy Seed(s)
  Filling (for pirozhki), 74
  Noodles and, Cabbage with, 179
  Torte, 286
Pork
  Stew, Ukrainian, 238
  or Veal Brawn, 41
Potato(es)
  and Herring Bake, 175
  Mashed, Casserole of, 180
  in Russian Salad, 45
  Salad, Estonian, 245
  Salad, Pink, 47
  Straw, 96
Pozharskie kotlety, 86
Prepared Horseradish, 216
Prunes
  Braised Chicken with, 237
  Stuffed with Cheese, 245
Pryaniki, 144
Pudding(s)
  Apple, Latvian, 246
  Cornmeal, 247
  Cottage, Russian, 192
  Fruit, Russian, 190
Puff Pastry, 77
Puree, Chestnut, 135

Queen Cake, 108

Rabbit, Braised, in Sour Cream, 91
Radish(es)
  Sandwiches, Open-faced, 54
  in Sour Cream, 185
Raisin Buns, 279
Raspberry
  Jam, Kiev-style, 213
  Soup, Cold, 67

Rassol'nik, 66
Rasstegai, 75
Rediska v smetane, 185
Red snapper, in Cold Fish in Aspic, 34
Relish(es)
  Black Currant, 212
  Cranberry-Horseradish, 217
Rhubarb Mousse, 119
Rice, in Uzbek-style Pilaf, 265
Roast Goose with Apples, 141
Roast Meat and Herring Soufflé, 37
Roast Whole Calf's Liver, 102
Roe, Salmon, Fresh, Caviar, 26
Rogaliki, 278
Romovaya baba, 110
Rose Petal Jam, 215
Royal Paskha, 129
Rozovaya paskha, 130
Rulet s klyukvoi, 284
Rum, Beef Stew with, 99
Rusks, Hazelnut, 276
Russian Black Bread, 168
Russian Caramel Torte, 287
Russian Cheese Pancakes, 191
Russian Chicken Pie, 81
Russian Cottage Cheese, 217
Russian Cottage Pudding, 192
Russian Easter Cheesecake, 128
Russian Egg Salad, 48
Russian Fruit Pudding, 190
Russian Gingerbread, 143
Russian Hot Chocolate, 149
Russian Lemon Soup, 65
Russian Liver Pâté, 36
Russian Pancakes, 135
Russian Pies, 67
Russian Salad, 44
Russian-style Hamburgers, 173
Russian-style Mustard, 215
Russian Tea Cookies, 272
Ryba zalivnaya, 34
Rye Bread, 170
Rzhanoi khleb, 170

Saffron Vodka, 25
Salad(s)
  Beet, 184
  Carrot, 185
  Celeriac, 186
  Cucumbers in Sour Cream, 183
  Egg, Russian, 47

Potato
  Estonian, 245
  Pink, 47
  Russian, 45
  Salade Bagratian, 46
Salade Bagratian, 46
Salat iz yaits, 48
Salat oliv'ye, 45
Salat "zdorov'ye," 185
Salmon
  Coulibiac of, 77
  Roe, Fresh, Caviar, 26
  Smoked
    Canapés of, 30
    Marinated, 30
Salted Mushrooms, 208
Sandwiches, Radish, Open-faced, 54
Sauce(s)
  Cherry, Sturgeon with, 93
  Dill, Herring in, 28
  Dried Mushroom, 181
  Egg and Butter, Cod with, 94
  Gooseberry, Spring Chicken with, 88
  Horseradish, Beef Stew with, 172
  Mayonnaise and Sour Cream, 35
  Mustard, Herring in, 29
  Plum, Kidney Beans with, 264
  Sour Plum, 256
  Tomato
    Basic, 50
    Cocktail Sausages in, 42
    Smelts in, 32
Sauerkraut
  Barrel-cured, 203
  with Mushrooms and Sour Cream, 182
Sausages, Cocktail, in Tomato Sauce, 42
Savory Kidney Beans, 263
Sbiten', 202
Scallion Filling (for *pirozhki*), 72
Selyodka marinovannaya, 27
Selyodka pod ukrophym sousom, 29
Selyodka s gorchichnoi pripravoi, 29
Selyodka v smetane, 28
Semechki, 226
Shafrannaya, 25
Sharlotka malakova, 113
Sharlotka yablochnaya, 111
Shashlyk, 255
Shashlyk karsky, 255
Shchi, 155
Short Dough for Sweet Pirozhki, 70

Siberian Dumplings, 233
Sibirskie pel'meni, 233
Sladkoye bezdrozhzhevoye testo, 70
Slivovaya nastoika, 224
Small Fish Pies, 75
Smelts in Tomato Sauce, 32
Smetana, 219
Smetannik, 105
Smoked salmon. *See* Salmon
Smorodinovka, 24
Solyanka sbornaya myasnaya, 160
Solyonye griby, 208
Solyonye ogurtsy, 206
Sosiski sous-tomat, 42
Soufflé(s)
  Cabbage, Steamed, Ukrainian, 236
  Roast Meat and Herring, 37
Souffléed Baked Apples, 188
Soup(s)
  Basic Bouillon, 199
  Beet
    Cold, 162
    Moscow-style, 159
    Ukrainian-style, 157
  Cabbage, 155
  Fish
    Clear, 64
    Stock, Basic, 200
  Fruit, Cold, with Dumplings, 165
  Kidney and Dill Pickle, 66
  Lemon, Russian, 65
  Meat and Vegetable, Cold, 164
  Mixed Meat, 160
  Mushroom and Barley, 161
  Raspberry, Cold, 67
  Sturgeon, with Champagne, 63
Sour Cabbage, 204
  see also Sauerkraut
Sour Cream
  Berries with, 117
  Braised Rabbit in, 91
  Cucumbers in, 183
  Herring in, 28
  Homemade, 219
  and Jam Pie, 105
  Mayonnaise and, Sauce, 35
  Mushrooms and, Sauerkraut with, 182
  Mushrooms in, 104
  Pastry for Pirozhki, 69
  Radishes in, 185
Sourdough White Bread, 171

Sour Plum Sauce, 256
Soused Apples, 209
Sous provensal', 35
Spiced Pickled Cherries, 211
Spread(s)
  Garlic-Cheese, 55
  Ukrainian-Style Cottage Cheese, 183
Spring Chicken with Gooseberry Sauce, 88
Spun Sugar, 115
Stew(s)
  Beef
    with Horseradish Sauce, 172
    with Rum, 99
  Lamb and Noodle, Kazakh, 266
  Pork, Ukrainian, 238
  Veal, with Cherries, 100
Stock, Fish, Basic, 200
Stolichnyi salat, 45
Strawberry(ies)
  Kisel', 190
  Romanov, 118
Straw Potatoes, 96
Studen', 41
Stuffed Cabbage Leaves, 176
  Jewish Sweet-and-Sour Style, 177
Stuffed Peppers, Moldavian Style, 248
Stuffed Whole Cabbage, 178
Sturgeon
  with Cherry Sauce, 93
  Soup with Champagne, 63
Sugar, Spun, 115
Sukhariki, 276
Sunflower Seeds, Toasted, 226
Sup iz osetriny s shampanskim, 63
Sushonye griby, 208
Suvorov Cookies, 274
Svekol'nik, 162
Svekol'nyi kvas, 223
Svekol'nyi salat, 184
"*Svekrukha*," 288
Svyokla v tomatnom souse, 50
Sweet Boiled Buns, 280
Sweet and Sour Beets, 50
Syomga marinovannaya, 30
Syr i chesnok pod mayonezom, 55
Syrniki, 191

Tart, Apricot, 285
Tartlets, Cottage Cheese, 277
Tatar Meat Pies, 249

Tea
  Cookies
    Meringue, 273
    Russian, 272
  Vodka, 25
Telyatina, tushonaya s vishnei i fasol'yu,
    100
Toasted Sunflower Seeds, 226
Toddy, Egg, 193
Tomatnyi sous, 50
Tomato sauce. *See* Sauces
Tongue, *in* Cold Meat and Vegetable Soup,
    164
Tort "evgenia," 107
Tort "tyanuchki," 287
Torte(s)
  Caramel, Russian, 287
  Eugenia, 107
  Mother-in-law, 288
  Poppy-Seed, 286
  see also Cakes
Travnik, 24
Treska s pol'skim sousom, 94
Tsarina's Cream, The, 116
Tsvetnaya kapusta pod mayonezom, 52
Tsvetnaya kapusta s yaitsom, 264
Tsyplyata tabaka, 260
Tsyplyonok pod sousom iz krizhovnika, 88
Turbot in Dill Marinade, 33
Turkey
  Breast with Apples, 90
  in Cold Meat and Vegetable Soup, 164
Tushonoye mayaso s romom, 99
Tvorog, 217
Tvorog Filling (for *vareniki*), 241
Tvorozhniki, 192

Uzbekskii plov, 265
Ukha, 64
Ukrainian Dumplings, 240
Ukrainian Honey Cake, 243
Ukrainian Pork Stew, 238
Ukrainian Steamed Cabbage Soufflé, 236
Ukrainian-style Beet Soup, 157
Ukrainian-style Cottage Cheese, 182
Ukrainian Sweet Braid, 242

Varenets, 220
Vareniki, 240
Varen'ye iz rozovogo tsveta, 215

Vatrushki, 277
Veal
  in Khlodnik, 163
  kidney, *in* Mixed Meat Soup, 160
  Pork or, Brawn, 41
  Stew with Cherries, 100
Vegetable(s)
  Meat and, Soup, Cold, 164
  see also Names of vegetables
Vereshchaka, 238
Vinaigrette of Beets, 51
Vinegret iz kartofelya i svyokly, 47
Vinegret iz sel'dereinogo kornya, 186
Vinegret iz svyokly, 51
Vishnya marinovannaya, 211
Vishyovka, 24
Vodka(s)
  Anise, 24
  Apricot, 24
  Black-Currant-Bud, 24
  Buffalo Grass, 25
  Cherry, 24
  Coriander, 24
  Garlic-and-Dill, 24
  Herb, 24
  Lemon or Orange, 25
  Pepper, 25
  in Plum Cordial, 224
  Saffron, 25
  Tea, 25
Vyalenaya ryba, 225
Vzvar, 138

Walnut
  Crescents, 278
  -Honey Filling (for *pirozhki*), 75
Wheat Berries with Honey and Nuts, 139
Wine Bowl, 150

Yablochnaya nachinka, 74
Yablochnaya zapenkanka, 246
Yablochnyi pirog, 283
Yabloki so smetanoi, 188
Yagody, 117
Yagody so vzbitoi smetanoi, 117
Yaitsa, farshirovannye gribami, 47
Yeast-raised Lemon Cake, 281
Yellow (Crookneck) Squash or Zucchini
  Caviar, 42

Zakuski
  Apples, Soused, 209
  Beet(s)
    Salad, 184
    Sweet and Sour, 50
    Vinaigrette of, 51
  Black Bread, Russian, 168
  Buckwheat Groats with Mushrooms and
    Cream, 104
  Cabbage
    Sour, 204
    Leaves, Stuffed, 176
  Carrot Salad, 185
  Cauliflower
    with Beet Mayonnaise, 53
    with Mustard and Horseradish
      Mayonnaise, 52
  Celeriac Salad, 186
  Cheese Pie, Georgian, 258
  Cherries, Spiced Pickled, 211
  Chicken and Mushrooms en Cocotte, 38
  Cottage Cheese Tartlets, 277
  Cranberry-Horseradish Relish, 217
  Cucumbers in Sour Cream, 183
  Dill Pickles, Barrel-style, 206
  Eggplant(s)
    Caviar, 40
    Cold Stuffed, 103
    Pickled, 210
  Egg Salad, Russian, 47
  Fish
    Cold, in Aspic, 34
    Dried, 225
  Flat Bread, Armenian, 254
  Fresh Ham Cooked with Hay, 134
  Garlic-Cheese Spread, 55
  Herring
    in Dill Sauce, 28
    in Mustard Sauce, 29
    Pickled, 27
    Roast Meat and, Soufflé, 37
    in Sour Cream, 28
  Horseradish, Prepared, 216
  Kidneys in Madeira, 39
  Liver Pâté, Russian, 36
  Meat, Roast, and Herring Soufflé, 37
  Mushroom(s)
    Caviar, 43
    Marinated, 44
    Salted, 208

Zakuski
  Mushroom(s) (cont.)
    in Sour Cream, 23
    -stuffed Eggs, 49
  Onions, Dilled, 54
  Pancakes, Russian, 135
  Pork or Veal Brawn, 41
  Potato(es)
    Salad, Estonian, 244
    Salad, Pink, 47
  Radish(es)
    in Sour Cream, 185
    Sandwiches, Open-faced, 54
  Russian Pies, 67
  Russian Salad, 45
  Rye Bread, 170
  Salmon
    Coulibiac of, 77

    Roe, Fresh, Caviar, 26
    Smoked, Canapés of, 31
    Smoked, Marinated, 30
  Sauerkraut, Barrel-cured, 203
  Sausages, Cocktail, in Tomato Sauce, 42
  Smelts in Tomato Sauce, 32
  Sourdough White Bread, 171
  Turbot in Dill Marinade, 33
  Yellow (Crookneck) Squash or Zucchini
    Caviar, 42
Zasakharennye abrikosy, 290
Zharenaya pechonka, 102
Zhavoronki, 137
Zhul'yen kurinyi v kokotnitsakh, 38
Zubrovka, 25
Zucchini, Yellow Crookneck Squash or,
    Caviar, 42

DARRA GOLDSTEIN's interest in Russian cooking began in her childhood when her grandmother, an émigré and a great cook, taught her various Russian recipes. Later when she was studying at Leningrad State University and had access to famous old Russian cookbooks, she began to adapt their recipes to modern kitchens. After her graduation from Vassar College she was guide on a traveling U.S. Department of Agriculture exhibition that toured the Soviet Union, and people from Odessa to Alma-Ate opened their homes to her and shared their cherished family recipes with her.

Dara Goldstein is Assistant Professor of Russian Literature at Williams College and lives in Williamstown, Massachusetts.